"If you're straight, the casting director looks at you as though you're a carbuncle on the seat of progress."

"I'll always remember the look on my father's face as I dangled my gold bracelets in front of him."

"While they were shutting bars in New York, I discovered they were far more enlightened in Chicago, St. Louis, and San Francisco."

"Being married doesn't make much difference. I hoped it would but every three months or so I look at some guy and he looks at me and that's it."

"One thing that gripes me about lesbians is how they manage to fool everybody while we have to go through so much pretense. But we're still in the same boat."

also by Jess Stearn
The Wasted Years

"There's no place for you unless you play ball with society."
—A GREENWICH VILLAGE HOMOSEXUAL

THE SIXTH MAN

BY JESS STEARN

A MACFADDEN BOOK

THIS BOOK IS THE COMPLETE TEXT OF THE HARDCOVER BOOK

A MACFADDEN BOOK.................1962

MACFADDEN BOOKS are published by
MACFADDEN PUBLICATIONS, Inc.
205 East 42nd Street, New York 17, New York

PRINTED IN THE U. S. A.

CONTENTS

THE
SIXTH
MAN

Foreword

THE SUBJECT of the sexual deviates in their homosexual manifestations is one that has only yesterday been heard in the market place. Hitherto what there was to say about the matter was said among a small coterie of scientific workers, the moralists and the makers and enforcers of penal laws. What they had to say was said in the peculiar idiom of their professions. It was a bold layman who had either the interest or the ability to master the esoteric language of those who wrote only for the edification of the fellow members of a closed corporation. Now all that is ancient history. All sorts of things conspired to throw open the public discussion of the varieties of sexual experience. Two world wars brought in their train what many call the inevitable decline in manners and morals that is the aftermath of every major conflict. Certainly the public outlook on war is not without its repercussions in the moral realm. And whether the active participation of more human beings in some form of homosexual relationship is another consequence of the war remains to be seen. A much more hopeful view seems to be that the general discussion of the subject has forced the presence of the phenomenon to the surface. That is all to the good.

Jess Stearn is an experienced journalist. He is a reporter of events and the men who make them. The good reporter is a man with no ax to grind, no point of view to impress upon his neighbor, no mission other than to record what he sees. He is a chronicler; and the good chronicler is able to make what he sees come alive. That's just what Jess Stearn does in this book.

The outward and visible signs of homosexuality, as these are worn by a small and to many a somewhat offensive segment of those so conditioned, have caused the public to view the homosexual as an effeminate individual whose every gesture and mannerism clamors for attention. It is by this stereotype of the homosexual—the effusive, preening, smirking exhibitionist—that the man in the street mistakenly judges all homosexuals. Mr. Stearn does well to point out that men such as these are the logical consequence of society's harsh dealing with those whose sexual behavior fails to conform to the standards that society has unsuccessfully attempted to enforce.

It becomes abundantly clear, as we read what Mr. Stearn has to say about the homosexual, that society's notion of his position is in need of a great deal of revision. It is always easy to single out those whose conduct is troublesome and pass laws against what they do. But Mr. Stearn shows there are all kinds of homosexuals. This must be stated again and again. If society is to solve what is called the problem of homosexuality, then it is first necessary to become accurately informed as to the causes and conditions thereof. It is easy to categorize behavior that fails to meet the approval of the keepers of the social and ecclesiastical traditions as immoral, illegal, or sinful. It is easy to persuade the populace that this behavior should be punished. Unfortunately, punishment solves no problems. Nor is it particularly successful in eliminating the behavior that called for punishment. Least of all does it provide society with any useful clues as to what is involved and what can be done to make men act differently.

Mr. Stearn has given us an objective presentation of the behavior of a little-understood and much-abused group. It is not necessary to agree with what he has to say; his main contribution, and this is important, is that he has added to the popular understanding of what is involved in the problem of homosexuality. To expect an early solution tomorrow morning at nine o'clock is a form of optimism best left to those who prefer to deceive themselves.

It is said that one of the greatest achievements of language was the invention of the words *on one hand* and *on the other*. In this book we are given some clear-cut notions of the case for and against the homosexual. Thus we are helped in our need for facts rather than opinions about what is needful for society to do to get to the heart of the matter.

Let what Mr. Stearn has to say speak for itself.

ALFRED A. GROSS
June 1960

CHAPTER I

The Impact

IN A VERY real sense, this book is the product of homosexuality.

It was inspired by the enigma of the rising homosexuality in our midst. It was put together with the aid of homosexuals and the people who deal with them. It is not an exposé or indictment of the homosexual, nor is it an apologia or justification. It is as unbiased a report on the homosexual world as a disinterested reporter could make it.

It is a glittering make-believe world—at times tragic, sometimes ludicrous, even comical. Like any other world, it runs the gamut of human emotions, and no two emotions are the same.

How did my reportorial interest in this world develop? I am not quite sure. Homosexuality did not obtrude into the regular course of my life. Like many others, I had been inclined to regard the homosexual as an oddity whose existence at no point paralleled my own.

There were, of course, always cases coming up in my newspaper work. I remembered that some years ago a young man of evident brilliance, leader of his college class, conspired with a classmate to poison his doctor-father and mother. Dubbed the "champagne cocktail killer" by the tabloids, he calmly explained to the authorities that he disliked his father and hated his mother because she had taunted him since childhood for being a homosexual.

The youthful killer was "good copy." He had long hair, horn-rimmed glasses, and read aloud from the pages of the *Oxford Book of English Verse*. But there was something rather sad about him, and one couldn't help wondering whether things might not have taken a better turn if there had been more understanding in the family.

Some time after that I covered the story of a wealthy middle-aged visitor to New York who had met a husky young man in a mid-town bar and taken him back to his hotel suite. The older man had been killed for his pains, and the younger claimed improper advances. I couldn't help wondering why he just hadn't walked out, if that was all there was to it.

On Fire Island, a sun-drenched resort near New York City, one homosexual killed another and the police explanation was simply "jealousy."

Gradually, other incidents, not particularly significant in themselves, began to take my notice. And my viewpoint began to change. The homosexual was nearer to home than I had thought.

Searching for an apartment, I discovered many superintendents were homosexuals, and not at all retiring about it.

At a Park Avenue cocktail party, given by a magazine editor, I was amazed to find that of all the males in attendance, I was the only nonhomosexual.

Walking in East Fifty-seventh Street, one of the city's pleasanter thoroughfares, I had to sidestep young homosexuals leading their dogs on leash, and watched as they paused to "admire" each other's pets; dog-walking was a way of making new friends.

At a dinner party given by a model I met two youngish men, one an interior decorator and the other a junior executive. They were describing the problems which had arisen from living together—as man and wife—in suburbia. They were quite amusing, even to relating how they shared their country-club membership.

I visited a well-known gymnasium with friends, noting with surprise the number of large-muscled young men who seemed so mutually attentive. Later my friends reported they had changed gyms. Too many homosexuals.

I was vaguely conscious of homosexuals in government and industry. Many had been forced out of the State Department, and I was intrigued by the efforts of some to reshape their lives.

There was another factor in the equation. More and more I heard—or overheard—attractive young women bemoaning the dearth of eligible males, complaining that "everybody's a homosexual now." And there were the young women who said they preferred the homosexual because he was such a "perfect gentleman." It was all very confusing at this point.

My work, too, seemed to be increasingly touching on homosexuality. In books and articles homosexuality somehow kept intruding. I had been discussing a book on juvenile delinquency with a sociologist priest when the subject of youth gangs came up. "These gangs," he observed, "have an obvious homosexual pattern, even when there is no overt homosexuality." Shortly thereafter I saw where a gang of marauding young killers, tracked down by police for a pair of senseless murders, calmly admitted they had become male prostitutes to finance their amusements.

Researching a newspaper article on the upsurge of venereal disease, I came in for my biggest jolter. "Some 65 per cent of our V.D. cases," a U. S. Public Health officer told me at one clinic, "resulted from male contact exclusively." One young man with V.D. had exposed ten pupils from a nearby high school.

Back in my office, still mulling over this statistic, I checked back with the clinic. "Yes," the health man laughed, "it's still 65 per cent." The homosexuality clientele was greater here than at other clinics. "We serve the garment and theatrical areas, and Greenwich Village," he explained. But the explanation only served to open new avenues of speculation.

I began toying with the idea of doing a book—about a phenomenon I knew enough about to know I didn't quite know enough about.

I discussed the project with a number of experts. All agreed that while the problem was by no means a new one it now had a new dimension. "It is a problem as old as the world," an eminent psychiatrist told me, "yet it bears comparison at this time to the decline and fall of Rome."

However, the more experts I talked with, the more questions there were unanswered. Some kept rattling through my head:

Was homosexuality becoming more prevalent, or was it just more open? And exactly how prevalent was it? If homosexuals preferred other males, why were so many married and apparently living contentedly with their wives and children?

Just how much impact did homosexuality have on the life of the city—and the nation? Was it really a mark of Western decadence or just something transitory washed up by the war?

I had written considerably about prostitution, addiction, juvenile delinquency and related social problems, but homosexuality seemed the greatest enigma—and the greatest challange.

There were many books on homosexuality—by sociologists, psychologists, clergymen, and homosexuals themselves,

11

but all with their own special approach. I thought of a report which would answer not only the questions in my mind, but would deal with everyday aspects of the homosexual's world—his social adjustment to himself, his job, friends, and family—but even more importantly, perhaps, the nonhomosexual's problem with him. It was a bigger job than I had anticipated.

My research took me to the homes and meeting grounds of homosexuals—the bars, parks, streets in which they converge. I not only talked to homosexuals, whose stories might be discounted as prejudiced, but to their wives, girl friends, mothers, boy friends, and social advisers.

I made a study of the fashion and entertainment industry, fields in which the homosexual influence is strong. I explored Hollywood and Broadway, talking with producers, actors, photographers, models, designers. I went to many of the places where homosexuals seek each other out. In Greenwich Village they lounged invitingly against the rails bordering historic Washington Square, in an area known as "The Meat Rack." In New Orleans it was a bar, in Los Angeles a park, near Washington a bus station, in Philadelphia a street corner, in San Francisco a public square.

I was soon moving in a world such as I had never dreamed existed. It was the thinking, above everything, that I couldn't identify or relate with—the blandness, for instance, with which grown-up, educated adult homosexuals compared their homosexual relationships to relationships of other people. "There's nothing we do," a homosexual businessman assured me, "that other men and women aren't equally guilty of."

Some even "married," with ceremonies duly solemnized by clergymen of sorts. Others, like the American Indian, cut their veins and mingled their blood—but not, like the Indians, as "blood brothers."

I had no problem meeting homosexuals. They were only too happy to talk to me. Some asked me to respect their anonymity. Others didn't seem to care. "I'm not sure my boss is one," a homosexual accountant told me, "so until I find out I'd like to keep my name out."

Learning that I was writing a book, some got in touch with me for the purpose, they said, of assuring an honest report. "Just don't make us out a lot of effeminate, mincing, weak-livered nances," a burly bisexual warned.

In all, I must have talked to hundreds of homosexuals, and observed many more. Some were gay, witty, and charming. Others appeared to be quite successful and pleased with themselves. Still more seemed to have solved the problem of comfortably living a double life. And yet with all the gaiety, brightness, and substance, I had the feeling at times that it was all a big mirage, and nobody knew it better than they. And toward the end of my research I became painfully aware of one thing: I had yet to meet a truly happy homosexual.

It was not only a problem for males. Women, too, seemed concerned by the subject, especially when their interest in males was not returned. "There are plenty of males in this town, but few men," an attractive young model said. "Even the truck drivers aren't for real these days." But, curiously, other women seemed to prefer homosexual companionship. Many wealthy dowagers, whose husbands are long dead, dote on the gazelle-like, effeminate creatures they know as "the boys" and are more than willing to pick up the bills as the price of an evening out with "an escort with a pair of pants."

But nobody speculated more about homosexuality than the homosexuals. One homosexual ran off the names of a dozen Hollywood stars whom he identified as homosexuals. Others cited stage stars and public figures by the score, but, generally, they were only repeating stories passed on by other homosexuals. "They seem to take satisfaction," a psychiatrist explained, "in bringing the great of the world down to their level."

As a rule, homosexuals, I discovered, feel that nobody knows anything about homosexuality but themselves. Their reactions to the solemn pronouncements of the men of science were often startling. I asked a young Philadelphian, a college graduate of twenty-five, "Isn't it true that where civilizations have become decadent, as in Rome or Greece, homosexuality has flourished?"

The homosexual, who passed as normal, grimaced and replied with an expression of scorn: "We hear that claptrap all the time but don't dare speak out because it might give us away. But who can deny that any nation was greater than Greece when its warriors gloried in their comradeship of arms and Alexander, a homosexual, led their conquest of the world?"

Others mention Julius Caesar and Frederick the Great as prototypes of homosexual virility, and balance out the picture artistically with Michelangelo and Leonardo da Vinci. The "incomparable Leonardo," they call the most versatile and complete man of all times, with the possible exception of Caesar.

As I went from one homosexual haunt to another, there were times when I wondered whether the whole world might not be homosexual. "Someday," a young homosexual told me confidently, "we'll outnumber you, and then you'll be the abnormal ones and we'll be the normal."

And while New York and other large cities might be havens for sexual deviates, it soon became apparent the problem was pretty much the same around the country. Charlotte, North Carolina; Worcester, Massachusetts; Pasadena, California; South Bend, Indiana—all had their homosexual scandals. Organizations dominated by homosexuals flourished in San Francisco, Boston, Denver, Detroit, Philadelphia. And just to make things cozy, there is a code by which homosexuals can contact other homosexuals in their travels around the country.

In smaller cities and remote communities homosexuals operate less openly, but no less actively. And colleges, too, have become convenient centers. Many youthful homosexuals, who have lost themselves in the indifference of the big city, have been introduced to homosexuality on campuses in Virginia, Vermont, Oklahoma, Iowa, Texas, California, etc.

Many communities refuse to acknowledge they have a homosexual problem until police step in and the sordid details are spread out on the front pages. Others would rather not discuss it, hoping, ostrichlike, that it will magically vanish. Still others have learned to their sorrow that even the most drastic police action does little more than intensify the problem.

Invariably, the revelation of homosexuality hits an unsuspecting community like a succession of shock waves. First, there is disbelief, then chagrin, and then shame. And it is a pattern that can occur across the length and breadth of the land. Only recently, for instance, at the same time one homosexual scandal was rocking the placid little community of Waukesha, Wisconsin, another was erupting a thousand miles away in the equally peaceful town of Northampton, Massachusetts, home of Calvin Coolidge's family and eminently respectable Smith College. In both instances, the accused were from virtually every walk of life—clergymen and educators on one hand, gasoline-station attendants and salesmen on the other.

Across the nation many homosexuals, either as groups or individuals, are quietly aware of one another's favorite

14

haunts and meeting places. And homosexuality is by no means a purely national phenomenon. With the possible exception of Russia, where even the word is taboo, the international set is well represented by these glitterbugs. Many turn up en masse at arty functions here and abroad, and sometimes take over. Homosexuals of many nationalities were so conspicuous at Italy's "Festival of Two Worlds," that an American critic observed that "three sexes" were painfully involved. Critic Irving Kolodin, writing in the *Saturday Review*, noted that the festival town of Spoleto had become "the happy hunting ground of 'the boys' who have previously made the ballet their particular, bloodless passion."

In some areas, trading on public acceptance, they are so bold and ostentatious that they violate the sensibilities and good taste of other homosexuals. For instance, even the homosexuals turning up for a recent ballet premiere were nettled by a young man flaunting his "individuality" in a shocking-pink shirt, designed to set off black-beaded eyelashes and gold earrings in pierced ears. "You know," one onlooker indignantly twittered to another, "*that one* will set homosexuality back a hundred years."

They have been prominent in the national scene, at times reaching high places even in government. At one point, while the late Senator Joseph McCarthy of Wisconsin, highly publicized foe of "fairies" and Reds, was riding high, the number of homosexuals in government in Washington alone was conservatively placed at about four thousand. In a matter of five years more than four hundred were drummed out of the State Department itself for "homosexual proclivities." The investigation of but a single office of the "Voice of America," an agency devised to put our best foot forward overseas, resulted in the dismissal of twenty-six at one stroke.

Around the country there is obviously a strong homosexual underground, raising its head in towns and villages as it dares. Recently, a pastor in a small Ohio community inserted a notice in a physical-education magazine, advising that he would counsel young men with problems of any kind on request. An unlooked-for avalanche resulted, and from an unlooked-for source. "He got letters from more than one thousand avowed homosexuals," a brother pastor reported, "and some even sent their pictures in various stages of undress."

How was the good pastor to know that many homosexuals are addicted to body-building and physical culture?

Even in the first stages of my research it was evident that

15

the homosexual population was far more considerable than I would have thought possible. I found whole beaches and entire community areas devoted almost exclusively to homosexuals. But these obvious, open homosexuals were only a small part of the growing homosexual population.

The great uncounted masses were the unknowns: those who went about their business every day posing as normal or straight, turning in a nine-to-five day at the office, occasionally dating a girl as a cover-up or because they derived some gratification from it, while clandestinely meeting male friends. And then there were the others—the bisexuals who married and had children; the latent homosexuals who suppressed or sublimated their desires; the male prostitutes and the so-called normal men who made a pretense of preying on homosexuals, while actually grappling with the problem themselves.

Toward the end of my research, after consulting with police, and health authorities, and just looking around, I was ready to accept the homosexual's own estimate of the overall homosexual population—one out of every six adult males!

It seemed staggering, but in New York City alone the estimates for overt homosexuals—those who had lapsed at one time or another—runs from a conservative 400,000 by police authorities to 500,000 from a fact-finding homosexual group. Indeed, the latter organization, the Mattachine Society, insists this figure may be low when one includes the homosexual who breaks out only when he is sure he won't be found out.

In the United States at large, according to the Mattachine, the homosexuals are just as numerous, if not as open. "There are fifteen million male homosexuals in the nation, actual and potential," a Mattachine officer estimates. "One out of every six."

And the figures are on the rise. "Not only are there about 400,000 homosexuals in New York City, based on a projection from the thousands of arrests we make every year," a high police inspector told me, "but they are gaining new recruits by the drove every day."

There are many reasons for the sharp upswing, and the decline of social disapproval is not the least. It has made open conversion less hazardous for all concerned. "Many no longer have to hide the fact they are homosexual," the inspector said. This has brought about a great change in their habits.

16

"Prior to World War II," he pointed out, "it was commonplace for them to live together, surreptitiously, as man and wife. Now they no longer feel the necessity for being so secretive or so easily satisfied and can pick and choose more exciting relationships, cruising streets and bars until they find what they want. Where once they contented themselves with one partner, they are now constantly recruiting."

Homosexuals can be anybody.

They are not confined or even concentrated in the artistic professions as has been commonly supposed, but are numerous in all fields and social classes, as one social agency soon learned when it scoured the Bowery for "underprivileged homosexuals."

However, because of social taboos, they must be careful in most walks of life not to reveal themselves, or else face exposure and ruin. But in the easy world of the theater and arts they find tolerance and acceptance, just as prostitutes and other characters would, and can show themselves openly. But the average homosexual, be he a lawyer, accountant, insurance agent, or day laborer, must live a double life, pretending he is anything but what he is. Consequently, because of their social vulnerability, the great mass of uncounted homosexuals live in a gray, shadowy world of intrigue and deception. Thus their very homosexuality encourages crime, making them prime targets for all kinds of criminals—muggers, blackmailers, thieves and petty grifters.

Consequently, they consider themselves badly used by society, and of all the injustices, fancied or real, that they fret about, blackmail rankles the most. For their exposure to blackmailers they bitterly blame the society which makes it necessary for them to keep their homosexuality a deep, dark secret. "We suffer," one told me, "for the world's hypocrisy."

While often hidden, the impact of the homosexual is constantly at work, influencing American thought and gaining greater acceptance for homosexuality. At times the influence is obvious. The homosexual, with his flair for clothes, has contributed heavily to masculine fashions. Preferring tight bulging trousers, he introduced the tight-cut blue jeans, which appealed to teen-age toughs, and the Ivy League pipe-stem trousers, which pleased the more refined. In pursuing talismans of virility he has been responsible for the popularity of leather jackets, broad leather belts, and identification bracelets. Flamboyantly colored shirts and open

17

high-cut collars are other homosexual innovations unwittingly adopted by rugged heterosexuals.

In the movies and on the stage the increased acceptance of homosexuality is reflected by the productions. Where the subject was once theatrically verboten, it has lately become fashionable. *Tea and Sympathy* and *Compulsion*, for instance, recently got both the Broadway and Hollywood treatment. *Suddenly Last Summer*, with Elizabeth Taylor and Montgomery Clift, played to smash movie audiences, and *The Third Sex*, a documentary, played first-run houses. And there are currently a rash of plays around (*The Best Man*, *The Hostage*) with this theme prominent.

Probably the strongest impact has been on the young. An easier attitude toward homosexuality by teen-agers and youngsters has become sadly apparent. Many teen-age converts, drawn by curiosity or money, seemed to think they were untouched because it was the homosexual who submitted. A blasé youngster reassured me with a shrug, "I can stop any time I want," he said. "I'm not queer."

Homosexuals find encouragement for their behavior in the loftiest places and on the loftiest levels. Condemnation of homosexuals is by no means universal. Many homosexuals, seeking justification of their conduct, often quote the most impeccable sources. One homosexual earnestly pointed out that an official English committee, made up of the best minds in the United Kingdom, had recommended that homosexuality, when practiced by adults, be stricken from that nation's criminal statutes. Another just as solemnly quoted a professor in this country who said homosexuality should be permitted without hindrance if neither participating adult imposed himself on the other.

Still another homosexual found moral support for his sex drives in the official journal of the Church of Scotland, which broadly defined homosexuality as "a condition of sensitivity which can enrich human relationships—or can be abused to the lowest depths."

But there is also an encouraging aspect of religious interest, based on helpful understanding. It expresses itself in an effort to throw out a life line to bring the homosexual into the stream of community life. But the homosexual still has to reach out for it. For as the Reverend Robert W. Wood said in a report to the New York City Association of Congregational Christian Churches:

"The sin is not in being homosexual but in failing to adjust oneself to the added responsibility in being so. The

18

homosexual didn't ask to be gay, but he is and the chances are he is never going to be otherwise. This leaves him but two choices: Either such a person becomes a slave to homosexuality, or he lives with it in a rational manner."

CHAPTER II

Origin of the Species

WHY ARE SOME men homosexual, and not others?

Why do so many homosexuals, despite the scorn of society, apparently continue to enjoy what they are doing and show no remorse or regret?

Is there actually a bisexual, and how is he different from homosexuals who have nothing to do with women?

Why do homosexuals marry and have children?

All these questions were teeming through my mind as I faced the brilliant psychiatrist who reputedly knew more about the emotional life of the homosexual than anybody in the land. Dr. George W. Henry was head of the George Henry Foundation, dedicated to helping homosexuals. He had pioneered in studying their habits more than twenty-five years ago, when the subject was distasteful even to psychiatrists. He was the first to have delved into the lives of unacknowledged homosexuals. When the courts, trying to learn about these men, directed them to Dr. Henry's attention, he soon discovered he was getting only a certain obvious type, not the brooders who kept their secret to themselves.

Long before World War II, Dr. Henry engaged a sociologist to help throw light on behavior of the so-called underprivileged homosexual. Disguised in old clothes, masquerading often as a skid-row bum, the aide haunted the Bowery and Greenwich Village, winning the confidence of down-and-outers.

From this research, which introduced many homosexuals to the foundation, came the first information about homosexuals who had kept their own counsel.

During the draft, preceding World War II, Dr. Henry was consulted about ways and means of screening homosexuals. "A few," he said, "would say they were homosexual to avoid being drafted. It really didn't matter, draftwise, whether they were or were not, because a person who would acknowledge homosexuality, when he wasn't, certainly wasn't acceptable."

For every known homosexual there are again at least fifty not known to any agency, court, police, or military services. There was no simple way of detection. "Just as many have been accepted as have been rejected," the doctor pointed out. "In many instances, enlisting for military duty was a homosexual's way of establishing to himself that he was as much a man as anybody else."

Like many students of contemporary Western culture, Dr. Henry feels that our civilization may be declining somewhat as the Romans' did. "Homosexuality, with its lack of responsibility for the procreation of the species, is certainly a factor in that decline. Where living is hard, there is less homosexuality, since it becomes a luxury for a nation pressed for helping hands. As a rule, however, as we travel east, into older cultures, from America to Europe and into Asia, homosexuality becomes more prevalent. Only in the Anglo-Saxon culture, as a by-product of our puritanism, is it automatically both a moral and legal crime. In many lands it is not concealed or even considered reprehensible, so it does not create the social problems which stem from our moral taboos."

"Then," I said, "homosexuality is not necessarily tied up with the so-called decline of the West?"

"In the lands where living is hard," he replied patiently, "where people must scratch the earth and devote their complete energies to feeding and sheltering themselves and their families, homosexuality is almost unheard of. In ancient Macedonia before Alexander, for instance, near a Grecian area of traditional homosexuality, the people had to make a rigorous effort to stay alive; the instinct for self-preservation, for perpetuation of the race was so strong, so near the surface that nothing was permitted to impede its own propagation."

Yet, I had heard of homosexuals having children, of others who actually fancied themselves ladies' men. And how about the undeclared homosexuals, the "closet queers"—strong, active, muscular men who flit from one woman to another, knocking them about violently and otherwise mistreating them. Were these the bisexuals we had been hearing about lately?

"By no means," he said. "They are the Don Juan homosexuals. They get no satisfaction out of women and really

20

degrade the normal relationship. They are trying to prove to themselves they are as virile as the next man, but resent the women they have to prove themselves with."

"What is the difference," I asked the psychiatrist, "between the homosexual and the bisexual—aren't they basically the same?"

A trace of annoyance swept over his aristocratic features. In a weary undertone he sighed, "Oh, how naïve we are!"

He turned to me. "Let me ask you," he said coldly, "is there any difference between day and night?"

I correctly assumed the question was rhetorical and he went on:

"There is no more similarity between the homosexual and the bisexual than between day and night—or between you and me. What so few seem to realize is that there are female and male components in all of us, so delicately balanced that no one can say for sure when the balance will be tipped."

"But," I said, "I have understood even from homosexuals that the bisexual is a homosexual who just happens to like women. Then there's the theory that he is a normal individual who turned to men when he became sated with beautiful women, as in Hollywood, with so many of our stars."

He gave me an almost pitying glance. "There is no mystery about the bisexual. Because of the combination of components there is a side to him that appeals to and enjoys men and women at different times. He gets something out of both relationships, as these components make themselves felt and as the circumstances indicate."

"If that is the case," I observed, "I can understand why so many homosexuals say that everybody should be homosexual—they would seem to have it made."

An associate of Dr. Henry's who had been sitting quietly, cut in. "Wouldn't it be opportune," he suggested, "to say that the homosexuals and the bisexuals are hedonists, enjoying the physical sensations of sex without reference to the responsibility involved in the relationships of love?"

"In a way, yes," the doctor said. "They never really attain the complete love which is possible only between men and women whose shared interests include the blessedness of children and grandchildren, which gives a grand purpose to the sex relationship."

Dr. Henry's associate again interposed. "Isn't it true, doctor, that the Don Juan homosexual and the bisexual are often confused?"

The doctor nodded. "Only by the uninitiated, which, of course, includes many homosexuals. The Don Juan is a homosexual who is constantly trying to show how much of a man he is. He engages in affair after affair with women, none of which gratifies or satisfies him. Frequently he beats these women, which is a way he has, unconsciously perhaps, of debasing them in his own eyes."

"If a man finds himself satisfied in a relationship with women," I said, "why should he risk social disapproval and possible ruin by mixing with men?"

"It all depends upon what you call satisfaction. Is satisfaction purely the physical release in sexual congress, or is it involved in the feeling that follows that act? Does the person feel more alone then, more unwanted, more melancholy than before?"

"But men feel this with women, and keep seeking women until they find the right one. Why turn to men for satisfaction?"

"It takes a mature man to work out a satisfying relationship with a woman. There are responsibilities, there is the need for compromise, and it is responsibility that the homosexual commonly shrinks from. By the same token, there are women who marry homosexuals because there is something about the heterosexual relationship that disturbs them. Perhaps it is the intensity of the male or his aggressiveness; perhaps the female components of the homosexual are more gratifying to these women."

"How can you tell when somebody reveals homosexual tendencies?"

"In what is not heterosexual there is always the possibility of homosexuality."

"Why," I asked, "do people go along for thirty or forty years of their lives and then show a tendency to become homosexual?"

He shrugged. "You can't generalize. Each case stands by itself."

"Take myself," I said confidently. "I've been married, have children, am over forty. Could I suddenly become a homosexual?"

He gave me a cold searching look. "I'd have to know more about you," he said, "but men with similar backgrounds have become homosexual."

He thought a while. "Homosexuals marry and have children, but a successful marriage is something else again. Marriage, of course, is the most rewarding of human re-

22

lationships. But it requires a mature male. It is especially trying these days because of the rise of feminism. Women work today, are independent, have acquired aggressive characteristics usually associated with the male. They have challenged the male, but it does no good for the male to bluster. He must assert his manhood through reason, patience, and love.

"If he gets a clout on the side of the head one day, he must be able to rise above it and enfold his wife in his arms the next day. He must be the stronger of the two.

"The woman, even if she is boss, must let the man think he is running things. Otherwise, she undermines his masculine role. It is the most difficult of situations, too difficult for the homosexual who finds it easier to go from one typically transitory relationship to the other."

"There are homosexuals who seem to have been cured," I said, "though some authorities insist this is an impossibility." Dr. Henry's associate sat up. "Dr. Henry," he said, "tell him about those cases you helped, those men from the consular service, and the minister."

"I do not like the word cure," Dr. Henry said. "However the cases speak for themselves. This man had been expelled from his job as a result of an investigation. He was young, about thirty, had never married, and was in a rather sorry state from the humiliation of having been exposed and rejected. His feelings of guilt were an additional complication." The doctor looked up. "But he wanted to be helped, and he had a goal. He wanted to be married and to have children."

The doctor didn't reveal the cure in this instance, but remotivating the patient was a factor. "Each case is different. I never tell a patient what to do. I try to point out the truth of the situation and let him find his own solution. In this instance, the young man as a boy had been involved in an incestuous relationship with an uncle, and it had apparently set up a pattern of fear as regards sex. This fear had to be dissolved."

The patient, for years, communicated regularly with Dr. Henry. He is happily married, has four children, and has never reverted to homosexuality. "So far as we know," Dr. Henry observed.

"Is there any way of telling," I asked, "when a patient has reached a turning point in therapy?"

The doctor's face showed impatience.

23

He turned to his associate. "Did you tell him," he asked, "about my eye?" The aide shook his head.

The doctor touched his right eye. "I lost the sight of this eye a few months ago. It was the result of a blow by a young man whom I had been treating off and on for some time."

He paused. "In the course of practicing psychiatry for over forty years, I have acquired a certain amount of understanding of cases. Yet the attack came as a complete surprise. The patient, who had a homosexual problem, had shown a certain attachment or devotion to me. Only a few weeks before, he had insisted on his devotion and had come to see me about a specific problem." The doctor touched his eye and impassively looked off into space before continuing. "On this occasion he had been sitting quietly at my desk when, suddenly, he launched his attack." The blow was struck before the doctor could defend himself.

"Later, of course, as I reviewed the situation, I realized that it was because of this devotion he had attacked me. He was striking out against the father image, subconsciously resented, of which I had become a substitute in his mind."

Dr. Henry turned to me. "Despite my years of practice, I had no way of knowing this. If I had, I would have been forewarned, or if it had happened once before, it would not have caught me off-guard as it did." He said dryly, "Does that answer your question about detecting the turning point?"

His mood changed quickly. "There are no turning points, or there are scores of turning points, varying in quality and subtlety—just as there are all degrees of homosexuality. There is no more of a common denominator for homosexuals than for heterosexuals."

I mentioned that many homosexuals seemed more intense about sex than even the most bullish male. They were forever casting about for new friends and seemed obsessed by the prominent people in the theater and public life whom they identified as homosexuals.

He smiled. "Yes, they pick up every little whisper and rumor in their anxiety to put the homosexual label on others. The average man doesn't care about the sex habits of other people. Homosexuals, however, have reasons for their interest. Feeling their equivocal position in society, many are prone to see others more highly placed brought down to their own level. If you listen to the average homo-

24

sexual, everybody is homosexual, overt, latent or suppressed. You will hear them say, 'Oh, he's a fairy, but he's too dumb to know it.' "

"They keep insisting," I said, "that the only difference between them and other men is that they like men instead of women."

"That," he said tartly, "as I have pointed out, is not the disease but the symptom."

I mentioned, too, that many male homosexuals appeared more at ease with female homosexuals than they did with heterosexuals. "They tell me," I said, "that there are as many lesbians as male homosexuals and that they get along like country cousins."

He sighed. "Again, what do you mean by the two terms? By lesbians, I suppose you mean women of all types who have the love relationship with other women?"

I nodded.

"If anything," he said, "it is an easier step for women, by their nature. They still can be very feminine and have a relationship with another woman, as witness the kissing and hugging between women which is considered quite normal. There is also no great guilt complex to compare with the male's from loss of his virility.

"And there are the usual number of women with latent tendencies, who, themselves, don't realize it. They associate their repugnance for sex with a virile male with an early unpleasant sex relationship, not realizing that any relationship would have been unpleasant. In some cases, these are the women who fill their need for male companionship by going with homosexuals or marrying them. The homosexual, by his very nature, represents no threat to their natures or individuality."

"But," I said, "so many homosexuals also seem to resent lesbians."

"There may be surface friction," he said, "but, essentially, they understand each other better than other people do. Both are homosexual, both prefer their own sex. In some circumstances they get along well. They may even marry and make it last, balancing off each other's shortcomings. The passive partner may cook and sew around the house, fluttering about as his aggressive wife gets home from the shop. It is a convenient alliance. While expressing their own personalities, they gain the social approval homosexuals secretly covet."

How was the homosexual created?

There are many opinions.

For a hundred years many researchers have insisted on a distinction between a constitutional or physiological-type homosexual and the psychological or psychogenic, the born or the developed. But a current view is that there is no such thing as constitutional homosexuality, that homosexuals are made early in life within the family group, encouraged either by an overly protective attitude by the mother, or by failure in identifying with a masculine father image. It sometimes seems the tendency runs in families, the son picking it up when exposed at a susceptible age to a homosexual father. However, the instigator is propinquity, not heredity. It could have been influenced by any other male, an uncle or guardian, some authorities say, with whom the boy was similarly identified in his impressionable pubic stage. The female homosexual also flourishes in a home where the father is either homosexual or overbearingly aggressive. When a well-known theatrical magnate came home and told his wife and four grown daughters he had decided to live openly as a homosexual, one of his daughters was already a lesbian without his knowing it.

For a while homosexuals were regarded as glandular freaks. However, recent research reveals hormone injections and even testicular transplants not only failed to alter a single homosexual, but resulted in intensifying the prevailing abnormal sex drive. W. H. Perloff, working in the endocrine clinic of Philadelphia General Hospital, found no connection between choice of sex object and hormone balance.

There is no such thing, observes the scholarly Reverend Thomas McGrath, S.J., as a homosexual who has no other personality problem. Fundamentally, the priest insists, the homosexual is a man of immature thought, incapable of meeting difficult situations.

"The homosexual," he observed, "is usually found to be satisfied with a sort of total arresting of his personality development. This apparently provides some form of pleasurable protection. He unconsciously clings to this immature level and ceases to advance to maturity—not just in choice of love object—but in almost all other areas of personality integration as well."

While many in the psychoanalytical school contend homosexuality is wholly acquired, others like Dr. Henry insist the genes still have something to do with it. "The seed must first be there," a prominent sociologist said, "and then it must be nurtured by parents before it eventually buds and flourishes."

Without meaning to, some experts say, many parents contribute to their children's homosexuality. Some parents show a preference for one child over another, causing the youngster to feel insecure or unwanted within his own family circle and depriving him of the understanding and feeling of belonging he so desperately needs during the emotional changes of puberty. Also, at this sensitive age, rejection at home often leads the confused youngster to look afield for a "protector" who is sympathetic and interested—and there are all too many of these older males waiting in the wings.

During the particularly vulnerable period of adolescence, when a youngster is ridden by his first sex awareness, the jealous mother is often so dominating and possessive, the experts say, that she subverts her son's normally awakening interest in girls his own age. "And this," a long-time observer adds, "frequently stifles a boy's psychosexual development at a time when it is so delicately balanced that circumstances can tip him either way."

All too often parents who want a girl and get a boy induce sexual inversion in susceptible children because they act as though the child were of the opposite sex. "When I was a child," an adult homosexual recalled for his analyst, "my mother kept putting me in dresses and braiding my hair long after other boys were in knee pants and had their hair decently trimmed."

The thoughtless naming of children has also contributed to their misery and, in many instances, to their differentiation from other children, some authorities contend. "Such 'sissy' names as Reginald, Percival, and the more ambivalent Shirley or Tracy, have resulted in many boys being taunted as effeminate during the sensitive years of their growing-up period. "And while effeminacy does not necessarily signify homosexuality, it does make a self-conscious boy wonder about himself," one expert says, "and often impedes the perfectly natural and healthy curiosity which leads to liaisons of gradually deepening degree with the opposite sex."

The effect of early seductions on the impressionable child, either at the hands of adults or somewhat older youngsters, can be a decisive factor in the making of homosexuals, particularly if there is no compensating example of masculinity in the immediate family. "If the boy can identify himself with a rugged male figure," an expert said, "this distasteful

27

experience can be put down as a bad accident that will never occur again; thousands of similar experiences happened in adult life to men who were forced through circumstances to live without women in prisons and wartime military areas. Unless they were homosexually predisposed, most were able to resume normal sex lives."

With a child, of course, the wound often cuts deeper and the scar may never heal without love and skilled attention.

Some graphic evidence supports the seed-parent theory. Recently, investigating a reported delinquency, authorities visited a middle-class home, ruled by an autocratic mother who insisted on putting dresses on her four boys. She also kept their hair long and in braids.

Intrigued, investigators temporarily put aside the burglary inquiry that had prompted their visit and began to explore family relationships. The oldest boy, fifteen, was already a confirmed homosexual and gaily showed himself off in woman's attire. But the youngest three, aged ten to fourteen, resisted the most persistent maternal pressure.

As fast as the mother brought out girls' clothes for them, they would throw them aside, despite the threat of punishment. One of the boys had once tossed his clothes out a window and defiantly paraded in the nude. Under questioning the oldest boy disclosed a deep resentment of the mother who had made him effeminate. The hostility of the others was more open but less pronounced.

Here was an enigma for the sociologists. Why were the four children, all exposed to a similarly grotesque environment, not equally affected?

The children were questioned together, and separately, and the mother was questioned again. "We finally discovered," an official said, "that the three youngest boys were blood brothers, and were adopted. None was related to the oldest boy, who had become queer. He was actually the only one of the four born to the mother."

CHAPTER III

Personality

WHEN THE Metropolitan Law Enforcement Conference met at Manhattan College recently to discuss the homosexual problem, some homosexuals became upset and "demanded equal time."

There is probably no more sensitive individual anywhere than the homosexual, and yet, as a rule, he wouldn't be anything but a homosexual. He talks of being a member of an ill-treated minority, but wouldn't sign up with the majority tomorrow.

He is a mixture of paradoxes.

He resents being put down as a faggot, queer, fairy, nance, pansy, fruit, or homo—preferring the euphemistic "gay" or "gay boy," and yet he uses these terms himself when describing homosexuals whose conduct fails to meet his approval. One young homosexual, for instance, referred witheringly to a well-known bookstore as "a fruit stand" because he disliked its homosexual clerks. Another, living a secretive double life, explained contemptuously that he didn't want to become a "miserable old faggot whom nobody would have anything to do with."

Many are privately scornful of "straight" people—heterosexuals—whom they dismiss as insensitive at best and brutishly obtuse at worst. They have no liking for lesbians, whom they distrust, but frequently find themselves allies because of a feeling that, fundamentally, they are in the same predicament. "The one thing that gripes me about lesbians," a homosexual told me tartly, "is how they manage to fool everybody while we have to go through so much pretense. But we're still in the same boat."

They have a different face for different occasions. In conversation with each other, they often undergo a subtle change. I have seen men who appeared to be normal suddenly smile roguishly, soften their voices, and simper as they greeted homosexual friends. When I commented on this change in inflection a homosexual registered surprise. "Doesn't your voice change," he asked, "when you speak to a woman?"

Many times I saw these changes occur after I had gained a homosexual's confidence and he could safely risk my disapproval. Once as I watched a luncheon companion become an effeminate caricature of himself, he apologized. "It is hard to always remember that one is a man."

Effeminate features or mannerisms, I learned, do not necessarily signify homosexuality. And, paradoxically, an inveterate homosexual may be the most masculine-looking person in the world. Still, teen-age effeminacy may contribute to homosexuality. All too often it makes the effeminate child conscious of masculine shortcomings and attracts older perverts. One homosexual, blaming his homosexuality on his childhood, told me, "Because I was a pretty little thing, my mother kept putting me in dresses and braiding my hair long after other little boys were in knee pants and had their hair trimmed." Bitterly, he recalled, "She kept telling friends that I was as cute as a little girl."

The latent homosexual is so confusing a type that he often confuses himself. He is constantly torn by doubts. He worries about being attracted to men, and he worries about being attracted to women. When he feels most concerned about his attitude toward other males, he may be pursuing women most assiduously, and often tries to buy their affection. "Any adult male who requires a new girl every day," an expert observed recently, commenting on a widely known millionaire's penchant for two prostitutes a day, "is primarily trying to impress himself."

Since the latents have not yet committed themselves to overt homosexuality, they are not driven to extreme measures of concealing their interest and may put off matrimony indefinitely. On the other hand, doubts of their masculinity may be resolved under psychiatric care or by some catastrophe such as unplanned fatherhood. "I always feared the worst about myself," a long-time bachelor said, "until circumstances forced me to marry, and then as we got ready for the baby I realized how much I had been missing."

But more often than not they go the other way.

Many an effeminate boy, treated as a homosexual, has reacted resentfully as he grew older. But few, fortunately, have been driven to the violent extreme of the "champagne cocktail killer." One boy, taunted for years by his father, finally paid him back dearly. "I will always remember," he recalled with obvious relish, "the look in my dear father's face as I dangled my gold bracelets in his face."

Many are as vain as peacocks—or women. When I mentioned casually to one homosexual that he didn't look old enough to have done so much, he began preening himself at the dinner table, almost purring, as he deftly combed back his hair. "I'm twenty-eight," he said, "but I'm taken for twenty-one or twenty-two all the time."

The love relationship is often complex. Reflecting the jumbled personality of the homosexual, it is often a mixture of affection and scorn. One moment a homosexual may be talking admiringly about his love partner, and the next be moved to ridicule or contempt. "He likes to think himself the male," one said in describing his roommate, "and I usually let him have his way. But he also fancies himself as quite the man with the ladies and doesn't think of himself as a fairy. But, of course, that's what he is—just as I am."

The homosexual contempt for the "faggot," the most obvious of homosexuals, is only too real. In it the homosexual reveals his gnawing fear of his precarious position in a "straight" world. "The last time I saw this faggot," a clean-cut-looking bartender, posing as straight, told me, "his cheeks were rouged and he wore a woman's hat. He was only thirty-five but he looked fifty-five. No self-respecting homosexual would have anything to do with him. His only chance was to buy what he wanted. But he hardly ever had any money, since the only work he could get was an occasional job as a 'female impersonator.' "

This type, he felt, was not only impractical but stupid. "They behave as though there were nobody but faggots in the world," the bartender said, "but before long they find themselves barred from everything. There's no place for you unless you play ball with society."

While they do so resentfully, many feel they have to pretend heterosexuality to win jobs and social acceptance. It isn't always easy. "One night," said the straight homosexual bartender, "I had to throw some faggots out of the place—the boss's orders—and I didn't know who I hated more—the faggots, the boss, or myself."

While he often says he prefers a lasting relationship, the adult homosexual seems quite ready to indulge in sex for sex's sake. And when he ventures forth on the prowl, he generally prefers somebody younger. This preoccupation with youth often borders on the pathological. One homosexual, a middle-aged businessman, chided an acquaintance his own age who had been arrested for molesting a thirteen-year-old youngster on a beach. "How could you do it?" the businessman said. "Think of the shame and disgrace!"

The other shrugged helplessly. "You can't imagine the thrill I got when I reached out and saw the look of disbelief, and then the horror, creep over the boy's face."

His friend drew back in dismay. "Why, you're not a homosexual," he shuddered, "you're a degenerate."

One day I was having lunch with a prominent sociologist and a dark, handsome youth he was trying to rehabilitate. "As long as I trust him," the sociologist said, indicating the smiling boy, "he won't let me down."

The young man nodded his agreement as his mentor fondly

continued. "I know," he said, "I could even trust him with a fourteen-year-old boy, because I did once as a sort of test and it worked out fine."

He turned for confirmation to the youth. "Now, couldn't I count on you?" he asked.

The youth, who had been recently asked to leave a New England college, smiled back calmly. "Oh yes," he said, "I would do nothing to disappoint you."

As the sociologist beamed, I inquired, "You mean you wouldn't be in the least bit interested?"

"Oh no," he said, "not unless I found him attractive."

To some homosexuals the laws which "discriminate" against them are part of society's hypocritical conspiracy to keep them from declaring themselves openly in every level of social or business life. "The straights are afraid," one told me bitterly, "of losing their sons."

Nevertheless, many insist they are as opposed as anybody else to homosexuals who prey on children, and yet justify relationships with teen-age boys by pointing out that many older heterosexuals are fascinated by teen-age girls. "How about Lolita?" one asked.

While they often talk of seeking help, they generally shy away from psychiatrists, ridiculing the contention that they are sick and can be helped by such therapy. "It is not we who are sick," a handsome middle-aged business executive assured me, "but that element of society which, through fear, refuses us equal status."

Honesty, to the homosexual, is a variable quality. To many, the man who gives up the comforts of society to declare his homosexuality reveals an honesty more admirable than Ben Franklin's. "How could anybody be more honest," one said admiringly, "than the two doctors who told their wives they were leaving them and their children—for each other?"

Out of defensiveness, perhaps, many homosexuals withdraw into an unreal world of their own. With an imbalance that is more than physical, their values and standards often become twisted out of all sense of proportion. Overly sensitive, many nurse slights or fancied slights to a point of utterly neurotic resentment. Some have turned against friends, family, and even their country because they have thought they were not properly treated. After the quite recent defection of two State Department aides to the Russians, it became known that one of the pair, officially described as homosexual, had become discontented and resentful to a degree where he lost all sight of reality. He was almost incredibly naïve politically and in his lack of hardheaded objectivity and stability fell prey to the transparent propaganda of the Russians. "He was blinded," an observer of the Washington scene stated, "by the intellectual arrogance which he had wrapped around himself as a protective cloak." And it was equally obvious that he had brooded long, before his fateful step, over the gap between his own extravagant self-appraisal and the more moderate—and practical—estimates of his superiors. "He was stewing about," another observer said, "in a world all his own."

Though maintaining they have only contempt for the effeminate, primping caricatures whom they charge with giving the whole group a bad name, many homosexuals are nevertheless privately indulgent of the capers of their brethren. Among themselves, for instance, many reveled in descriptions of the audience activity at the showing of a motion picture on homosexuality, laughing till the tears rolled down their cheeks.

"Most of the ushers were homosexual," one related, "and they seated the heterosexuals and other squares downstairs. They sent the homosexuals and sailors upstairs, where they camped it up and had a good time generally while occasionally looking at the movie." Some homosexuals "saw" the movie four or five times.

Many homosexuals have a sense of comedy which is distinctively their own. It is often self-mocking, reflecting itself in jokes ridiculing the dignity of the homosexual or his pretensions at being a respectable member of society. For instance, one story with wide currency among homosexuals goes like this: A young homosexual was brought before a judge on a morals charge. The judge, appraising the clean-cut, manly-looking figure before him, remarked: "I can't understand how a young man like you could become involved in something like this."

The young defendant responded, "It wasn't my fault, Your Honor. I was ruined by an older man when I was quite young."

"Oh yes," the judge said sympathetically, "and how did that happen?"

The homosexual explained that as a boy he had been walking through a park when the older man jumped out of some bushes and forced himself on him.

"Well, why didn't you run?" the judge inquired.

"I did, Judge, but he overtook me."

The judge was incredulous. "How could an old man catch up to you?"

The young homosexual shrugged. "I don't know, Judge. I ran as fast as I could, but my high heels kept getting in the way."

While it is true they are not always welcome in hotels, bars, restaurants, and other public places, homosexuals are generally tolerated unless they make themselves conspicuous by their dress and antics. However, there are dozens of bars in every large city in the country where their trade is more than welcome, no matter how they dress, primp, or otherwise "camp it up."

In a Greenwich Village bar, for instance, a reporter overheard one manly-looking homosexual introducing two friends. "Your friend is sweet," said one. "And you're sweet, too," responded the other, circling his arm around the shoulder of the third, "if you're a friend of his."

Homosexuality occasionally is found in several members of a family. However, homosexuals, understandably, resent any imputation that the quality is inherited. One homosexual, for example, was telling me about a younger brother who liked to dress in "drag"—women's attire—and camp it up at dances and other functions. "Funny thing about my brother," he said, "he wasn't homosexual, but he liked to go out with the gay boys, go to their parties, and dance with the worst faggots."

"Well, what makes you think he wasn't homosexual?" I asked.

"Because he wasn't," he said flatly. "I would have been the first to know since I watched him closely."

"Was anybody else in the family homosexual?" I asked.

He gave me a look of annoyance and said with a rasping voice, "What do you think it is—a contagious disease?"

As homosexuality is perhaps the greatest of all social taboos, homosexuals with standing in the community must be correspondingly discreet to maintain their position. In their approaches to other people many homosexuals strive to make their point without irrevocably committing themselves, and leave a road by which they can safely retreat if the advance is rebuffed or ignored. As a gimmick, some, in dealing with unknowns, tentatively bring the conversation around to homosexuality, then watch sharply for the slightest reaction. If the response is not unfavorable (no violent diatribes or hard suspicious stares), it may be considered safe to make the next overture. These approaches are made almost anywhere, at any time. In one instance, a young, attractive lawyer was sitting in his dentist's chair, when the dentist, pausing in his exploration of cavities, began casually to discuss the rising number of homosexual bars around the city, one or two in that very neighborhood. Wrapped up in thoughts of his aching gums, the patient nodded perfunctorily, hardly aware of what the dentist was saying. Apparently taking this gesture for interest, the dentist proceeded on his discourse of the bars, ridiculing them mildly, and then suggested that it might be amusing to make the rounds of a few of them—together. Just as he was about to say he wasn't interested, the lawyer patient was aware that the dentist was studying him with an odd intentness. "And when his hand casually dropped to my shoulder," the lawyer recalled, "I decided that I needed a new dentist."

To many homosexuals the bisexual is a fraud. As a matter of fact, they insist he is only a homosexual who is trying to fool himself and the ladies. The expression "A.C.-D.C." (alternating and direct current)—which is generally applied to bisexuals—draws only knowing smiles from the homosexual fraternity. "The bisexual," a homosexual told me, "is only a homosexual who lacks the courage of his convictions."

Nevertheless, I did meet bisexuals who appeared genuinely interested in men and women, who seemed to return their interest. For many of these women the bisexual provided a pleasant contrast to the all-masculine male. "After an unhappy marriage or love affair," said one divorcée, "many women seem to prefer less realistic relationships."

Although sneering at bisexuals, about half the homosexuals I met acknowledged some intimacy with women. But for the most part these were brief, desultory relationships from which they derived scant pleasure. The motivations were varied. Some were designed as cover-ups, others sprang from vanity.

Many homosexuals have even less patience with the latent or suppressed homosexual than with the bisexual. "He's too dumb to know what he is," a photographer told me, describing a married colleague. "But someday he'll wake up."

Attracted to their own sex, suppressed homosexuals frequently inhibit their desires to the point where they get into serious difficulties with themselves and sometimes with society.

They are not content with punishing themselves but seek also to punish their neighbors who so offend, a well-known authority said. "One should be extremely suspicious of the loud-mouthed habitué of a bar whose denunciations of homosexuals are frequent, vociferous, and persistent. Why is it so necessary for him to protest masculinity so loudly?"

Many homosexuals drink to excess. Many are alcoholics. As a matter of fact, some will commit an act of homosexuality only under the influence of liquor. "It numbs me," one homosexual observed. Many authorities see a definite tie between alcoholism and homosexuality. Some point out that many latent homosexuals, constantly at war within themselves, turn to alcohol for the "Dutch courage" they need for normal heterosexual relationships. And many homosexuals quote a survey, still unpublished, which allegedly indicates that 95 per cent of the alcoholics under study have a homosexual problem, secret or overt.

Younger homosexuals, groping in their confusion, are often trying to establish a sexual identity. "At first," a teen-age homosexual related, "I had no idea I preferred men—all I knew was that I didn't enjoy women."

For years, without consciously thinking of themselves as homosexuals, many young men indulge in homosexual practices. "I just did what a lot of other kids were doing," a high school senior said, "without classifying myself as anything, and then one day a girl I knew said, 'The trouble with you homosexuals is' . . ."

Lowest on the deviate's totem pole is perhaps the "rough trade"—male prostitutes who prey on homosexuals. "Today's rough trade," one said, "is tomorrow's competition."

Homosexuals seem to have no trouble recognizing one another. The old saw "It takes one to know one" proves itself a thousand times daily. There is the notably masculine stride, the lank haircut, the lingering look and handshake, and the subtly changing quality of voice and mien, with the inflection noticeably dipping or rising as circumstances warrant.

Among their own kind they nourish a quality of togetherness. This is often exemplified by the way they help one another when they can do so without stirring suspicion. "In some business concerns they favor each other for jobs not only because they prefer one another," an astute female observer noted, "but because it gives them a social recognition or status denied them by others."

They have a morbid preoccupation with homosexuality, concluding, almost automatically, that anybody showing interest in their problem—policeman, sociologist, psychiatrist, or newspaperman—is suspect himself.

So positive are they of this themselves, that they even caused an eminent researcher to doubt himself. "I began to wonder about my own masculinity," this researcher told me, "and one day I drove out to a deserted beach and sat staring out into the ocean, until common sense reasserted itself."

On a hair trigger emotionally, many homosexuals are given to temperamental outbreaks at the slightest provocation. To the *cognoscente*, familiar with their tears and tantrums, the expression, "He's a bitchy one," has acquired a connotation of the homosexual at his worst. Once, during the making of a picture, a well-known Hollywood star, a homosexual, was informed by his director that a friend of the star's, a daily visitor on the set, was to be barred thereafter as a distracting influence. The star flew into a frenzy and, jeopardizing a million-dollar production, furiously stomped off the set. "I won't be back," he pouted, "until you apologize to my friend."

The homosexual personality has been discussed frequently by the experts. At the Metropolitan Law Enforcement Conference, which drew homosexual protests, Brother Aquinas Thomas, F.S.C., a distinguished sociologist, underlined many of their distinctive traits and characteristics. "They do not like games of body contact," he said, "yet they may display some skill in events of individual co-ordination. They are usually helpless in a combative sense and are seldom known to fight. Yet they are known to flash rank to squelch smaller adversaries, and these outbursts of rage often take on the pattern of a tantrum."

In affairs of the heart, Brother Thomas indicated, they are equally unstable. "They are usually quite jealous," he said, "especially when there is competition for their particular friend. They develop noticeable crushes and, like a clinging vine, seem to need the approval and supportive strength their particular friend affords them. In this company they develop signs of sophistication, but if frustrated, easily pout."

He urged his audience of professional sociologists and penologists to be patient in dealing with this homosexual type. "We might contribute to maladjustment and psychic damage," Brother Thomas said, "by forcing such a one into combative sports or related athletics. In a quiet and not too obvious way we can break up particular friendships, and we can see to it that our passive activities, such as drama, speech, music, and arts, are not too much cluttered by these mortals."

CHAPTER IV

Cross-Country

THERE IS A universality about homosexuality that makes it almost endemic around the country. There is hardly a community of any consequence, homosexuals say, which doesn't have a park or bus station where strangers can soon become friends. In some cities the busiest street corners and the smartest hotels are contact centers for the curious wayfarer as the homosexual underground, a rather loose camaraderie of homosexuals, keeps apprising its growing membership of the best way to enjoy a strange town.

Meeting in their bars and clubs, homosexuals exchanging reminiscences pass on to one another pertinent details of homosexuality in America, warning against police and blackmailing hazards in some communities, praising others for the easy tolerance on which they thrive.

Before leaving town—any town—homosexuals check friends thoroughly for interesting addresses in the communities they were visiting. Traveling for pleasure, they prefer the carefree irresponsibility of transitory relationships in cities of distinction. Many gravitate to picturesque New Orleans, the lively home of the Mardi Gras, cosmopolitan San Francisco, which some call the Pearl of the West, and the holiday paradise of Miami. But they are equally at home in Chicago, Kansas City, Denver, and Detroit, where a good time can be had by any homosexual with a sensitized antenna which can distinguish friend from foe.

It is a matter of knowing where to go, and how to go about it. In New Orleans, where some stores have been facetiously known as "fruit stands," the gay set savors the rich continental flavor of the French Quarter. In San Francisco a large square opposite the St. Francis Hotel, in the heart of the downtown district, is rated by many as a busier recruiting center than Times Square. In certain cities in Texas and Missouri homosexuals head for the bus stations. In Boston they flock to famous Scollay Square—not far from the Common—which is a favorite haunt of sailors. Pershing Square, in Los Angeles, near several big hotels, is a popular meeting ground, and in Washington, the nation's capital, where deviates have been under intermittent attack, the well-dressed quietly frequent bars in the northwest sector. For activity, some Denver bars far exceed anything for which Manhattan bars have been closed tight. And in San Francisco even homosexuals have registered surprise at scenes in waterfront bars. Visiting in Philadelphia, the original City of Brotherly Love, homosexuals often make a beeline for stately Rittenhouse Square and Fairmount Park. In Florida, Miami's beautiful Bayfront Park has been well publicized by the homosexual underground, but is currently considered too well policed for comfort.

Not all homosexual havens abound in large cities. Even in dreary little by-stations in the Carolinas and Georgia, enroute to Florida, homosexuals report interesting encounters. "I've never been any place in the country," said a veteran traveling salesman, "that I couldn't find a place. If I stood around a bus terminal long enough, and looked interested, somebody else would invariably get interested, too."

Often a community is the last to suspect that it may be a harbor for homosexuals. Long before a stunned citizenry of Waukesha, Wisconsin, was aware of what was going on regularly in one of its most beautiful parks, the homosexual underground was fully alert to the situation. After the arrest of ten men in a series of raids on the park, which was also frequented by families on innocent outings, flabbergasted Waukesha police learned that in public washrooms as far away as Milwaukee and Detroit, was scrawled this advice for the knowledgeable: "Try Frame Park, Waukesha."

Those arrested in the park represented virtually a cross section of America. There were a priest, schoolteacher, dentist, accountant, waiter, business executive, athlete, and a respected educator.

Even the district attorney and the chief of police were admittedly shocked by not only the incidence of the homosexuality itself, but by the prominence of the accused. For many in the community it was a shock from which they would not easily recover. "I was always so sure I knew everyone in the community and they were such fine people," a Waukesha housewife said. Then she added with a mournful shake of her head, "I was so sure—now I can never be sure again."

To many homosexuals making quick stopovers, time is of

39

the essence. "We don't have time to go rooting around," a homosexual traveler reported, "when we're on business." Anticipating a brief visit to New Orleans, a homosexual brought along a list of interesting bars in the Quarter, supplied by friends. Somehow he mislaid the list. Forgetting the names, but remembering some descriptions, he decided to explore the Quarter for himself. Poking his head into several places, he had covered three or four blocks before he tentatively edged into one spot and was confronted by a bartender with bleached blond hair and earrings. "Come in, girl," the bartender said reassuringly, "you're in the right place."

The homosexual laughed about it later. "I guess he'd seen a thousand like me come up to the door."

In some cities the fashionable areas are highly popular with homosexuals. In the City of Brotherly Love two homosexuals were standing around Rittenhouse Square, watching a crowd mill around curiously, as a visiting potentate checked into a nearby hotel. With an expression of utter boredom and distaste one homosexual said to the other: "Why are these people making all that fuss about a prince, when there's a queen on every corner on the Square?"

Other cities, known for conservatism, have shared in the recent homosexual trend. Absent for years from Baltimore, a homosexual returned to find his favorite haunt had disappointingly disappeared. But before he even had a chance to reconnoiter, he observed two obvious swishes mincing along a downtown street. "I just followed them for a few blocks," he observed blithely, "and they led me into one of the gayest bars I've ever seen."

Many homosexuals, who thought New York the only real center of homosexuality, have been pleasantly surprised by the tolerance in other areas. "While they were shutting bars in New York," reported a middle-aged homosexual who made a recent cross-country tour, "I discovered they were far more enlightened in Chicago, St. Louis, and Carmel by the Sea."

In San Francisco, in a rough bar near the waterfront, the traveler saw the kind of activity which had endeared Frisco to the less conservative of his cohorts. "As you walked in," he said, "it looked like any other waterfront spot, with a lot of characters standing around drinking beer. But then, with my friend who was known locally, we walked downstairs. The room was dark, hazy with smoke, but you could see well enough to look twice. At the bar everything possible was going on between gay boys, while a few tables away men sat sipping drinks and not paying any attention. As I watched the gay boys, I was almost equally amazed to overhear the next table conversation. In all of this they were discussing politics, and one chap was saying, 'Do you honestly think Rockefeller will ever make it?' And the other, frowning deliberately as though he were in the library of the Union League Club, and, shaking his head, 'A good man, but a little on the liberal side.' "

In Denver, which had little of San Francisco's reputation for liberality, he was even more surprised to find a similar lack of restraint in a cellar bar to which friends had taken him his first night in town. "There was only one difference," he said. "Nobody was interested in Rockefeller or Nixon."

Even in staid old cities like Quebec gay boys report pleasant interludes, in areas which homosexuals seem to have marked off for themselves. "From my first look at Quebec," a homosexual salesman reported, "I felt doomed to a dull two weeks of business. However, visiting a hotel bar, I overheard the promenade along Dufferin Terrace favorably mentioned. The next day, strolling down the promenade, my eye caught that of a young fellow passing in the opposite direction. I stopped, turned, and smiled as I saw he had done the same. Retracing our steps, we got to talking and a half hour later we were having tea in his apartment. I never did get his last name straight, but he was a medical student, brilliant, and I found the next two weeks very interesting. I shall always remember Canada fondly."

Homosexuals find college towns particularly interesting but complain it is often difficult for outsiders to break into student cliques. Fear is the great dissuader. "Many of these kids are so fearful of exposure," a middle-aged homosexual explained, "that an occasional fling with a stranger is all they will risk."

Nevertheless, outsiders frequently invade the halls of ivy. In one southern college city of some size a professor reported that one of the men's washrooms in a campus building had become a rendezvous for downtown deviates preying on students. "In one month," he said, "with guards posted near the only entrance, three hundred and fifty homosexuals were caught, and only two had any connection with the university." In some strange way, he pointed out, the homosexual underground had established the room as a rendezvous, even though it was hard to get to and pretty much of a trap.

41

When homosexuality becomes so flagrant that complaints begin to appear in the letter-to-the-editor columns, police crackdowns usually follow. In Los Angeles, homosexuals say, the police are especially tough, possibly because the film industry attracts so many potential homosexuals who have flocked to Hollywood to sell their looks and talents. Failing in their aim, many young men, turning to "hustling" homosexuals, have sought easy money elsewhere. "More gay boys have been mugged and robbed in L.A.," a well-traveled homosexual said, "than any city in the country. And if the pretty boys don't get you, the cops will."

Wherever they are, homosexuals watch for the least glance or gesture which will indicate whether their interest is returned. "Homosexuals have a sixth sense nonhomosexuals can never develop," said a homosexual with friends all over the map. "Normally, when I hit a strange town, I head for the best hotel, entering the bar during the cocktail hour. There are always a few of the boys milling around with the rest. I take a few minutes to single them out, strike up a leisurely conversation, and eventually inquire where the activity is." Occasionally, the strangers are so responsive that the search ends there. More frequently, another bar, in a different area, is recommended. Only once did he receive a false steer. "I had gotten around to the usual question," he recalled, "and, following directions carefully, wound up in a lesbian joint." He was sure his instinct had not failed him. "They were gay and they knew what I wanted, but I guess they were telling a stranger to keep off their ranch."

In rummaging around the country for new contacts experienced homosexuals are particularly careful not to say anything that could be used against them. "Even if you've figured it right, you can still be wrong," a homosexual pointed out, "if the 'right' man turns out to be a cop."

Confident they can tell a homosexual anywhere, in any street or hotel lobby, some homosexuals claim they can name at least ten for every one spotted by a sharp-eyed heterosexual. Many idly pick out random gay boys for their private amusement. Sauntering up Fifth Avenue from Fiftieth Street to Fifty-ninth, at Central Park, and then wending their way slowly back, two office workers kept a mental tally of passing homosexuals. Their walk concluded, they jotted down the totals and compared them. Each, independently, had counted to one hundred, presumably verifying the other's judgment. Pleased with themselves, they were smiling benignly when, suddenly, one's smiled faded. "I wonder," he said, "how many times we were counted?"

But even the least fallible acknowledge they may slip up in appraising the unpredictable English, by mistaking manners for effeminacy and more. "I had met this handsome young Englishman vacationing in Italy," a gay American reported, "and we became friendly. After tennis he'd come back to my room and sprawl over the bed in shorts, talking in that odd way of his." Thinking the young man was being rather obvious, the American decided to oblige. A look of utter disbelief crept over the Englishman's handsome features and he broke up in laughter. "You'll have to excuse me, old boy," he said finally, in his piping voice, "but do you really take me for a Nancy Boy?"

While many homosexuals prefer to lose themselves in the anonymity of the big city, smaller communities have been rocked by scandals which indicated homosexuality was commonplace in everyday life. In Michigan revelations of widespread homosexuality among teachers and students were made following the arrest of a Bay City, Michigan, principal and two teachers. Many Michiganders, who had considered homosexuality outside the pale of neighborly behavior, were shocked by state-police charges that the teachers, functioning as a loosely organized ring, had wrongfully instructed many of their students.

After looking away for years, officials at Provincetown, Massachusetts, finally made a concerted effort to rid the Cape Cod resort of its "homosexual element" when conservative summer visitors began packing their bags. Some of the town fathers thought the situation sufficiently urgent to warrant a house-to-house appeal, warning that the community was "faced with a situation which bids fair to undermine our morals, our business, in fact, our very existence as a respectable summer resort."

Calling for a public crusade to eliminate the deviates corrupting their youth, the selectmen chided townspeople for apathy and shortsightedness. "Unbelievable as it may seem," they said, "they [the homosexuals] have their friends, defenders, and supporters among our own people. Many who run lodginghouses willingly house them. The night-club operators cater to them."

The agitation, long building up, was touched off by a mother who said she was leaving the community after many happy years. She said her sons—and others—had been seduced by deviates who cavorted on the beach and sand dunes during the day in questionable bar and "literary clubs" at night, cajoling innocent youngsters with marijuana and other narcotics.

For sheer eroticism New York has had nothing to rival the homosexual ring in South Bend, Indiana, where two exclusive clubs, presided over by queens, operated for the benefit of young aristocrats and the working class. Drawing recruits from as far off as Chicago and Detroit, the membership had swollen to several hundred before police cracked down on deviates for widespread seductions of teen-agers.

Even the police were astounded by the club rules. The upper class, priding itself on its intellectual activity, did not mingle with the proletariat, though both groups, according to police, were dedicated to the common purpose of "satisfying their own lust and recruiting younger boys as members."

The intellectuals combined their intellectual pursuits with the most debasing forms of eroticism. Lacking these intellectual interests, the workingman's club practised even cruder forms of diversion.

None of this comes as a surprise to homosexuals. According to the best informed, there are hundreds of Bay Cities, South Bends, and Provincetowns in the country. "Just skim the surface of almost any town," a widely traveled homosexual observed, "and you'll find the homosexual underground."

The homosexual underground is really more of a grapevine, by which homosexuals contact one another, and it works swiftly and wonderfully.

In New York a magazine was anxious to reach a young sportsman with whom an editor had discussed an article on hunting. Not having an address or telephone number, the editor phoned an elderly publicity man who had introduced the sportsman weeks before. The publicist, a recognized homosexual of the Old Auntie type, had no idea where the young man was but promised to get in touch with him, saying, "I'll drop around and see the bartender tonight."

The editor was mystified. "The bartender," he exclaimed, "what would he know about it?"

The publicity man became vague. "Oh," he said, "many of Richard's friends patronize the bar, and the bartender can ask them."

Less than twenty-four hours later young Richard phoned

the magazine editor from a hunting lodge in Canada. "I understand," he said, "you want to see me about the article."

Out of curiosity the editor inquired of the publicist how the young man had been found so quickly in the wilds of Canada. The publicity man explained. "He left word with friends. The bartender told the friends I was interested." He smiled. "Of course, they would tell *me*."

Parting from New York has not been such sorrow as many homosexuals have thought. Temporarily assigned to so wholesome a midwestern, middle-class municipality as Kansas City (Missouri), a Manhattan businessman, a confirmed homosexual, found the prospect a cheerless one. But not long after his transfer he discovered the Missouri city could be as hospitable as his home town. "It was a bit quieter," George recalled, "but there were bars where you could meet in the heart of town." And the need for secretiveness enhanced the excitement of encounters in a community where a known homosexual might well have been ostracized.

In time George shared an apartment with a homosexual and found himself wrapped up in a circle of new friends. Some were of distinguished family and enjoyed common intellectual pursuits, openly; other pursuits, less openly.

"It was a very informal group," George recalled. "One day this chap, whom I had seen around, but had never talked to, came to our flat and asked for my roommate. Roger was away, but this boy put his foot in the door and said, 'You know, you are most attractive. I don't think Roger would mind.' I found him equally attractive, and I was sure Roger wouldn't mind, since I had no intention of telling him. However, I don't think he would have been shocked. I remember his telling me that he once woke up in a rooming house and found the landlady's husband in his room. It didn't bother him."

While acknowledging that the most immoral woman might have bridled at such casualness, George felt he was only being honest. "Gay boys," he observed, "don't see much point to playing games. Why lose all that time?"

Directness seems to be the most effective approach. In downtown Baltimore, just out for an airing, a salesman exchanged searching looks with a passing youth. The youth promptly paused, edged toward a store, and began window-shopping. Soon the salesman was peering at the same window. "Look," he said lightly, "don't let a couple of old hands like us waste time in preliminaries."

It worked.

In resort areas, particularly where the beach is the major attraction and life is more informal, homosexual identification is usually bolder and more dramatic. Walking five abreast on the Atlantic City boardwalk, homosexuals clad in bright shirts and flannels spotted a group approaching from the opposite direction. As they passed, they traded searching stares and the respective end men, without breaking stride, simultaneously cried out, "Swish." As one explained later, "It was a spontaneous sort of greeting, like two Americans recognizing each other abroad."

There are many ways homosexuals recognize one another when away from their home base. In Pittsburgh, for instance, "Grandma Williams" is the name of a well-known male dowager who has enjoyed some celebrity in homosexual circles throughout the state of Pennsylvania. Two older homosexuals, cruising partners, catching the eye of a younger man in a "mixed" bar in Philadelphia frequented by both homosexuals and heterosexuals, talked to him guardedly for several minutes without being able to classify him. The conversation was getting nowhere when one of the older men asked the younger where he came from. Looking the other squarely in the eye, he said: "Pittsburgh. My grandmother lives there."

Immediately, all reserve vanished; the three finished their drinks and left together, arms intertwined like old friends or lovers.

Many homosexuals are remittance men, paid to stay away from home. From all over the country they pour into such centers as New York and San Francisco, where they can live as homosexuals without embarrassing or ruining their families back home.

Fresh from Atlanta, Georgia, one scion of wealthy family was maintained in a luxurious town house on Manhattan's East Side by a father eternally grateful that his son and heir had seen fit to lose himself in a city far from home. From time to time the son dutifully visited the family's old manse but was always glad to hurry on to New Orleans or get back to New York. He objected to Atlanta's stiff "segregation" policy. "Homosexuals and heterosexuals have separate bars," he lamented, "and never the twain shall meet."

Traveling abroad, American homosexuals find themselves equally at home in the great capitals of Europe. London, Rome, Berlin, Athens, Copenhagen, and others have the lavender carpet out for the eager visitors. In many of these centers male prostitutes make a special appeal to the rich tourist trade and openly patrol areas frequented by Americans. In a few capitals, such as Lisbon and Madrid, where public displays are drastically discouraged by police action, touring Americans report discreet activity in bars, restaurants, and hotels, which are soon known to the venturesome travelers.

Very few homosexuals, save for a handful of defectors, show any desire to holiday in Russia, where living is anything but easy, and the government, concerned with perpetuating the species for its farms, factories, and armed forces, has little patience with homosexuals or homosexuality. "You don't even dare mention the word there," an American traveler said, "but they do have some in the ballet."

In London, touring homosexuals get a warm welcome from the numerous fraternity there. The choice of friendships and meeting grounds is wide and varied. Some visitors savor the Bohemian flavor of the quaint bars and coffeehouses in Soho, where beatniks, prostitutes, and would-be intellectuals hobnob with a fine indiscrimination. Others patronize elegant restaurants and bottle clubs in Mayfair and Kensington, where introductions are arranged through the universal language of homosexuality—the long stare, the short nod, and the middle-size, enigmatic smile.

After the necessity for caution in the United States, the visiting American finds it's a refreshing change to be able to comport himself without much caring what anybody says or thinks. "It is wonderful," a middle-aged American businessman said, "to be able to travel about in Denmark, Holland, Sweden, and the rest, where people are so civilized they don't give a damn what other people do. Indeed, the only people who seem to care at all are the straight Americans you meet abroad—and they look down their noses at you."

Although Rome is a favorite spot for the vacationing gay set, the fraternity found it strangely subdued at first sight last summer, when the Eternal City was playing host to the 1960 World Olympic games and the streets and hotels were thronged with sports lovers from every corner of the globe. But below the surface it was the same old congenial Rome, homosexuals reported, with swarms of male prostitutes within easy reach of the main hotels and pensions. "While some of the more conspicuous spots were shut down for the duration of the track and field events," a homo-

47

sexual reported, "there was as much activity as ever around the Spanish Steps in the heart of Rome."

Many homosexuals were disappointed by the temporary closing of a Turkish bath not far from the Spanish Steps, which had long been a favorite hangout of the international embassy crowd. The landmark was shuttered, just as the throngs were beginning to pour into Rome for the games. The only explanation offered visiting homosexuals was a sign which announced: Closed for repairs.

Elsewhere in Italy, in Venice, the reception was warm enough to please the most exacting. As in other years, the tables bordering picturesque St. Mark's Square were adorned with impromptu welcoming groups. By no means were most of these male prostitutes. However, returning homosexuals reported that many young Italians, while distinctively handsome and gracious, made a point of getting paid, even when they didn't seem to be impelled by gain. "They would come up to your hotel room," a puzzled American related, "and then make a little speech about how they were naturally not doing this for nothing." Some, though disdaining money, would still walk off with a trinket or an article of clothing, or even a small bedside clock, anything that was lying around handy. "I got the idea," an American traveler said, "that in this curious way they justified their behavior, by telling themselves they had behaved this way for material reasons only, and not because *they* were in any way homosexual."

Nevertheless, many visiting Americans felt that the European youth, out seeking touring homosexuals, was more amoral than homosexual, more concerned with making money than friends, and not much caring what anybody thought of them. "They thought of themselves as being as much in the business of supplying the tourist, as were the small shops and street hawkers," one homosexual observed.

In Paris, the City of Light (and of Love), many homosexuals were surprised to learn that comparatively little homosexuality was carried on openly, and the Parisians, when they did prowl, were fascinated by good, old-fashioned feminine pulchritude. With Parisians, it seems, *viva la différence* is still the ticket.

Across the continent, in Greece, birthplace of Western culture and democracy, American homosexuals had no trouble getting to know modern Athens. Reception committees, informal, of course, were out early and late. The cab drivers were the first to make the visiting deviates feel at home, a few minutes after they had landed at the airport or pulled into the train depot. The cabbies were a fount of information, once they had satisfied themselves their passenger was the right type. "First," a homosexual recalled, "they'd talk about girls, prostitutes usually, and then they'd inevitably get around to the other thing. They'd tell you where to go for anything, what to pay, and usually wound up offering themselves."

But touring homosexuals didn't have to look farther than Constitution Square, right in the heart of Athens proper. "All you had to do was sit down," a homosexual recalled, "and somebody would be along presently."

The "password" was often a door key, which the strollers would keep tossing in their hands as they talked to Americans, indicating, one homosexual explained, that a room went with the key.

All too often, Americans abroad were dismayed by the crudity of the foreign approach. One day, in Constitution Square, a visitor from the States was enoying a warm sunny day when a dark youth stopped in front of his bench and said without preliminary: "You English?"

The visitor shook his head. "No, American."

Encouraged by even this brief response, the young Greek's eyes brightened.

"Ah, American," he said. "You got American cigarette then?"

After lighting the proffered cigarette he inhaled deeply and then smiled warmly. "You know," he said, in faltering English, "I live in America one time. San Francisco. Work with merchant marine. Great city, San Francisco. Live there four, five weeks, like American."

The American nodded, and the hospitable young man, seeming to warm up to his task, then offered his services— out of the common bond of their Americanism—as interpreter, guide, or general handyman. "Anything you want I get you," he volunteered brightly, "even me."

Some homosexuals reported distressing experiences. While male prostitutes did not make extravagant demands, rarely insisting on more than a few dollars, they were, like their American counterparts, adept at the art of blackmail. "They would keep coming back to your hotel," a homosexual said, "and if you didn't pay them again and again, they would stand outside your room in their underwear and howl until they raised everybody in the hotel."

CHAPTER V

Paradise Island

IN GREEK MYTHOLOGY Narcissus was a beautiful youth who fell in love with his own reflection and pined away until he was transformed into a flower. Steeped in narcissism, many homosexuals are body worshipers who chase the sun—and excitement—from one gay resort to the other. In Europe the international gay set frolic quietly on the Riviera, mingling almost unrecognizably with other elements of society. In Cannes, Juan-les-Pins, and Nice they are happiest disporting themselves on the beaches. Clad in male versions of the bikini, displaying supple expanses of skin, they congregate off Naples on the sunny island of Ischia, sometimes known as the "isle of men," and in beautiful Capri. They cavort blithely in the bathing resort of Lido, washed by Venetian waters, and are moving into lovely Majorca and the islands that speck the seas off Greece.

In the States they have invaded family resorts like Provincetown and have taken over until they wore out their welcome. And they made the Pacific sand strip at Santa Monica justly famous as "Muscle Beach" from their fanatical devotion to body-building. But nowhere, at no time, not even in the declining days of ancient Greece and Rome, have they played and gamboled with greater freedom and frivolity than on a small splinter of an island some forty miles from New York. Known as Fire Island, it is only a few miles south of Long Island, which it parallels, and is easy to get to by train or car, and ferry.

This lush resort, with the best beaches in the world, has become such a haven—and heaven—for homosexuals that the vast majority of colonists, who are conventional heterosexuals, often wince defensively when "confessing" where they summer. For though the homosexual colony is confined to two or three of the many lush, green communities dotting the narrow island, the impact of their behavior has been overwhelming. The most lurid resort by far to which homosexuals have swarmed from less tolerant island communities is Cherry Grove, the clump of cottages most New Yorkers think of when they speak of Fire Island.

It has been often said of Cherry Grove (or Fire Island) that anything goes. Staid business executives from all over the country, artists, actors, truck drivers, clerks, hairdressers, educators, and sundry other professionals all lose themselves and their inhibitions on the transforming island. Prominent men, spotting each other on the Cherry Grove beach or walk, have simultaneously come to their first realization that the other was gay. The weekend home of a television executive is pridefully pointed out as the place where many a young career has been launched. And in some reverence homosexuals point to a shoddy cottage where, they say, a noted playwright gave the first assist to a budding young actor who climbed to fame with this break. Others insist it was Provincetown—so fleeting is fame.

Attracted by reports of Roman-like Bacchanalia, thousands of curious, ferrying the few miles from the mainland, swoop down on the tiny community, watching with mingled fascination, delight, and revulsion as the true habitués of Cherry Grove gaily remove the mask they have patiently worn all week in the city.

The island, with its cozy air of intimacy, or perhaps the feeling of togetherness derived from being in the majority, seems to do something to the weekenders. Five minutes after they get off the boat young men who had seemed quite normal and inconspicuous on the way across are taking mincing steps, bending their wrists, and simpering as they talk. They can hardly wait till they get to cottages to change from ordinary business suits or slacks into colorful costumes. And they are soon laughing and talking loudly among themselves as they head for the center of mass activity—the beach.

The broad beach and the quaint wooden walks are common pickup places, as are the restaurants, hotels, bars, and even grocery stores. On the dance floors it is common to see young man clasped together, swaying rhythmically to the music in close embrace. Lipsticked and rouged like loose ladies of the Old West, some are garbed in women's attire, and others sport bikinis. Whatever their regalia, they blithely brandish their homosexuality to each other—and a gaping world.

"Here we are the majority," one explained seriously, "and we can do as we like."

Each seems to outdo the other in flaunting his bizarre costume as a badge of distinction—and deviation. It is not unusual to see homosexuals, wearing bright purple or orange shirts, tight pirate trousers, and brilliant scarves strolling arm in arm down to the beaches, occasionally turning to peck the other on the cheek or lips. Walking by one spacious home, set back in the bushes, I distinguished two beautifully muscled young men clad in trunks, looking like movie idols with their lithe tanned torsos, standing in the open doorway, one holding his arms around the other, bending him back in a Hollywood-like embrace and then leaning over to warmly kiss his partner squarely on the lips. As I stood transfixed, hypnotized in spite of myself, the dominating figure spotted me on the crosswalk and leisurely reached out with one arm and swung the door slowly shut, without once relinquishing the other arm.

Many of the residents, and their guests, present such garish figures as they stalk in drag down the narrow walks that other homosexuals are often moved to wonder. One elderly homosexual who sported a gay parasol was ironically dubbed "Mr. Clean" because he appeared to have scraped the closets clean for his whimsical getup.

The beach itself, with its broad expanse sloping down to the breaking surf, was clogged with nonparticipants. Nobody made any pretense of athletic activity, including bathing. They had come to sit around and admire the surrounding wildlife.

Surprisingly, there were a few women on the beach, sitting in small knots by themselves. Three or four beautiful young girls, with trim figures, nodded to several coolly watching gay boys. "Lesbians," a gay boy explained, "models. They come out here because they don't want to be bothered by a lot of men."

Hunched together in campfire-like circles, the homosexuals chatted and took stock of the beach; occasionally preening themselves in the sun, combing back their hair, buffing their nails, or sauntering stiff-legged to the edge of the water, much as the male animal seeks to impress susceptible young females with his manliness. Other homosexuals were idly flexing muscles or zealously applying sun-tan lotions to each other's bodies. Meanwhile, they kept up their lively chatter gossiping about "heartthrobs" and "lovers" as though they were girls and occasionally ribbing one of the group who had met with an unexpected repulse.

"Didn't you know," one inquired with a giggle, "that he was taken?" All joined in the laughter, as though it was a good joke at the rejected one's expense. Their target responded goodnaturedly with a play on words that evoked further laughter. "He may be taken yet," he promised, with a droll wink.

Another conversation, occupying a smaller group, carried easily a dozen feet away. The subject was a youth of twenty-five or twenty-six with a slight, almost frail form, delicately white in contrast to the supple brownness around him. On approaching the group he had been greeted by a mocking barrage of gaily waving handkerchiefs.

"Look who's here," one youth cried. "Little Boy Blue."

"Whaddya doing, slumming?" another called.

The new arrival looked aggrieved. "I'm sorry, fellows, but I found I just couldn't stay away. I guess it was nostalgia or something, but I had to come out here again."

"Who asked you?" another young man said.

The youth flushed. "You boys don't understand. I didn't stay away because I wanted to. I got married."

"Married?" There were incredulous gasps. "But who would marry you, Harold?"

Harold shrugged. "Oh, I guess I had to. My family kept after me, mostly my father, and so I finally did it."

There was a ripple of laughter. "Well," one said, "where is your wife?"

"I left her home. I didn't think she'd understand." This brought on new gales of laughter.

"I just couldn't keep away," Harold said. "I thought of all of you out here enjoying yourselves, and I just had to come out."

"Then why did you get married?"

"Honest, boys, I couldn't help it. I had to please Dad. But I kept thinking of you guys, and so here I am."

"All right, Harold," one boy said. "Sit down and tell us all about your wife."

At that laughter was so loud that other nearby groups glanced over curiously. The bridegroom dutifully sat down and tried to check the fusillade that followed. The banter went on for hours, until the sun glazed over and they all straggled off to their cottages.

There is a soft sensuous beauty about the island which seems to communicate itself to the homosexual colony. After dark, while some sun worshipers gambol indoors, others flock to the moon-washed beaches and groves, their senses sharpened by the tang of salt air and ocean breeze. So absorbed do revelers become in their carousing that on one occasion, at least, a house burned to the ground before anybody turned in an alarm.

Merrymakers roam the walks and beaches, sipping from beer cans, and gaily invite passing boys to parties not yet started. Traveling by beach buggy, safaris from neighboring Fire Island communities swell the ranks of the celebrants. For the average straight visitor one trip was usually enough. However, some made the excursion so regularly that friendly observers warned: "One more visit, and you may never get back."

Though visitors are tolerated, habitués prefer to hobnob among themselves, retiring in the early hours to cottages they rent from old-stock natives across the bay who do not permit their distaste for their tenants to keep them from taking their money.

The community itself is a conglomerate of small cottages which bring lavish rentals and resplendent homes finished off with rare delicacy and taste by the artistically inclined. As many as a dozen homosexuals occupy some cottages, appropriately named in keeping with domiciliary humor. For example: Sin-erama, Roman Holiday, Queen for a Day, Trade Mark, Man Trap, Hothouse, Les Boys, and dozens of others as homosexuals laughingly point out that it pays to advertise.

Although a hopeless minority, some heterosexuals cling to the island through business necessity. And though most seem impervious to the Mardi Gras-like procession, a few are sorely tried explaining it away to unsophisticated menials, house servants, and baby sitters they are afraid of losing. Many consider little white lies justifiable in the circumstances. The teen-age nurse for the children of the community doctor, brought up from the South, watched wide-eyed the parade of oddly dressed males and finally turned to her mistress with an uneasy giggle. "What's all that, ma'am?" she asked. The doctor's wife, loath to discuss the complexities of homosexuality with a sixteen-year-old girl of modest education, fell back on a euphemism. "Oh, they're having a masquerade party here tonight, Amanda, and they're all getting ready." Satisfied, the girl later went shopping at the community grocery store. On her return she was bubbling over with fresh tidings for her mistress. "Oh, ma'am," she said, "they're having a masquerade party over at the grocery store, too."

Sporadically, local people at Sayville, a crossover point on the mainland, and surrounding Fire Island communities protest the wanton exhibitions and demand greater decorum. Once, following a homicide which climaxed a lovers' quarrel, a police crackdown discouraged such flagrant activity for a while. But the reform movement soon lost out to economics. "The business people ask us to clamp down," a police official said, "and then complain that we are keeping business away."

Even homosexuals, in the wealthier, more conservative brackets, shrinking from the excesses which threaten to tar them with the same "faggotty" brush, have shown their distaste for transvestism and other effeminate aspects of deviation by moving to the mainland, beginning new, discreet colonies in the fashionable East Hampton and Southampton areas. "They don't have to behave like that," said a homosexual who had moved to exclusive East Hampton, "but they're just dying for attention."

Mindful of this exodus, which is a continuing one, a few restaurants and inns have tried to reverse the trend by discouraging homosexuals who feature female attire, make-up and hairdos. "We want only nice boys here," said a lady proprietor who runs an ocean-front restaurant with her husband, "none of that riffraff that gives a place a bad name." New arrivals, particularly strangers, are scrutinized closely as they come through the door.

When a group of four homosexuals entered the dining room, wearing slacks and so made up they could hardly be distinguished as male, they were allowed to stumble around by themselves until they finally found a table. The waiters, good-looking young homosexuals, so clean-cut they resembled lifeguards, passed them disdainfully, heads high. While everybody pretended not to notice, they nervously sat there trying to look unconcerned. Finally, a captain suggested that if they wanted to be served, they should try the hotel across the street. "We don't serve ladies without male escorts," he said dryly.

Without a word, but glancing coolly, almost defiantly about them, they slowly wended their way out the door, presumably for the recommended hotel.

There is a saying in Cherry Grove that all wildlife eventually winds up at The Place on a Saturday night. This Saturday was no exception. The bar itself was jammed with homosexuals, lesbians, curiosity-seekers, and tough townies from nearby mainland communities.

The townies could be picked out of the crowd by their surly stares with which they greeted each newcomer. Many jammed the long barroom which led through a hall into the main dining room, cleared for dancing. There bedlam prevailed, volatile emotions at trigger point after hours of drinking. The scene was one long to be remembered.

To music blaring from a record player, males danced together, some in bare feet with bracelets dangling from arms and ankles, mocking the way couples ordinarily dance. They giggled as they pressed cheek to cheek or clashed together in rhumbas and sambas. On the edge of the floor, forming a semicircle, spectators were watching the performance with amusement. Several of the town huskies, making a Saturday night of "watching the queers" sat grimly on the sidelines, baiting the performers. With a single exception the dancing duets didn't even turn their heads.

One heavily muscled young man, evidently new to the island, angrily broke off from an ardent embrace with his male partner and turned menacingly at thinly veiled jibes about his virility. Gleefully, the townies sent up a chorus of mock falsettos, piping mockingly, "Look at the big muscle man." Their target, face flushed with drink, advanced belligerently, breaking away from the restraining hand of his partner, a sensitive-faced, blond boy who might have been described as beautiful had he been a girl.

As he recklessly moved forward, the leader of the toughs, a much heavier man, crouched to meet him, snarling, "C'mon, muscle man, I'm waiting for you."

It quickly became apparent that the homosexual, despite his beautiful physique, was no match for the townie. A bully-type streetfighter, he soon knocked his adversary to the dance floor and flailed his face and body with fists. In a wild frenzy, straddling his helplessly writhing victim, the townie battered the lighter man unmercifully, banging his head against the floor with a sickly thump. When spectators and friends moved in to intercede, the bully's pals deftly smashed the tops off beer bottles and faced the crowd threateningly. "Take that, muscle man," the townie kept snarling as he continued to pound his victim's head against the hardwood floor.

Only when all fight and consciousness left the homosexual and his body sagged limply did the townie halt his savage attack. The guards then lowered their jagged bottles and horrified companions moved in, raised their semiconscious friend, and tenderly carried him to the house where he was a weekend guest.

The house, a lavish affair, was spacious, decorated by

ornate statuary, busts of early Romans and Greeks perched on costly mahogany pedestals. There was a fountain in the middle of the floor. Animal skins were strewn about. Two beautiful poodles, fashionably sheared, looked on curiously, barking furiously as each newcomer bustled into the house. "Silence, please," somebody admonished shrilly.

The victim was carried into a small bedroom, off the main living room. The host, a handsome, healthily complexioned man in his forties, blanched when the body was brought in. A doctor was immediately summoned, and while the examination was proceeding the host, an advertising executive, delivered a stirring indictment of the townies. He explained to the doctor that Frank was "a nice, sweet young man. He's a gentle boy and would never cause any trouble."

Frank's dancing partner, the young, beautiful blond boy, clad in Bermuda shorts, hovered tearfully around the bed, where the victim, now conscious, was wildly muttering what he would do to his assailant.

"If I live," he said, "I'll kill that Brownie. I'll get him, I swear, I swear."

The blond boy, called Max, tried to quiet him. "Just think of getting well," he said.

The host, who was obviously embarrassed and ill at ease, cut in, "Oh, so that's who it was, Brownie."

He turned apologetically to the doctor, who was now applying cold compresses to his patient's head. He seemed anxious to explain. "That Brownie and his gang keep coming over from the mainland, Sayville, begging for trouble, knowing that nobody will do anything about it."

"Do you know this boy very well?" the doctor asked.

The host, Ernest, hesitated, and then said, as three or four other homosexuals looked at him, "Not very long, but he's a splendid fellow."

"Well, this boy has been hurt badly," said the doctor. "I think somebody here should notify the police."

The homosexuals laughed harshly. "They wouldn't do anything about it," Ernest said.

"Well," the doctor said, "you could always bring charges yourself."

Ernest grimaced. "You don't understand how they are out here, doctor. Just because a man sleeps with another man, he has to put up with all kinds of insult and injury. These townies know we can't afford the publicity, that's what encourages them."

The doctor shrugged. "Well, keep putting the cold compresses on all night, and we'll decide tomorrow whether we should put him in a hospital."

Tears began to stream down Max's cheek. Ernest fidgeted nervously. He turned to the other homosexuals. "That Brownie," he said, "he's been coming over here for two or three years causing trouble."

"Yes," one called Charles said, "if it wasn't Frank, it would have been somebody else. He's always looking for trouble."

Ernest laughed. "It isn't hard to figure him out. He's always screaming about homosexuals. The poor boy ought to see a psychiatrist."

Charles sneered. "He might not like what he hears."

Max looked up interestedly. "Do you mean he's fighting it?"

Ernest replied impatiently. "It's simple psychology. He'll be a lot more agreeable when he makes up his mind to what he is."

The doctor, poker-faced, gave the moaning patient a sedative. "That should keep him till morning," he said.

As he picked up his bag, Ernest approached him anxiously. "He'll be all right, won't he, Doctor?"

"I'm sure he will," the doctor said. "It just looks like simple concussion to me. I don't think there's any hemorrhage, but we'll know more about that in the morning. The important thing is that he rest quietly."

He brought out a pen and slip of paper. "I better get his name for the record." Ernest looked confused. He stammered a bit. "It's Frank . . . oh, Frank." He turned in some confusion to Max. "It's so stupid of me," he said, "but Frank's last name skips me completely. And I knew it so well." He put his hand to his head. Max became flustered, too. "I don't know it myself," he said. Charles looked at the others blankly. "I wouldn't know," he said crossly, "I just met him this weekend myself."

As the doctor left, Charles strolled down the walk with him. "Really," he said, "I don't know why they make such a mystery of it. We all met Frank only this weekend on the beach, and Ernest, who's quite rich and successful"— he spoke mincingly now—"invited him to spend the night."

"Oh, I see," said the doctor noncommittally.

"Oh yes," said Charles, watching the doctor closely. "I suppose you'd call him a male prostitute."

58

CHAPTER VI

Fashion and Beauty

SIGHING OVER ELEGANT clothes she can't wear, the average woman little realizes that current smart fashions are often the product of homosexuals who have no appreciation of well-rounded curves.

Under the mass pressure of the homosexual clique dominating the style world, the face of beauty is changing, too. No longer is it fashionable to be rosy-cheeked and laughing-eyed, with a healthy tan and shining round face. Dramatic planes, with high cheekbones and hollow, haggard cheeks, are the coveted ideal, and circles under the eyes add to the sweet mystery of it all.

Legs with calfs half gone out of vogue, and though busts are fighting their way back to popularity through the valiant effort of the movie queens, they still have no high place in the fashion field.

It is all, observers insist, part of a homosexual design— male and female—to demean and degrade the traditionally American concept of soft, lovely, feminine beauty.

The plot to defeminize the female face and form usually begins with the homosexual designers, who fit their clothes for gaunt, emaciated women. It extends to homosexual or lesbian magazine editors, who hire boyish-looking girls to show these clothes, and is supported by fashion photographers, homosexual or otherwise, who use these models out of preference or to stay in tune.

In Manhattan's Seventh Avenue garment center, often called dressmaker to the world, bosomless designers' models form a prototype of long-legged, lean-shanked, and flat-chested models who set the style for the rest of the country. "A girl with a bust just doesn't have a chance in high-fashion modeling," a leading photographers' representative pointed out, "because even if there is a straight photographer or editor who will give her a chance, she doesn't fit the clothes originally styled to a gaunt form."

To look like a high-fashion model, a girl must go hungry. Not only fashions but the unhealthy dieting vogues of recent years have been inspired by the prominence of the emaciated models, whose pictures adorn the pages of the "smarter" women's magazines. One of the top models, for instance, was recently featured in a bikini in a double-page spread in one of the leading fashion journals. Males were aghast at the vast uncovered expanse of skin and bone, and dubbed the picture "The Cadaver." But many young impressionable girls, who had made this actress-model their idol, wondered admiringly how they, too, could achieve the flat hips and flat chest that created this lathlike effect.

As a matter of fact, many models, who would normally have healthy, well-rounded figures, diet to the danger point themselves, spurred on by the rich rewards, which bring many $50,000 a year and more. One female fashion plate dieted to such excess that she became seriously ill. After convalescing in the deserts of the Southwest she returned triumphantly to the studio circuit. Gaunter yet and hollow-eyed, with a concave chest, she is now more popular than ever with the homosexual clique. Drawing down modeling fees of $60 an hour, she earns close to $75,000 a year and is booked weeks ahead by the admiring phalanx of homosexual photographers and editors who rate her the greatest beauty since Garbo.

She maintains a semblance of life on a diet of orange juice, black coffee, and cigarettes. Bravely she staggers from one studio to the next, weighed down with her heavy modeling kit and painting as though the next lurch will be the last. Although she stands five feet nine inches in her bony feet, she barely weighs one hundred pounds—and much of this seems to be make-up. Nevertheless, her figure is extoled as a paragon by the model-agency head who fattens on her, commission-wise. But not all agency heads feel the same. "She looks," said one, "as if she should be in a hospital." And yet he added, "But just the same I wish I had her."

When young fashion models balk at the drastic dieting regimen, they are constantly nagged at by homosexual photographers. homosexual editors, and homosexual designers.

Many beauties go throug startling shanges to keep the figures homosexuals love to photograph. One of the most radiant beauties on Broadway, lured by the big money of the fashion field and tired of dancing in night clubs seven days a week, decided to switch into modeling. Besides being exotically beautiful, in a healthy midwestern sort of way, she was divinely shaped, with a tall statuesque form. With her smile and verve she had helped bring back the day of the stage-door Johnnies and appeared to be ticketed in time for a Hollywood career.

A critic who had seen her perform proudly on stage, discharging waves of electricity as she moved majestically about like some fine thoroughbred, had commented enthusiastically: "She's a throwback to the most glorious of the old Ziegfeld beauties."

Six months later that critic happened by chance to run into the same show girl in a photographic studio. He saw a girl, vaguely familiar, sitting across from him. And she nodded, appearing to recognize him. However, even when she stood up, he couldn't place her. His only impression at first was that she was ill and should be home in bed rather than wandering around the city. Her face was dead-white, there were blue hollows under her eyes, her shoulders sagged, and her chest caved in. Even her hair and teeth had no luster, and when she smiled it was no more than a cheerless distortion.

As he looked at her, he wondered what held the poor creature together.

Suddenly, with a sort of start, he realized she was talking to him.

"I see you don't remember me," she said, with a dull smile.

He shook his head, murmuring a polite apology.

She then identified herself as the former dancer whom he had once so admired.

Could this be the lovely, vivacious girl who had made him think back to the most famous beauties in the world? The bloom was gone from that apple-blossom cheek, the ruby-red lips were now a straight hard line, and from the look of her once full-blown frame he was afraid that she was going to collapse momentarily in his arms.

With an effort he concealed his dismay.

"What are you doing?" he asked.

"Oh, I'm modeling now, and doing very well."

"But aren't you a trifle thin to be working?"

She smiled pityingly. "Oh no," she said, "my agent would like me to be even thinner." She sighed. "I've lost thirty-seven pounds, but I should get down a few more."

She was slightly under five feet ten inches in her stockings, and weighed 108 pounds.

"You should eat more, and watch your health," he said.

She laughed, and he thought the effort, leading to a spasm of coughing, might carry her away then and there. But she recovered after a while and said: "Oh no, I couldn't do that—the photographers love me just as I am."

Even those photographers who appreciate a pretty girl with curves discover that they have to get on the homosexual bandwagon if they want to stay healthy economically. One heterosexual photographer, new to the fashion field, for instance, had sent a lovely rosy-cheeked girl with a well-rounded figure to a female magazine editor for approval for a series of fashion pictures. It was the last time he made that mistake.

"She told me," he recalled ruefully, "that if I ever sent over another girl-type girl, I had had my last assignment for that magazine."

The fashion editors, many of them lesbians, have their own ideas of what a model should look like. Generally, they resist anything that even smacks of femininity. "These editors," an agency head analyzed, "are not interested in pretty girls. They are interested in shock appeal, and the more bizarre the model and the pose, the happier they are. And they dote on photographers to whom a woman is acceptable only when her womanliness is downgraded or satirized."

Of course, not all models are the sickly, skeletonlike fashion type. There is the wholesome commercial type, popularized on television, where the advertiser picks out the girl. And a more natural type is also featured in commercial-advertising magazines and newspapers, where the advertiser again insists on somebody who reminds him of the girl next door. They even model some clothes, but nothing elegant or exotic.

The high-fashion fields, as a rule, are closed to these girls, many of them glowing with a healthy, animal beauty. However, the more ambitious, unfortunately, do try to melt off poundage, and lose their glamorous glow in the process of cracking the fashion-magazine field.

This metamorphosis has had an unhappy effect on some model marriages. For while a model's income may go up, as the homosexual contingent cheers her on, the danger of her losing a husband rises commensurately. Many young husbands, ruefully reviewing the rag-and-bone-and-hank-of-hair that was once their wife, have served their partners with ultimatums to gain weight. But others are happy to share their wife's wealth.

The conspiracy to debase the feminine form flourishes on social as well as business levels, helping to cement ties that bind the fashion field into one big homosexual complex.

Some time ago a reporter attended a cocktail party honoring one of the most famous young designers in the business. He had been invited by a friend, a model-agency head, who explained that her husband was busy and she needed an escort.

A suite in a fashionable East Side hotel had been engaged for the occasion, with a number of hired flunkies on hand to see to the drinking comfort of the guests. Never, the reporter thought, had he seen a more glittering group of women—socialites, models, actresses, designers, decorators, and magazine editors. And, numerically, there was a man for each. This included the guest of honor, who seemed to typify the males present.

He was a short, slight young man, with a jacket two sizes too small for him, sharply creased charcoal trousers so snug they gave his legs a kinked stovepipe effect. Head bobbing, he walked around the room with a little mincing step, smiling brightly at everybody. Occasionally, he would buttonhole a male guest, the two dangling their cigarettes, and bending their wrists limply as they conversed. As the reporter looked around, he saw the scene repeating itself everywhere. With a start he suddenly became aware he was the only heterosexual at the party.

Later, he asked the agency head why he had been invited. "Well," she said, "I had to come, or they might have gotten the idea I was uppity, and my husband just wasn't up to another one of these things."

Not all designers, of course, are homosexuals. One of the outstanding exceptions has squired beautiful women for years and was once married to a lovely screen star, renowned for her quiet sex appeal. "As a result," a stylist observed, "his dresses and gowns are for women with curves where curves should be."

It is no accident, photographers say, that many of the world's most beautiful models go along with the effort to defeminize their beauty. "Many of these girls," a fashion photographer reported, "are lesbians or have such tendencies." And that, he explains, is why so many turn to modeling, where they are centers of attraction. "It is all part of the Narcissus urge which drives them on," he said. "Their beauty makes them the cynosure of all eyes, including their own. And many, becoming enamored of themselves, turn logically to the person or persons who most resemble them, obviously another girl."

63

There are more direct examples of how beautiful young girls have turned to modeling careers through lesbianism—either theirs or another's. One of the loveliest show girls on Broadway had been troubled for some time by conflicting sexual desires. Only nineteen years old, she was still young and impressionable enough to be shaped one way or the other. In the show she met a girl whose blond beauty contrasted with her own brunette loveliness. This girl had already had relationships with her own sex and openly mocked the intentions and integrity of the male sex. She took her young friend to Greenwich Village, showed her how much girls enjoyed dancing with each other in the night-traps catering to this trade. She almost managed to win her over. But not quite. She still had to compete for her convert's attentions with a small army of stage-door Johnnies who kept trying to woo her back to normalcy.

To eliminate this competition, she prodded her protégé into entering the high-fashion modeling field, where, she reasoned, the male competition would be relatively nil. The beauty dutifully applied at a modeling agency and was promptly told she would have to lose thirty pounds. Aghast, she pushed aside thoughts of this new career, but she reckoned without the determination of her lesbian friend who kept after her until she finally got down to the required poundage with a health-draining diet.

She was no longer one of the most luscious-looking brunettes on Broadway, and masculine interest waned. But the lesbian, ironically, had been more successful than she planned. Although the girl was little more than bones, her face took on a new haunting beauty (probably from being hungry all the time) which attracted many girls in her new profession. If anything, the competition was now keener than ever—if different.

In the male field many models are openly homosexual, though few are effeminate in bearing. Others pose as paragons of virility, masking their own homosexuality with violent diatribes against the "minority" which has stereotyped their profession. Indeed, the homosexual tag is so strong that many male models defensively identify themselves as actors, socially.

Many homosexual photographers make no secret of the fact that they prefer to work with male models. "Why not?" said one well-known photographer. "As a minority group we ought to stick together. Besides, I have a better working rapport with other homosexuals. And if they want to stay over later, what's wrong with that? Straight photographers do it with the girl models all the time."

Although many male models openly avow their manliness, some homosexual photographers are often loath to take them at their word. One robust male model, showing friends a skinned fist, explained, "I had to fight my way out of that faggot's studio."

In a field where sexual abnormality seems normal, almost anything seems possible. Some girl models, for instance, have gone into light housekeeping with male models, just as they would with another girl. Such designs for living, while novel, are casually assumed.

Two, for example, got together while posing for a cigarette ad. Conversing idly, shapely, lovely Joan, who already had all the male admirers she wanted, mentioned she was looking for a small apartment, without a lease. The male model, a virile-looking blond with wavy hair, promptly observed he had an apartment he was willing to share.

At first Joan was not quite sure what was being proposed.

"It's an idea," she said, "but no funny business."

He laughed. "Don't worry your pretty little head about that."

In the beginning the arrangement worked out notably well. "We seldom got in each other's way," Joan recalled. "In fact, Sam was a big help. At times, when I felt like going out dancing, but couldn't stand the thought of defending myself at the door against some aggressive male, we'd slip out together for an evening."

Neither intruded on the other's privacy. "He slept out on the roll-away in the living room," Joan said, "and I took the bedroom. The only intimate moments came in passing each other en route to the bathroom in the morning."

Homosexual friends accepted the arrangement for what it was. However, Joan knew her suitors would not be as broadminded. "They would never have believed the truth," she said, "because they were so damned male and suspicious." Consequently, she kept her own dates waiting downstairs or in the hall.

His friends usually called at the apartment but rarely lingered. There was one notable exception. "On this occasion," she said, "we were all going out together. But some time passed without Sam coming down. I finally went back to see what was keeping him. There he was, in the middle of the living room, embracing his friend. I started to duck out, but he winked over the other boy's shoulder, and I knew he was only playing, and told him to hurry along."

As time wore on, it developed the two did not balance each other off. Sam was not the homemaking type. He didn't like to cook or straighten up, and neither did Joan. "He was the chorus-girl type," she recalled, "always giving his sweethearts a rough time."

They would exchange yarns about their dates and laugh together over the discomfiture they had caused. Occasionally, they double-dated, and this was where the trouble started. "I did it for Sam," Joan explained. The foursome included an older man, enamored of Sam, and a pretty friend of Joan's. "The older man was very prominent," Joan explained, "and he couldn't afford to let anyone think that he liked my little roomie."

Ostensibly, Joan's girl friend was the older man's date. And through this cover-up he was able to pay court to Sam. But in the end the plan boomeranged.

As it developed, this convenient setup proved the undoing of the happy housekeepers. "We had all been out together four or five times," the model recalled, "when the older man began showing an interest in me. I guess he was one of those bisexuals, or just a homosexual trying to make an impression. Anyway, my little roommate began to get jealous —and one day ⌐ ⌐ I got home there was a little note telling me he had a new roommate."

And what was in the note?

"Nothing much," said Joan with a derisive laugh. "The nasty little boy tried to hint that I was a lesbian. Can you imagine anything like that?"

CHAPTER VII

Smell of Success

WHILE THEY LIVE in apparent glamour, mixing in a giddy world of beautiful women and talented men, many homosexuals are anything but happy. Behind a gay, indolent, sometimes saucy front often lurks a haunting feeling of make-believe and a lack of purpose which compels many to seek oblivion in drink and sex.

No matter how successful they seem, many are embittered by the nightmare of not belonging. And the more sensitive they are, the more cruelly they feel the cold contempt of polite society. But with success and prominence some learn to mask their feelings behind a façade of indifference or disdain.

The world-famed photographer, who sat across from me, was no exception. "I am only seeing you," he apprised me coolly, "because of our friend."

Looking at him, I saw no indication of creative artistry. He was medium-aged, medium-sized, and his protruding eyes, a dull blue, were his only distinctive feature. He was bald except for a fringe on the sides, and his face was faintly purple. A dark polo shirt revealed white flaccid arms and a small paunch. His shoes were scuffed dirty. He was independent financially, but he looked like a man who had watched the parade go by. "I don't like newspapermen," he said. "They're uncouth."

I shrugged. "Not any more than anybody else." I smiled and said lightly: "Essentially, they're rough diamonds."

He spoke sharply. "Yes," he said, "and they have their share of homosexuals, too." He proceeded to name a few.

Still hostile, he turned on me sharply. "Tell me," he asked, "how did you pick on me? I have no interest in the subject of homosexuals."

"According to our model friend, you consider homosexuals the world's most misunderstood group."

He grimaced. "That's a woman for you. I may have said something like that, but it certainly wasn't for publication."

"There's no reason," I said, "why you should discuss anything if it makes you uncomfortable."

His lips drew down tightly. "It is not a question of discomfort," he said, "but these things are always getting misrepresented."

"Well, if you'd rather make it another time," I said, "that's fine with me."

The less interest I showed, the more interested he appeared in having me stay. "No, that's all right," he said, his voice becoming friendlier. "I'll mix you a drink."

Sitting down, crossing his legs comfortably, he said, "What do you want to talk about?"

"You, and the modeling business," I said. "I think your work might be interesting."

He nodded agreeably. "I work mostly with women," he said, "but I use male models, too."

"What kind?"

"Oh, the virile type," he said quickly.

"You don't favor models, then, because they're homosexual?"

He smiled coolly. "Of course I do, as long as they're the manly type."

"Some photographers told me they never play favorites."

He laughed harshly. "That's so much nonsense," he said. "I hire homosexuals whenever I can. And so do the rest. Why shouldn't I? Don't the straight photographers pick the girls they like?"

His manner again froze. He seemed alternately aloof or gracious, as though he couldn't make up his mind whether I was friend or foe. But when he did loosen up a little, the vanity characteristic of many homosexuals became apparent.

Generally, he kept his personal and professional life separate. And he kept clear of the cocktail circuit. "I have no desire for the social life of the art or fashion worlds," he said frostily. "In fact, I have nothing but contempt for the straight people and the fags who push into it. They're filthy little climbers, trying to get rid of their inadequacies and confusion in chatter."

He was equally unimpressed by the beautiful models who made their way in and out of his studio. "Many of them," he said disdainfully, "are lesbians, you know."

While he brushed the ladies aside lightly, he appeared quite serious on his choice of male models. "They are by no means pretty boys," he said. "That type is rather dated. I prefer homosexuals who are manly-appearing. And," he added with a note of pride, "when you look at it without prejudice, I don't think there's anybody more masculine in bearing than homosexuals."

He got up from the divan on which he had been sitting, swishing noticeably for the first time as he led me into an adjacent room. Framed photographs of handsome-looking young men, head shots and full figure, nude or plainly dressed, hung around the walls. "This is my picture gallery," he said, pointing pridefully around the room. "Did you ever see a more manly-looking group?"

He pointed to a picture of a handsome young man whose face looked strangely familiar. "A top magazine just featured him on the cover as God's gift to girls," he said, snickering. "Funny, isn't it?"

He showed me around the gallery, watching intently out

of the corner of his eye, to judge my reaction. "Yes," I admitted finally, "they're good-looking enough, but they all have the same look about them."

He nodded agreement. "The manly look."

"I don't know about that," I said. I pointed to a picture of a particularly well-developed-looking figure, nude save for a loincloth, astride a horse. "For all those muscles," I said, "there's something unmasculine about that one."

"Oh, that." He put his hand to his mouth. "Oh, that must be my fault. I insisted on posing him that way."

The trip around his private gallery seemed to do something for his personality. He had become friendlier with each drink, but now his reserve appeared to melt away. He leaned over to confide, "Because I do admire virility, I can't stand all those queens with their perfumes and powder. But otherwise, I have no prejudices. As a matter of fact, I admire the primitive quality in some racial groups. Elegance is greatly overrated."

He thought a while. "In the long run I find it simpler to pay for what I want. Most homosexuals won't admit they're driven by lust, but they are, whether they admit it or not. They see somebody they like, and they can't wait to be with him, no matter what it costs or what's involved." He shook his head. "I don't know why they make it all so complex, when it's really very simple. It all gets down to getting what you want, when you want it."

It was difficult, studying this disillusioned, cynical man, to picture him as ever having been part of the social fabric. Yet he came of a New England family, proud of its Pilgrim tradition. But even in his teens, in his small community, he became increasingly aware that he was different from other young men. At first he didn't know what to do about his uneasy, prurient impulses, and then, looking around, he became convinced that a surprising number of men had similar impulses which they were burning to express, if only there was no danger of discovery.

While in his teens, this belief was encouraged by his sister's fiancé, a college athletic hero, who seemed just about as masculine as anybody could want to be. And yet one night when his sister wasn't around, they shared quarters together. For two years the relationship continued, without the sister knowing and without the two principals mentioning their own intimacy to one another. "Somehow," he said, "it seemed less real, less of a problem if we didn't talk about it."

He had just gone to the other's room to borrow a book. And then as their hands inadvertently touched, he felt a thrill. He looked up, and sensed immediately that the feeling was mutual.

Their being together provoked no comment. Both were at the same university; the photographer in his freshman year, his prospective brother-in-law a graduate student. "People just thought it was nice that we should be friendly," he recalled.

Even now, though he had photographed multitudes of the world's best-looking men, he could remember nobody who had impressed him so much as his old college hero. "Nobody would have taken him for a homosexual," he said. "He was the most beautiful man anybody would want to see. What a physique—a champion rower, decathalon star, and just bursting with raw vitality."

The engagement with the sister was eventually broken off, without explanation, and each married elsewhere. The photographer left the college town, back in the West, and moved on to New York to make his fortune. But years later, revisiting that area, he called his old friend.

He was now a distinguished professor with a large family of growing children. He had just sat down to dinner at home when the call came. "All I did," the photographer recalled, "was mention my name. That was all that was necessary." They met less than an hour later at a down-town hotel. "He stayed for two or three hours," the photographer said, his face brightening as he thought about it. "He was still a handsome man, and nothing had changed."

He closed his eyes, musing dreamily. "It was just like always. We didn't find it necessary to say a word at any time. And later when he left, we knew we'd probably never see each other again, but what difference did it make? We had borrowed a day as it was."

I was puzzled. "Why," I asked, "would it have been so horrible to have said anything to each other about what you were doing?"

My question seemed to jar him out of his euphoria. "I didn't say it was horrible," he retorted testily. "All I said was that it would have made things a problem if we'd sat around and gabbed about it, and the first thing you know, the two of us would have been having all kinds of guilty feelings."

He looked up. His eyes, reddened from steady drinking, were bulging more prominently than ever. He stirred him-

70

ity or talent others claim for them. Instead they attribute their popularity in recent years to an ever-increasing public preoccupation with a morbid emotional pornography nourished on decadence and degeneracy. "Today," a critic observed, "playgoers like to dig under rocks and then gloat over what's crawling around underneath."

As homosexuals have become increasingly powerful in the entertainment industry, their influence has spread itself to both sides of the theatrical curtain. Indeed, the impact of the unsuspected homosexual, cast in heterosexually appealing roles on stage, screen, or television, may be more extensive than any can imagine. For just as film stars of the last generation set up a male prototype for adoring young females, so now have these disguised gay boys become the romantic ideal of the immature female.

To many in the entertainment business, it seems a cruel mockery that the love image of some sighing teen-ager should be formed by some beautiful young man who wants nothing more himself than another beautiful young man.

And the social effects of this mass burlesque can be devastating. Where girls before the war had for their ideal the he-man personified by Gable and Cooper, their daughters now model their dream man after some pretty boy with wavy hair whom they have admired on the screen and television. "Searching for this type off-screen," a veteran showman pointed out, "they find only too often—and too late—that what they think is masculinity, is only homosexuality."

On some screens the homosexual attitudes of stars are so noticeable that audiences are audibly amused. Love scenes can be especially laugh-provoking. In a current picture a voluptuous screen siren dangles her charms tantalizingly before one of these new types of male impersonators. Though he supposedly returns her affection with passionate adoration, he is obviously hard-pressed to register the slightest interest. As a ripple of appreciative laughter ran through the movie house, a moviegoer observed caustically, "He looks at her as though she's a wilted anchovy."

The homosexual touch is often apparent in the homosexual production. In plays by homosexuals women generally fare badly. There is no mystery or romance about them, no sweetness or light. They are heartless mothers and wives—sluts, slatterns, and slobs. Rarely do they enjoy any degree of compatibility with the bull male, and even more rarely are they partners in a happy marriage. Homosexually speaking, they are an unattractive lot.

At times, the preponderance of homosexuals in show business seems almost the product of a vast conspiracy. The author of a recent motion picture, for instance, was an avowed homosexual. He was assisted by a well-known writer who made no secret of his homosexuality. And the male star of the movie? The darling of the homosexual clique! The picture itself, to round out things, smattered of homosexuality.

On some television shows homosexuals are so numerous that many legitimate actors have asked querulously what they had to do to land a job.

"If you're straight," a veteran performer said resignedly, "these casting directors look at you as though you're a carbuncle on the seat of progress." Things got so bad that *Daily Variety*, the show business paper, commented trenchantly on a deplorable situation which extends beyond the twenty-one-inch screen to casting directors and story editors, whose personalities are reflected in the television fare served up to millions.

The dean of television and radio editors, Ben Gross of the New York *Daily News*, discussing this trend, has expressed the dismay felt within some branches of the industry at these inroads. "What is beyond understanding," a producer told Gross, "is the choice of so many incompetents as the screeners of stories. And what is even more incredible is the ever-increasing number of homosexuals who are placed in these positions. While one accepts the customary stage 'dahlings,' 'sweethearts,' and similar endearments which have crept into show business as part of the language, it becomes nauseating to find that someone really means it."

On Broadway homosexuals are powerful not only as performers or playrights, but as producers, directors, composers, choreographers, even as backers of many productions. Backstage, they often outnumber heterosexuals, abandoning in the security of numbers the pretense which often masks their activity elsewhere.

Their importance startles even coldly ambitious show girls and actresses, used to different hiring conditions on the Coast. "It's the first time," said a blond Hollywood starlet, auditioning for a musical, "that I didn't get the casting-couch treatment."

In some shows virtually all the dancers are homosexual. It is so standard a Broadway pattern that it was used for a laugh in the play *Two for the Seesaw*, with Henry Fonda and Anne Bancroft. Fonda is jealous because the girl, Bancroft, had been seeing a dancer. "Did anything happen between you?" he asks approximately. She looks at him in disbelief. "Didn't I tell you," she fairly screams, "that he's a dancer!"

Dancing has special appeal for many homosexuals, as the theater does generally. It caters to the artistic sense so many have cultivated, and it throws them into a tolerant, ultrasophisticated world, where emotions are notoriously unstable, even among straight people, and abnormalities are looked upon as the normal thing.

Not all dancers are actually gay when they join the ballet companies. Broadway agents estimate that possibly one third are homosexual and the rest get that way. "Boys with homosexual tendencies," an agent pointed out, "are especially drawn to the glittering life of the theater with its emphasis on pretty things. After they get into ballet dancing, many want to become completely part of their new life. They discover, too, that homosexuality is an open sesame to jobs since so many of the choreographers are that way and the ballet masters, by tradition, have their pick of the little boys."

Homosexual dancers flirt and flutter around together backstage, gaining new friends and converts, and forming one big happy family in which nonhomosexuals are clearly intruders. Some directors just can't bear the sight of a straight dancer in their companies. But occasionally, through oversight or error, one may slip through. One Broadway director, horrified at the presence of a lone holdout in his show, went to every extreme to make him quit. He singled out his dancing for criticism before other members of the cast, accused him of ruining numbers when it was obviously not his fault. He even ridiculed the way he wore his costumes, claiming he was out of tune with everybody else, which of course, he was. It became a war of nerves, with the dancer, knowing he would be supported by Equity, determinedly sticking it out.

When the show went on the road finally, it was the director —not the dancer—who stayed behind. "He aggravates me so," the director explained, "I can't bear the sight of him."

Relationships between producers and personnel are usually fleeting. One famous producer hired a talented choreographer, whom at first sight he found charming and handsome. Before the show came into New York from routine road tryouts, the producer became bored with his attachment. He began picking flaws in the choreography. He finally fired the choreographer, engaging still another homosexual to redo some of the dancing sequences previously considered flawless. "He went to all this expense," an associate pointed out, "just to justify getting rid of somebody who had become embarrassing to him."

While many homosexual directors put on a respectable face publicly, in the theater they make no secret of their curious whims. Even though he was a homosexual, a dark, black-haired singer with a fine voice couldn't get an audition in a musical comedy auditioned by a homosexual. "I prefer blond boys," the director blandly explained.

Some tryouts have a tragicomic quality. As one youthful actor, a nonhomosexual, waited in the parlor of a director's Park Avenue apartment, a young neophyte walked nude out of a bedroom elatedly holding a playscript in his hand. "I got the part," he cried, "I got the part."

In Hollywood, where beautiful young actresses—and older ones too—bewail the lack of "eligible young men," homosexuality surprises no one who has been around. Make-believe marriages are commonplace, with stars and would-be-stars often marrying for their own convenience and the edification of their doting fans. Divorces are correspondingly common, influenced by the absence of a compelling sexual relationship. Only recently, a well-known Hollywood star, formerly on Broadway, was divorced from his partner of many years. His wife had married him knowing there was another well-known star in his life—a male. The marriage had ticked along conveniently for years while the movie magazines raved about the "idyllic" union. But more realistic Hollywood observers marked time. True to form, the marriage was finally dissolved. The competition had become too much for the wife, who had resigned herself to one long-standing rival but couldn't accept new ones.

In Hollywood the performers dominate the homosexual picture, as many producers and directors strive to live up to a well-earned tradition as wolves. Almost as openly, but not quite as sincerely, many homosexual actors have cultivated a reputation as Don Juans. However, they seem to fool nobody but their fans and the succession of pretty girls who provide a convenient cover-up.

Sometimes defying propriety, Hollywood stars have consorted openly with other males, occasionally marrying to offset insistent gossip. In one of the worst-kept Hollywood secrets of all time a prominent Western star shared quarters with a matinee idol, who had married several times without finding the serenity he knew with his roommate. But gossip, which might have damaged both their careers, eventually parted them for good.

Like homosexuals elsewhere, many Hollywood homosexuals have turned to women in a desperate attempt to prove themselves. One major star, tormented by his "inexcusable weakness," plunged headlong into one affair after another. Finding no lasting interest in these liaisons, he finally tried a more permanent arrangement—marriage. Close friends predicted, "It won't last a year." Less than a year later, though a child came along to complicate matters, he made good their prediction, violently breaking off a relationship he hadn't wanted in the first place.

Many onlookers question the underlying sincerity of all this apparent effort to change over. "Nearly all homosexuals want to stop being gay at some time," one agent pointed out, "and feel they can be a man exclusively if they marry and have children. Some talk of going into psychoanalysis, and discuss others who have been helped that way. But it is nearly all talk, except for the fact they do marry."

On Broadway, as in Hollywood, the sexual ambivalence of performers forms a bizarre matrimonial mosaic, which veteran observers have analyzed down to the last divorce and annulment.

Finding a wife is in itself no problem. Many attractive girls of good family and background, who find the theater a challenge, often turn to homosexuals as an escape from wolves. "They meet a lot of people, in and out of the theater, who go after them just because they're women, not individuals," a Broadway personality observed. "That makes them ripe for the manly-looking homosexual, who is the thoughtful opposite of the lecherous male who wants to possess their beauty, instead of sitting around and admiring it."

Sometimes these alliances work out beautifully. One illustrious Broadway actress, married to a homosexual, boasted openly of having a marriage far superior to a previous union with an aggressive male. Unlike her earlier try, there was no personal rivalry or competition. "My new husband," she told friends, "gets more of a kick out of my success than I do." He haunts the wings, fretting over her like a mother hen, making sure she is comfortable, picking out her clothes. "His taste," she confided proudly, "is much better than mine."

Homosexuality is obviously no social barrier on Broadway or Hollywood. Actors are judged by their prestige and success, not by their rating in Kraft-Ebbing. In the film colony a performer's ambivalence is hardly considered worthy of discussion. But many newcomers to the scene, neither so broad-minded or well informed, have not been able to achieve a similar casualness. In fact, a well-known chanteuse, fresh from Broadway, making a picture on the Coast, began brooding about her lost sex appeal after a number of handsome young males seemed immune to her charms.

Several nights passed without anybody calling her for a date. A curly-haired, middle-aged feature player, working the same picture, finally restored her confidence somewhat by asking her to a plush dinner party. Dancing gaily with her charming partner, she was beginning to feel her old feminine self when a youthful Hollywood star stepped onto the floor and made for the dancing couple. Just as she thought—thrilled—that he was going to cut in, he flung his arms about her partner with shouts of joy. Without looking at her, the pair walked off, arm in arm, happily jabbering away. "That's the last I saw of either," she recalled sadly. "They just got lost together."

Hollywood stars are usually circumspect in public, much more so than the English contingent, some of whom have stirred ugly scandals through their open activities in their native land. Even in this country a few make no secret of their homosexuality. Filming a picture here recently, an English star of a liberal turn of mind became involved in heated political discussions on location with an older, more conservative Hollywood star. One night the debate was raging, when the Hollywood conservative threw up his hands in disgust and snapped.

"I don't know why I'm wasting my time with you. You don't even know what you are."

The younger man eyed him scornfully. And then mimicking the other's high-timbered voice, said coldly:

"That's where you're wrong. I know what I am—I'm a homosexual. It's you who doesn't know what he is yet—Duchess!"

In Hollywood, as in the theater, homosexuality is a fact of life which must be kept in the background. The managers of some homosexual stars, trading on masculine appeal, have tried to get around this fact by marrying off their stars to lessen the possibility of scandal. But the best-intentioned efforts have sometimes boomeranged.

In the case of one rising film idol an enterprising personal manager persuaded the young man to regard favorably the advantages of a marriage—in name only. For a convenient bride the manager had turned to his own crisp, efficient secretary, a young woman whom he suspected of lesbian tendencies. It was to be the perfect arrangement. "She won't give a damn what you do," the manager insisted, "and you won't have to worry about people talking about you hereafter."

With some misgivings the actor agreed. The wedding came off without too much ado, and the country's teen-agers duly sighed over another lost matinee idol.

However, the manager had underestimated the charms of his ersatz screen lover. The secretary, whom he thought impervious to males, had suddenly fallen for her "hunk of man." She began to make demands on him, as would any normally affectionate wife, became jealous when he showed interest in anyone else, and berated him when he stayed out late.

The actor cast a jaundiced eye on the manager who had gotten him into this predicament, and ordered him to do something about it. Feeling his influence waning, the manager searched his brain for a solution and finally came up with a proposal for an annulment. But Mrs. Matinee Idol wouldn't have it. She enjoyed her new status of Hollywood wife, regardless of domestic problems, and felt these could be worked out if the manager was eliminated. That was all the star had to hear. Booking passage immediately, the actor flew to Europe, deciding to make pictures there until his wife would listen to reason. When it became obvious he wasn't coming back, she finally agreed to a divorce, demanding "a percentage of everything he makes for the rest of his life."

As the manager sputtered indignantly, his former secretary observed with a careless shrug, "I'll bet the fan magazines would be interested." She laughed. "Can't you just see it—the real-life love story of the great screen lover!"

The manager immediately became reasonable. A compromise settlement was worked out. The ex-secretary now follows the career of her ex-husband with the touching interest of a true partner. Thanks to her old boss, the manager, she will never have to work again.

In Hollywood and Broadway there is always a place for outsiders who are attractive, charming, witty, and "masculine." To avoid gossip, or blackmail, however, new friendships must be formed with care. Show-business homosexuals, because of their prominence, cannot afford to frequent homosexual bars or approach strangers in straight bars. However, they do occasionally sponsor get-togethers where they can meet young men, usually on the fringes of the entertainment industry, who have been first carefully screened.

Often the prospect is screened without his even realizing it. Billy, a burly young bisexual, working with an advertising agency, was asked by a television producer to join him at cocktails with a well-known Hollywood star. They made small talk for an hour or so, and Billy went back to his office wondering what it was all about.

Two weeks later the same producer invited him to a party in a fashionable Fifth Avenue hotel. As he walked into a large suite, he spied several well-known performers, including one sometimes billed as this generation's answer to Clark Gable.

There were about fifty males milling around, with the ladies conspicuous by their absence. About half the group seemed outsiders like himself, the others were busily greeting one another. Their conversation was in general terms. Not once was homosexuality discussed openly.

Looking around, Billy spotted the actor he had had cocktails with a short time before. The actor nodded and with an older actor sauntered over to Billy. Once the introductions were performed, the younger star moved on.

"As soon as we were alone," Billy recalled, "he made his pitch. However, it was all very subtle and would never have incriminated him. He was leaving town that night but would be back in two weeks and would like to get together for a drink. There was no leer or innuendo in his voice, and if it hadn't been for the circumstances, I might actually have thought he liked me for my mind."

Nothing ever came of it as far as Billy was concerned. Like so many bisexuals, he couldn't visualize a relationship in which he wasn't at least an equal. The invitation came, but Billy didn't respond. "I wasn't going to be one of their pretty boys," he said.

For some homosexuals on the lower rungs of the talent ladder the theater is a happy hunting ground. "Many gay boys and lesbians have no real ambition in the theater," an agent pointed out, "but use it as a device to get next to their betters. In one case, this boy only had to pay his union dues and it was an open door to a world of beautiful girls who dabble in the theater." He married one of them, a lovely heiress, and though a child was born, the marriage soon broke up. But the actor, who was no actor, besides demanding a million-dollar divorce settlement, had gained enough prominence to set himself up as an interior decorator for the wealthy people he had met through his wife.

Even without marriage advancement often comes rapidly for the young homosexual.

One Broadway agent who disliked the more aggressive Broadway characters hired a socially elite youth of twenty-two, just out of an Ivy League college, to be his Boy Friday —running errands, answering the phone, etc. Since the boy had theatrical ambitions, the agent changed his name, giving him one with a theatrical roll to suit his personality.

The youth began getting invitations to the right cocktail parties, became acquainted with people in the theater and designing set, and soon became much sought after by influential homosexuals because of his blond male-type beauty. He found many interested in him, including one of the country's leading designers, a man about twenty-five years older. Not long thereafter, he quit as errand boy at the agency and joined the designer's concern—as a full partner. "It was remarkable," the agent said, "how this designer discovered executive qualities I had never before recognized."

Many music and theater lovers are all too aware of the growing influence of "the third sex," but there is little agreement on what, if anything, should be done about it. Kolodin's controversial article on Spoleto in the *Saturday Review* brought many suggestions from playgoers. One recommended that an "ax" be taken to the "queers." Another proposed that they be permitted their pursuit of happiness, just as anybody else.

CHAPTER IX

Interoffice

LIFE IN THE sophisticated New York City office can be difficult and sometimes ludicrous for the normal male who finds himself surrounded by homosexual co-workers. In many offices, particularly in the theatrical and garment district, the homosexuals are so numerous they form their own little cliques. They seek preferment for their own kind through office politics and often sport their homosexuality like a badge, donning or removing it as suits their convenience. When even the breath of suspicion might jeopardize their jobs, they often keep their deviation a deep, dark secret. In less conservative areas they flit around unabashed and unashamed, almost defiantly revealing to fellow workers what they are, yet not making any admissions which might cost them their position in society.

They are sprinkled liberally through the mid-town-Manhattan sector, in the publishing, advertising, travel and communications fields, and in ordinary commercial offices and department stores. There are so many of them, and they make themselves so conspicuous, that they even offend other homosexuals at times. "They give people the mistaken idea," said one middle-aged conservative, "that all homosexuals are irresponsible, giddy little fairies."

In many offices homosexual cliques maintain luncheon groups, shoot out together to assignations in Turkish baths and bars, and mingle almost exclusively with each other after hours. Quite often they belittle office career girls, particularly those in competitive jobs, and either avoid or downgrade normal males who are hostile or indifferent. Some have married, but pay diminishing attention to their wives and children as they become absorbed in their new friendships.

In one travel-service office, for instance, a young man of thirty, who had brought his wife and infant child from France, sent them back after six months when he became fond of the mustached office manager.

Even "camping" around offices, they are not readily identified by unsophisticated office workers, who either are slow to recognize all but the most obvious or just don't realize that homosexuals often resemble any other male, except when they choose not to.

In many offices the conservative homosexual, trying to adjust to convention, quietly practices a double life, even dating girls around the office in whom he has not the slightest interest, so as to avoid suspicion of being unmasculine. "The homosexual who wants to live and work in normal society, with a minimum of headaches and heartaches, must acquire a dual personality," observed a forty-five-year-old executive who had protected his secret from colleagues for years. "On his own, with his own, he can let down as he pleases, but in an office, where he may be the only homosexual, he must do nothing to disturb the office routine—or give homosexuals a bad name."

Hardly fitting the popular swishy stereotype of the homosexual, this executive looked like the average successful middleaged businessman with thinning hair, graying at the sides.

He was slight, of medium height, with the start of a paunch, and he was neatly dressed in banker's gray, white shirt, dark blue tie and matching socks. His features were nondescript, and he would have never been picked out in a crowd.

Nobody thought anything of his sharing an apartment with another man. Loneliness and economy often serve to bring people of the same sexes together in an indifferent and expensive city.

His background was upper middle class, and his career had been creditable without being distinguished. A former infantry officer in World War II, he had seen combat duty overseas, acquitting himself well. After the war he joined a concern in Rockefeller Center and was rapidly advanced to his present authority.

We lunched together several times, meeting under the giant Atlas in the Center's International Building. At first, until he felt he could trust my discretion, he did not let me know where he worked. One day as we threaded our way through the crowded Fifties to a restaurant, he was greeted by several persons. I wondered whether they suspected he was homosexual. As though reading my thoughts, he smiled. "They're all people who work in the area, all normal, so far as I know, and they think me the same." He looked sideways at me. "That's the thing I have to be most careful of—that nobody knows what I am. I feel it's none of their business, so long as I do my job and don't embarrass the firm."

"How about friends?" I asked. "Do you have any in the office?"

"Oh, there's a couple of girls I take out occasionally, when there's an office shindig of some sort, and one or two fellows I lunch with occasionally." He smiled. "I don't encourage this, because you never know when you might make a slip that someone might get to thinking about."

He made few phone calls to homosexual friends. Even the man with whom he had lived for years seldom phoned, and then only to convey innocent messages. "You never know," the businessman said, "when somebody might be listening on another extension."

In the restaurant, a small sophisticated rendezvous for romantically inclined couples, we faced across a wide, narrow table. He had suggested I sit next to him, smiling when I said I would be more comfortable facing him. "I was only thinking of the convenience," he said.

I nodded. "Do you think," I asked, "that it would make

any difference to your employers if they were to find out you were homosexual?"

He permitted himself a smile. "Frankly," he said, "I can't say. I have often wondered about it. If they had discovered it when I was new, it wouldn't have been tolerated. But now that I have been there so many years, regarded as one of the pillars, it amuses me at times to think of the potential reactions." He laughed mirthlessly. "I'm not sure I'd want to put it to the test, but I think I might be accepted for the simple reason that nobody would quite believe it. They have one concept of me built up, a chap like themselves. If they were suddenly asked to believe I'm a fairy, they might not be able to accept it. Their idea of somebody gay is really a caricature of a human being, a screaming faggot who prances around like Mae West and is constantly after small boys and cute teen-agers."

"But," I pointed out, "there are homosexuals like that."

"Certainly," he said, "and there are straight people who murder, rob, and rape; but that doesn't make the rest of them criminals." He glanced up. "The thing you've got to get in your mind is that many of us are no different than other men, aside from the fact that we prefer men to women. Why, I went all through the war without anybody knowing I was homosexual."

"Anybody? How about other homosexuals?"

He replied easily. "Oh, one or two might have known but"—he held up a finger—"only because I wanted them to."

Unless he should make a slip himself, there is little likelihood of his being found out. "I have never married," he said, "and somebody might start speculating about that. That is why I sometimes go to office parties when I don't feel like it. But it's fashionable these days to say everybody is homosexual, so that suspicion, without proof, most likely would be put down to routine gossip." He looked up at me with a grin. "Not that I am in the least ashamed, but I realize that society is not ready to accept homosexuals as people just yet."

We went into his specific situation.

"Would you prefer working among homosexuals?" I asked.

"Well, if they were all homosexuals," he said, "it would certainly be easier to relax. But if there were only a few, some might be indiscreet enough to let themselves be known, and it could only lead to trouble, with all homosexuals eventually suffering."

He looked at me with a faint smile. "So far as I know," he

said, "I'm the only one in my place, and it might be just as well for me if it stopped there."

"You mentioned that homosexuals like yourself were different in only one aspect," I said. "But it seems to me that even conservative homosexuals are inordinately preoccupied with sex. Sometimes it seems to be the only thing they are thinking of, whereas the average man can love a woman and still enjoy a baseball game or a prize fight."

He looked up blankly. For a moment I thought I had offended. "I don't understand," he said.

I explained:

"Well, even when a man's in love with a woman, he thinks of her other than physically, and he thinks of things like a home and children."

He sat waiting, and I went on. "A man thinks in terms of things he can share with a woman he loves: plays, movies, museums, just walking together and feeling spiritually joined. It isn't just all sex."

He looked at me pityingly. "What makes you think we don't have these things together? Why, I go to plays and concerts regularly with my roommate, and we constantly do things for each other—cooking, sewing, and helping out when the other is sick."

Looking very much like the cat who had swallowed the mouse, he scanned his watch and said he would have to be getting back to his office. He shook my hand with a friendly smile and said, "I'm sure you'll discover a lot more activity in other offices. Mine is quite tame."

Actually I had heard from many young men and girls of rampant homosexuality in offices. This often offended their sense of propriety or upset them so much that they were disturbed by their own reactions, so strong at times as to give them a queasy stomach. Often office schisms developed not only between homosexuals and heterosexuals, but within the ranks of the homosexuals themselves. In other instances, homosexuals schemed and maneuvered to get their leaders into positions of power, not only making their working conditions more comfortable, but also deriving satisfaction in gaining prestige for their own kind in an unsympathetic world.

When they are numerous enough, homosexuals may "take over" an office. Sometimes surreptitiously, other times quite openly, depending on their unity and strength, they operate to achieve their ends in a way that serves to win some straight colleagues as friends while often alienating others. At times things are so bad that even pretty stenographers, who traditionally complain about office wolves, frequently sigh for the good old days when they were not competing with males for male attention.

And some of the alienated males, who consider their manliness beyond reproach—and approach—are often stirred to action, however ineffectual. One day, for instance, Robert, a young travel agent of my acquaintance, called at my office and suggested a newspaper exposé of the "disgraceful conditions" in the offices of New York, generally, his own, particularly. Since he was ordinarily a quiet, well-mannered, rather self-effacing individual of thirty or thereabouts, who did some painting and sculpting in his spare time, I was rather surprised at his display of emotion. "I am so disgusted at all this," he said, "that I wouldn't mind being quoted by name."

He seemed rather vague about how the problem should be approached, but as he warmed up to his subject, he became so excited I was afraid he was going to burst. A devout churchgoer, he even quoted from the Scriptures to emphasize the evil that he felt lurked behind so many innocent-appearing desks and typewriters.

"I detest them so much," he said, "I want them to know how I feel."

He was connected with an overseas airline which drew its personnel not only from this country but from Latin America and Europe, where the attitude toward homosexuality was more tolerant. He had taken inventory of the office homosexuals, giving each an appropriate name. There was the Diplomat, named for his languid Old World air and his relationship to an actual ambassador. There was the Groper, rather obviously named, and the Ballerina, who had been glimpsed pirouetting gaily on his tiptoes one night while the office teletype vainly clacked its message from overseas.

As he described the events of a typical day, I asked why he didn't just quit and get himself another job. It seemed so much simpler than what he was putting himself through. He hesitated. "Well," he said, "there's a girl there, and I don't know whether you'd say I was in love with her or not, but I'd like to go on seeing her."

From the beginning my friend had made a hit with the homosexuals, while the girl made a hit with him. His retiring personality, his slightness, together with a baby face and a natural grave courtesy, may have intrigued the gay set. "During the first week there were so many passes," he said, "that I began to wonder whether there was something about me which I wasn't aware of."

He had worked there only two days when young men were brushing against him in the seclusion of the filing cabinets. He pretended not to notice. About a week after his arrival he was invited out to lunch by a clerk at a neighboring desk. They were joined, unexpectedly, by other co-workers and the conversation somehow got around to homosexuality. He had the uneasy feeling he was being covertly studied. He was particularly conscious of the Diplomat's appraising stare. He had given Robert a piercing glance and remarked with a mocking smile, "It all depends on you whether we *use* or *abuse* you."

Robert felt a curious twinge in his stomach and was annoyed because he suddenly felt defensive. "I don't care if anybody is homosexual or not," he said, "as long as they leave me alone." They laughed, and a bantering voice sang out: "They say it takes one to know one."

Robert lost his appetite. Later there were apologies, but the attentions continued. At times he could hardly concentrate on his work. Whenever he looked up from his desk, he found this one young man smiling at him. When Robert took pains to discourage his overtures, mentioning falsely that he was engaged, the young man said incredulously, "You're not thinking of getting married, are you?" As Robert nodded, he added derisively: "You know, those mixed marriages never work."

Meanwhile, Robert had gained a new admirer, the Ballerina. Tête-à-tête at a nearby luncheonette, the Ballerina asked what Robert thought of him. Robert replied, tactfully, that he was impressed with his theatrical presence. Almost instantly, the Ballerina's manner became confiding.

"Do you know that I've saved almost all of your drawings?" he said. "I've got a bookful of them at home."

"What drawings?" Robert asked.

"Oh, you know, those drawings you do absent-mindedly on pads, when you're on the phone. I suppose you would call them doodles."

Robert felt that queasiness in the stomach again. But the Ballerina continued brightly, "I even dig them out of the baskets when you're not looking. Did you know that?"

Even interoffice communication reflected the homosexual influence. One day Robert received a business message from a colleague which read: "Robert: Flight 212 is late, will arrive at 8:15. Love and kisses, George." Another went: "All flights canceled—nobody flying tonight."

For Robert there was another disturbing factor: the discourtesy shown girls in the secretarial pool. However, the homosexuals in his office found their match in a comely young Spanish girl. Irked by disparaging remarks about her rather obvious charms, she perched on a desk, defiantly dangling her long shapely legs, and shouted scornfully: *"Son todos maricones."* There were many red faces as an office linguist translated her contemptuous "They are all fairies." Stung, one young man, flipping his coattails, shot back in a pretty falsetto, *"Puta, puta."*

"Even if I were a whore," the girl flared, "I'd be more man than any of you."

I asked Robert how anybody got any work done. "It isn't easy," he acknowledged, "but there are a few of us who carry the load."

Wearying of the continual pressure, Robert launched a counterattack of his own. One morning he turned up with a classic work on homosexuality, *All the Sexes,* by Dr. George W. Henry, and planted it conspicuously on his desk.

"I thought it would be amusing," he said, "to see who noticed it." A dozen young colleagues, including the Groper, expressed a wish to borrow the book. "That's a wonderful book, you know," the Groper said.

"Oh, have you read it?" Robert asked.

"No," this former chorus boy said, "but some of my friends have and"—his hands fluttering—"and they loved it." He looked at Robert with revived interest. "I think you'll make a lot of friends around here with that book."

Despite all the interest in Robert, he was interested in the pretty secretary, a socialite from Philadelphia's Main Line. But he had keen competition from—of all people—the Diplomat.

"Why," he asked the Groper, "does the Diplomat take her out when he's not really interested?" That was the day the Groper, drunk, had stumbled into the office, slumped over his typewriter, and announced to Robert, "I love you."

"That's nice," said Robert. "I like you, too."

"No," the Groper said, "you like the Main Liner."

"Yes, but she likes the Diplomat."

The Groper laughed uproariously. "She's crazy about him. But he's crazy about you." And then the Groper leered drunkenly, "Play your cards right and you may do well all around."

Revolted, Robert felt like walking out, but, he told himself, he could not forsake the girl. Besides, seriously beginning to wonder about himself, he decided it would be better to stay and fight it out.

"We never waste time on real straights," the Groper had said.

Robert remembered, too, the Diplomat's cynical observation: "Those who make the greatest show of resistance often crumble the easiest." He would show them how wrong they were. On his desk he planted a copy of the prayer of St. Michael, as a warranty against the forces of evil and grimly resolved to stick it out.

In other offices, where homosexuality is less common, many wisely refuse to accept rumors of a co-worker's deviation without more substantial evidence than gossip. Indeed, the fair-minded, deploring character assassination, often take it upon themselves to verify such reports. In one instance, a worker for a large publication, criticizing colleagues for slandering a young editor, was ridiculed in turn as a Pollyanna. Angrily, he took it upon himself to spike the ugly rumors once and for all.

There certainly was nothing in the editor's appearance to indicate that he was anything but a normal young heterosexual. He seemed interested in the attractive young girls in his immediate working vicinity, dated occasionally, and lived comfortably alone in one of the pleasanter residential areas of the fashionable East Side. He was interested in the theater and the arts, but these interests were certainly shared by others in the office and were in themselves indicative of nothing more than normal intellectual curiosity.

"If he were homosexual," his defender said, "I certainly would sense it." When the others laughed, suggesting the "acid test," a tête-à-tête outside the office, he agreed with alacrity.

As casually as possible Charlie suggested dinner to the young editor one night. Though surprised at the invitation, George expressed his thanks with equal casualness. That week they met for cocktails in a bar in the East Fifties, then adjourned to a restaurant nearby. After dinner, puffing at an old meerschaum, George began yawning.

"Would you like to drop up for a nightcap?" Charlie asked. "I'm quite close by."

George considered, then shook his head. "Too many late nights," he said. "I'll take a rain check."

Charlie was beginning to glow with vindication. All night he had been searching without success for some telltale glance, movement, an expression, a phrase, anything that could be classified as suspicious. And now, without more ado, George was ready to call it a night.

As they came out into the street, George said, "Shall we walk? My place is only in the next block." In front of his apartment, as courtesy would indicate, he asked Charlie if he would like to drop up a moment. After briefly hesitating Charlie decided to accept the courtesy invitation and add a final clincher to his report. "Yes, we were alone," he would say, "and there was nothing, nothing."

The apartment was what might be expected—pleasant and cozy, expensively decorated without being ornate. There were water colors and oils on the living-room walls, all in good taste, though none were by artists whose names he recognized. George poured the scotch and politely inquired, "Water or soda?"

They sat for a while chatting. Then Charlie, having expressed his admiration for the small gallery, looked at his watch and announced he must run.

"My best painting is in the other room," George said. "Would you care to see it?"

Charlie trailed after George as he stepped through a doorway. The room was faintly lighted by a small lamp shining on a large picture over the bed.

George stood quietly, waiting for Charlie's verdict. In the dimness Charlie could make out a large figure perched on a fence, in an indolent pose. As his eyes grew used to the light, he realized, with a start, that the figure was nude, and then as he edged closer, he recognized, with a sharp constriction of the stomach, that it was George.

He almost dropped the glass he had been holding, snatched up his hat and coat, and virtually ran for the door.

The following morning he was besieged by co-workers anxious for a report. "Well?" he was asked. He shrugged. "Nothing, absolutely nothing," he said. "All we did was have dinner and look at pictures."

CHAPTER X

Keeping Fit

THE GYMS OF New York are paradises for homosexuals. Here they come to posture, flex muscles, and establish an intimacy among themselves in apparently conventional surroundings. Not all gymnasiums welcome or want them. In fact, many take steps to discourage their trade. Some arbitrarily bar the most obvious. Others are put through such rigorous routines that they are only too glad to look elsewhere for their exercise and fun.

For those who prefer the great outdoors there is always Riis Park, a beautiful bit of sand strip on the Atlantic. Here the weight-lifting, muscle-happy colony rivals Santa Monica's old "Muscle Beach," and police have learned to keep a watchful eye out for those leaving their weights long enough to forage among the bathing thousands.

But the gyms get the vast bulk of the trade. In some gyms, particularly on Manhattan's more effete East Side, there are so many homosexual muscle men that the ordinary male interested in keeping fit gets the feeling of being surrounded.

In one health center, well known as a mecca for the gay set, they virtually monopolize the exercise room—and in the security of superior numbers, "let their hair down." Some waltz in with Capezios, instead of the customary sneakers. Others fancy ballet slippers. Nearly all sport bikini-tight shorts, which leave little to the imagination. And their shirts, when they wear any, run the spectrum from shocking pink to deep purple.

They smile brightly at one another as they mince, swagger, or toddle through their calisthenics, revealing an inclination to work in teams. Intimate physical contact between partners is common. They find it almost routine to touch one another, often caressingly, but usually unobtrusively, as though the contact was accidental. "They pass weighty bar bells and dumbbells to one another with endearing smiles," an observer said, "and when help is needed for the precise performance of a difficult calisthenic, they often make it more a labor of love than an exercise. Instead of holding down a companion's knees with one hand so he can do a situp without bending the knee, they sit down and straddle one another's legs, facing each other, smiling, as though this were the most natural thing in the world."

In some clubs their activities are well-organized.

In one gym, where their numbers discourage nonhomosexuals, they are supervised by a big-muscled "queen" who struts through the ranks of straining gymnasts as though he were a king. He pats one youthful homosexual on the backside encouragingly, corrects another, stops to chat with still another, discussing a current Broadway play or exchanging witticisms about a mutual acquaintance. He is an imaginative taskmaster. Once, when his disciples seemed to be lolling about indolently, hardly stirring, he clapped his hands and said brightly:

"Now let's do a few of these things to the rhythm of a cha-cha-cha."

There was a responsive laugh, and the boys gaily whipped into a fenzy of bench presses, jerks, snatches, chins, pushups, and knee bends as a smile of satisfaction crossed their leader's beaming face.

Though many homosexuals work out with favorites, they are not averse to making new friends in the course of common pursuit. The experience is unsettling to some who only want the exercise. One startled heterosexual, a rather unimaginative salesman, recalled his first brush with these exponents of "the body beautiful." Looking up in the calisthenic room, he noticed a young fellow watching him swing the pulleys. "I thought he was just being friendly," the salesman observed. "Everybody seemed to be watching everybody else, and I thought he was only being kind to a newcomer. So I smiled back, and the next thing he tells me I'm not doing the exercise right. 'You should pull up and out more,' he says, 'like this.' He grabs the ropes and is showing me how, and I can't seem to get the knack. So he clucks with his tongue a few times, smiles patiently, and says, 'Go ahead and I'll help you.' Now he's behind me and his hand is on my arm, the next thing his arm is around my waist and he's showing me how to twist my torso. I'm beginning to feel funny with this guy breathing down my neck, and his arm around me, but I didn't want to make a federal case out of it."

After the lesson the impromptu teacher, a trim well-muscled figure in his thirties, said with a friendly smile: "The next time I'll show you how to do the situps."

More conversation than calisthenics often seems to occur in the gymnasiums where homosexuals flourish. In one establishment where the gay boys outnumber heterosexuals, they seem to do everything but work out, engaging in rapt tête-à-têtes, sitting together in window seats in skimpy gym costumes, eyes glued on each other, and carelessly touching hands.

Impervious to eavesdroppers, one homosexual, interrupting another's weight-lifting routine, suggested a visit to the steam room in another part of the building. The other, a heavily muscled young man in his twenties, put down a hundred-pound bar bell and twittered: "Why do I always do what you want me to?"

The other responded with a pleased smile and they sauntered off together, to research the hot room, arms companionably about each other's shoulders.

Offended by such displays, many straight men have carried complaints to proprietors. Others have tried other gyms when the complaints for some reason went unheeded. Like some bars, there are gyms which seem blind to their customers' activities. "Give us proof," one health director challenged, "and we will be only too happy to get rid of them."

"How about the way they keep billing and cooing and petting each other?" an irate young man exclaimed.

The director shook his head sadly. "That's not evidence of anything."

After the disillusioned young man resigned, he happened to be walking near his old club one day with a friend. The friend waved at an older man with a mincing walk who abruptly turned into the club building.

"Who's that swish?" the young man asked.

His friend laughed. "He's one of the directors of the club."

The other groaned. "And they told me they didn't have evidence!"

There are many reasons why homosexuals go in for bodybuilding. Psychologists attribute it to an overwhelming Narcissus complex. Others see their obsession with musclebuilding as a compensation. As with other homosexual activity, they are motivated, too, by the desire to meet like-minded homosexuals.

"I'm convinced," said a veteran masseur in a well-known health center, "that they go in for all this gym work because it gives them a chance to look each other over."

Most, he pointed out, visualize the male form as normal men would a woman's.

"Just imagine," he said, "the ordinary Joe having a chance to work out in a skimpy gym suit with Marilyn Monroe or Elizabeth Taylor and then trooping off to the showers with them." He whistled. "What a turnout you'd have."

Even formidable health attendants, who were once boxers or wrestlers, have had their difficulties with the "effeminate Atlases."

"It used to make me laugh," said a burly ex-heavyweight in an East Side massage parlor, "to see these fruitcakes waltz through here, but, believe me, it can get you down after a while."

As he was bending over a massage table, plying his art, a handsome young man, looking very much the Athenian god or Hollywood movie star, brushed by on his way to the showers. His towel trailed lightly after him as though it were a robe.

At the sight of this Adonis, parading through the hydrotherapy room, the masseur's body stiffened and his face became a deep purple. He gave the new arrival a baleful look. "You left that shower running the last time," he shouted, "and it swamped the place. Next time I'll throw you out on your tail."

The young man reacted mildy. "I don't think it was I," he said. "It couldn't have been. I'm always so careful when *you're* here." The masseur became even angrier. "Never mind that," he roared. "Out you go the next time."

The young man still tried to be conciliatory. "I'm sorry *you* feel that way," he said, fidgeting with his towel, "but I want *you* to know it couldn't have been me. *You* really must believe that."

His abject apologies only seemed to fire the masseur's wrath. "Never mind the hogwash," he bellowed. "Just remember I'm watching you."

With a helpless sigh the youth glided into the shower room, carefully closing the glazed glass partition behind him. The masseur kept looking his way angrily, muttering under his breath. "What were you so excited about?" a customer asked.

The masseur mopped the perspiration off his face. "I don't like those fruitcakes messing around here, getting water all over the place," he said.

"It might have been an accident," another customer said conciliatorily.

But the masseur wouldn't be mollified. "He's no good," he said warmly. "And I mean it, I'll throw him out the next wrong move he makes."

The customer on his table started up in protest as the masseur's powerful hands dug into his relaxed muscles.

"Sorry," the masseur mumbled, resuming his normal rhythm. "Do you know what that fruitcake says to me the last time he's here?" He looked around indignantly. "He tells me what beautiful muscles I got." He was beginning to get angry all over again. "Can you imagine a crack like that? I told the bum if he came near me, I'd throw him out."

The masseur had reported the "overture" to his superiors.

"We can't throw a fellow out," he was told, "unless we have something more tangible than a compliment."

That was his last complaint. "I ain't going to do any reporting next time. Just let this fruitcake make one move, I'll knock him through the wall and report later."

"I understand now," the customer said, "it wasn't the running water after all."

Still belligerent, the masseur said, "I keep watching him. If he's in the steam, I duck in every once in a while to make sure he ain't causing trouble. I don't want him talking to anybody in there."

Not all health clubs are as lenient. In many, prospective members are carefully checked. "There must not be even a suspicion of sexual irregularity," one official reported.

However, even in the strictest places, a homosexual will occasionally slip through. In one East Side gymnasium catering to leaders of industry and the arts and sciences, suspicion focused on a slim, middle-aged customer of distinguished bearing who backed Broadway plays as an avocation. "Despite my years of experience with homosexuals," the owner said, "I had no misgivings when he started coming to the place. Then he turned up with two or three guests, and I began to wonder. They were young actors, and they were laughing and gamboling all over the place, bothering everybody. I revoked guest privileges, and we started to watch him. At first I didn't notice anything. Then one day I walked into the exercise room and saw him with a tiny poodle.

"The instructor was putting him through his paces, and the dog was littering up the place. I didn't know who to throw out first—the dog, the customer, or the instructor.

"I told him we didn't permit animals, and I gave the instructor hell. I thought of firing him but he'd been with me for years."

A new exercise program was worked out for the customer. "We told the dog fancier we felt he could use some boxing lessons, to develop timing. After one lesson with another customer, a onetime boxing champ, he didn't come back for any more lessons."

The club also lost its instructor. "The dog lover," the owner reported, "had set him up in a business." He sighed. "No matter how well you seem to know somebody, you can never be sure."

Despite the derision of heterosexuals, many of these muscle-building gay boys seem to be as tough as they look. For in the lusty tradition of Richard the Lion-Hearted and Frederick the Great, vaunted bisexuals of another day, the homosexuals seem to turn out their share of warriors.

CHAPTER XI

Bisexual

ALTHOUGH BISEXUALS HAVE flourished in the West since Achilles and Patroclus warred—and loved—together before the gates of Troy, they are still little understood, even by other homosexuals. Many homosexuals have never been intimate with a woman, either from shyness, indifference, or revulsion. Others have experienced limited relationships through curiosity or as a cover-up, but without pleasure or gratification. However, the bisexual is that singular paradox, a homosexual type who enjoys women pretty much as he does men.

In the modern vernacular they have been called switch-hitters, "A.C.-D.C.s, BIs (rhymes with pies), double-gaited;

and, almost contemptuously, they use these terms themselves. Many are married, with children, and live as seemingly normal citizens.

But rather than being the most favored of men, as some might think, the bisexual appears to have greater emotional and social problems than other people. He is in constant conflict with himself because of his very ambivalence, and no homosexual feels greater pangs of guilt. And no one has greater problems with himself and society. For the bisexual, unlike so many homosexuals and heterosexuals, does not know where he belongs.

I had been working on this book only a short time when a stranger phoned me at my office. He mentioned the name of a young lady who was a mutual friend and said he would like to discuss my book with me. There was an almost feverish intensity in his voice as he related he was with a prominent public relations firm, as though this were assurance of his good faith and substance. "I could meet you anywhere you want tonight, tomorrow, or next week," he said. I wondered a bit at the urgency in his voice.

"Do you know what the book is about?" I inquired.

"Oh yes," he said. "That's why I want to talk to you."

"Okay," I said, suggesting a popular mid-town restaurant convenient for the two of us. "I'll meet you at five-thirty."

"I'll be wearing a tan suit," he said, "with a tan tie."

"I'll find you."

Shortly after hanging up I called the girl, a magazine writer who had been interested in my book because of an unfortunate marriage with a homosexual. She was the brisk, forthright type of female so prevalent in the business world today.

"A friend of yours called," I said.

"Oh yes," she said. "He's a switch-hitter. I don't know what to make of him myself. He's got a wife, two kids, goes after the girls like mad, and likes the boys." She sounded wryly amused. "Have a nice time."

I was a few minutes late, and people were already milling around in the cocktail lounge. I could see no unattached, single men at the bar or at any of the tables in the lounge. Suddenly, I saw a youngish man, about thirty, heavy-set, get up from a small table and show a lovely blonde of twenty-one to the door. He was dressed in a tan suit and matching tie and looked like a professional football player. On his way back to the table he stopped and with a friendly smile inquired whether I was his man. He explained casually, "I slipped over early to have a drink with the girl. She's such an eager young thing, so anxious to please. One drink tonight, and tomorrow night we'll have a few more and it'll be over with." He winked, and it was quite obvious what he meant.

As we turned to our drinks, I could see his casualness begin to wear thin. He was nervously puffing at a cigarette, picking at a paper napkin, and hunching around in his chair. But mostly it was his eyes. They were covertly studying me as he asked the nature of my book. "What kind of story are you planning?" he asked. "The exposé type of thing?"

I shook my head.

"No," I said, "what I'd like to show is the impact of the over-all problem, not only as it affects the homosexual himself but society, his family, the people he works with, his girl friends, his wife, if he has one."

Stu nodded knowingly.

"You know, I suppose," he said, "that I'm married with two kids." He spoke hurriedly, gulping his martini. For a moment I thought there might be some mistake. He certainly wasn't the popular conception of the homosexual. There was nothing effeminate about him. He was of medium height, with big capable-looking hands. His face looked rugged, with deep-set eyes, a square jaw, and a prominent nose.

He laughed nervously, correctly reading my surprise. "Hell," he said, "being married doesn't make much difference. I hoped it would, but every three months or so I look at some guy and he looks at me and that's it."

That led to the question: Did his wife know?

"No, we live out a ways, and she doesn't have reason to suspect. And you've got to remember"—his brown eyes rested on me almost pleadingly—"I dig girls, too, and they dig me."

He drew a deep breath. "My wife wouldn't understand," he said; "no woman possibly could. And yet I feel she loves me and the children enough to stick anyway."

I couldn't help but wonder as we sat there why he was confiding in a complete stranger. Certainly as a responsible young executive, he was in no position to risk exposure. "Would it bother you if she found out?" I asked.

"Not really," he said, "but I just don't like her knowing. You never know about women. This way I'm the man, and what I say goes."

There seemed very little pattern to what he was saying. One moment he would be talking about the office, and the necessity of keeping his secret; another, describing his interest in girls; and then the young men; and again back to his wife. And his parents. It was certainly a free association of ideas in the best Freudian tradition, but there was no therapist in the neighborhood.

In his office only other homosexuals recognized him for what he was. "That's because I'm so strong with the girls," he said. "I always have one in the office on the string—they like the idea of living dangerously with a married man, and not getting tied up."

He glanced across the table. "Don't get the idea that all homosexuals don't like girls. I like them fine, but every once in a while, like I said, something happens." His voice suddenly became defensive. "It isn't just sex—it's like falling in love, I can't help myself.

"There's this one guy, for instance. We get together every three or four months, spend an evening together, and then do what we have to do and we go back to our wives and kids. He's a good family man—four kids and he's one of the top executives in his business. Besides," he shrugged, "what harm does it do?"

It had given me a start to hear this hunk of man speak unashamedly of an infatuation for another man. "What's the point of being married?" I asked.

He smiled for the first time. "I like it," he said. "I'm bisexual, and I guess that's the way the cookie crumbles. I'm not the kind of a guy who goes around hating women because he's trying to get even with his mother. I just dig women—and men—and if it weren't for all the guilt deal and the rest that I grew up with, I'd probably be having a helluva time."

"If that's the way it is, why feel guilty?"

He grimaced. "Hell," he said, "that's like telling a virgin not to cry about her lost virginity. I was brought up a Catholic, and you know how the Church stands on homosexuality." Expressively, he slid a hand across his throat. "I don't know how much of a Catholic I am today, but it does intensify the conflict."

There was no lack of congenial companionship for Stu, whichever way he turned. Like many of his friends, he was always on the lookout for other homosexuals, and he haunted cocktail parties, charity benefits, and other social functions for the telltale glimpse. "There are ways a homosexual

99

knows another homosexual that nobody else could even begin to know," he said. "First of all, effeminacy doesn't mean anything, because a lot of straight guys have effeminate manners, and some of the worst queers look like the young girl's dream of Mr. America.

"But at a party a homosexual will make a remark which would be meaningless to the average person but which another homosexual will either pick up or show interest in, and without giving himself away he'll remember who looked up when he made his remark."

"What kind of a remark?"

"Well, take sea food for instance. That's almost a code word, thrown in when it's not quite the right word and yet it's not too far off to lift other eyebrows. Suppose somebody's talking about whales or sardines, and you say, 'I like sea food.' Well, sardines or minnows aren't exactly sea food, though they're fish, and if anybody looks up on this then both know they have made a connection."

In his office, he said, there is a group of homosexuals known for sure only to themselves, though one or two who were obvious might be suspected by others. "They might wonder, but so long as they don't know," he said, "you're safe." And three or four times a week they would meet at a bathhouse and take the steam together.

I must have looked puzzled.

"Haven't you ever been in a steam room?" he asked. "They're quite foggy."

He gulped down another drink. "I don't like that kind of jazz myself," he said. "There's no privacy or dignity to it. Why parade it all—even in a steam room?"

"Have you any ideas how it all started?" I asked.

"I'm not sure," he said, "not even after $2700 for psyciatry. It helped calm me down a little and understand myself a little better, but I'm still not sure."

He looked up. "Maybe it's the broken home. Anyway, I blame it on my mother." His face clouded over, and he seemed lost in thought.

"When was the first time? Do you mind telling me about that?"

Ordinarily, I had found these difficult questions, but Stu seemed grimly resolved to talk about everything.

"That didn't amount to anything," he said. "I was fifteen then, and there was a painter around the house. He got me curious. But that was just a kid incident. There wasn't anything else until I went to college, one of those cow col-

100

leges out west, and I saw this guy at a fraternity rushing party. We just looked at each other across the room, our glances held, and we both knew it was it. A year later it broke up when I went in the Navy and served in the Korean War."

"Couldn't the service doctors tell with their various screening examinations?"

He laughed. "That's a joke. Anybody with any mind at all can answer the questions. As a matter of fact, they recommended me for submarine service, which is just about the last place they should have anybody like me—let's face it."

The conversation came back to Stu's mother. "I always resented the situation she put me in and I still do," he said. "When I was sixteen, my parents broke up. I dug my father, I really did and wanted to go with him. I was all set. But there was my five-year-old brother, and mother said she wanted to keep the family together. It was for me to decide where my brother and I would go. I hated having to make this decision for my brother because I felt that, being so young, he should stay with Mother and so I stayed, too."

Just thinking of those days seemed to stimulate Stu's drinking. He downed a double martini in one swallow, and then plowed ahead bravely. "It wasn't very good. My mother married again—a lush—and she began drinking, too. I spent a lot of time with my father and his second wife. She was a lot younger, nearer my age, and the first thing you know—my dad was away a lot—I was sleeping with her. I felt so guilty that I finally went off to college, but after I got to thinking about it, I couldn't help but think what a sap my dad turned out to be."

His earlier affection for his father had soured over the years, unconsciously perhaps over the wrong Stu had done him, but consciously over his father's inability to handle sympathetically a problem that baffles virtually all parents affected by it. Learning about Stu's homosexuality from his own lips, the father had counseled against entangling others in the web of homosexuality.

Even now, as he thought of that day of ignominy and confession years before, Stu's face darkened. He could still see his father sitting there, studying him. "I'm with you in whatever you want to do," he said, "but never marry. You'll wind up ruining not only your life but lots of others."

Stu, then eighteen, didn't make any promises. He just sat there, hanging his head in embarrassment, and he could

101

hear his father, "I don't care what you've done. You're still my son—nothing changes that—not even if you'd murdered somebody."

As Stu thought then about his father's reaction, he became resentful. Where did his father get off comparing him with criminals? What help was he? He had been looking for something, he didn't know what, and he got a slap in the face. His father was never again a major influence in his life.

Both at college and in the Navy Stu was constantly testing his masculinity with girls. The more the thought of his homosexuality bothered him, the more he became involved in attempts to prove his virility to himself. At one naval base he was attentive to an officer's wife, secure in the knowledge the officer was at sea. But the officer, advised by gossip sent back word that he would kill Stu on sight. I got so scared," Stu recalled, "that I carried a gun and accidentally shot myself. I was so nervous I'd jump if somebody closed a door or dropped a spoon. I felt as if I was going to jump out of my skin."

This experience, together with the deepening inner conflicts, shattered him so that he looked desperately for help.

"Finally," he recalled, "I went to the psychiatrist. He wasn't much older than I, and he'd sit there behind the desk, nodding wisely and saying: 'Yes, yes, go on, and then what happened?' I found myself fighting him, but I could feel my nervousness leaving me. I had somebody to talk to, to get rid of my fears, to talk about my mother, that guy in college, the painter and the girls. Soon I began looking forward to the sessions, and then I found myself watching him, studying him. Suddenly, the realization came to me that he was a beautiful man, and I had never even thought of him that way before. I felt an urge one day, as he was talking to me, to put my arms around him and kiss him. He seemed to sense what I was thinking and smiled over at me, saying, 'Let's talk that out now.'"

Shortly thereafter the doctor felt he had done all he could for his patient. "Essentially, all he tried to do," Stu observed, "was to make me feel more comfortable with myself. He was not trying to change me, except to get me to realize there were thousands and millions of people just like me and there was no reason to hate myself for it."

Through it all, tantalizingly, the notion of marriage lurked in a corner of Stu's brain. After leaving the psychiatrist, who had talked him out of his infatuation, he decided to marry. "I guess," he said, "I never gave up rebelling at my father's advice." The girl he finally fastened upon was no more attractive than a dozen others he had known. But he thought they could get along. "She excited me physically," he said, "and that was always important with me. And I guess I was looking for social approval. I felt if I married and raised some kids, the other urge would leave me. I thought it had, until one day I ran into this fellow. Instead of feeling depressed about it, I felt glad, exhilarated. I thought of fighting it, then thought what for? As a matter of fact, after relaxing with him it was easier to go home to my wife."

I couldn't help thinking Stu's life rather complicated. "How do you find time and energy for so many people?" I asked.

He shrugged. "Bill makes the difference for me; he gives me what I don't get out of marriage, the emotional stimulation I need."

This was a new name. "Bill?"

"Yes, Bill, the one with four kids. I mentioned him before."

He has been seeing Bill, a suburban dweller, for years. They have their private jokes together. Bill recently got a community award for father of the year. "We got quite a belt out of that one," Stu recalled.

There was no mistaking who was the paramount influence in his life. "Bill," he enthused, "is the only person I've ever met who was good for me. He has a clear, cold appraising mind which takes me out of my confusion and restores my calm."

As in nearly every homosexual relationship, Stu pointed out, there could be no permanence unless a pair complemented each other. "That's the kind of relationship I have with Bill," Stu said. "But you see these nances breaking up after a few nights or weeks all the time, and there's no helping it because there is nothing to keep them together. These things can last only if there is balance—if one is aggressive and the other passive; one working and earning money, the other cooking and keeping the home."

Bill clearly asserted his superiority in the intellectual field. "But in the bedroom," Stu explained, "I was supreme. I knew because of his superior personality I would have to register my domination early or the relationship would founder. So when he started to toy with me, shortly after we met, I picked him up bodily by the thigh and shoulder,

103

raised him over my head, and said: 'Look, don't mess around with me or I'll waste you.'

"He said, 'Let me down,' as quietly as anybody could, and we have never had any question since as to who rules in what realm."

That was by no means the only interview. Stu called several times thereafter, and we met at convenient bars. He seldom mentioned his wife but talked freely about everybody else. Wondering about his confiding so completely in a stranger, I once asked how he had happened to call in the first place. "For all you knew," I said, "you were exposing both your marriage and your job—if your confidences weren't kept."

He nodded. "I know that, but I had to talk to someone."

"How about one of your many girl friends?" I asked.

He made a wry face. "Tell one of those dames I'm a faggot and she'd laugh in my face."

"Well, how about your homosexual friends?"

He guffawed loudly. "That," he said, "would be like talking to myself."

"But why me?" I persisted.

"Since you're writing a book," he said, "you're bound to know something about the problem."

I nodded. "And since you're a newspaperman," he went on, "you're morally bound to protect your sources."

Again I nodded. "Well," he said, "since I had to talk to somebody, and couldn't afford a psychiatrist any more, I thought I'd try you." He grinned broadly. "That's all a lot of homosexuals want anyway—somebody to listen to them."

CHAPTER XII

Nonconformist

SOME HOMOSEXUALS NOT only don't mind being homosexual, but think everybody else should be. While they feel no physical attraction for women, they frequently enjoy their company, and may laugh and jest with them and pleasantly discuss cosmetics, styles, lingerie, and hairdos. The female component appears rather strongly in their make-ups, and they become passive figures, not only in relationships with other homosexuals, but in patiently enduring the slings and arrows of prejudice and scorn.

Although many are from respectable, even prominent families, they have no social status themselves, no hopes or aspirations, and seem to drift aimlessly in the stream of life. They wear their homosexuality casually, analyze it without rancor, or even interest, and consider journalistic attempts to understand it so much balderdash. "Why not go out," one suggested, "and ask heterosexuals why they like women?"

Many lose themselves in the Bohemian world of Greenwich Village, dabbling in art and literature, calling themselves poets or painters when they are often no more than vagrants. Even possessing talent, some still lack the discipline to accomplish anything and are content to impress other homosexuals with their "wit." Quite often they do not know where they are staying from one week to the next, sharing friends' apartments until the hosts tire and they have to move on. In their little Bohemia, they become caricatures of the Village genius, with unkempt hair, rumpled clothing, dirty hands and face. They look with mocking eyes—some gently, others fiercely—on what they call the materialistic world and seek to justify their own floundering by the utter futility of this antlike striving.

I suppose Hamilton, who was known to friends as the poet laureate of Greenwich Village, was of the gentler variety. He was mild, unobtrusive, quietly sardonic. Tall, stooped, angular, he looked like the proverbial sharp-faced Yankee, though his roots were in the Far West. He wore no hat even in the coldest weather, bending his shaggy head to the breeze, and his shabby coat, billowing in the wind, always seemed to be missing two or three buttons. He was thirtyish and had been in the city for ten years without becoming part of it. I ran into him frequently on the Village streets, and he was always alone, scurrying somewhere with a portfolio of his prose and verse under his arm. Though he appeared shy and diffident, he could usually stand a joke at his own expense. Once, looking down at his meager portfolio, he said laconically, "Have poems, will travel."

He generally looked as if he could use a good meal, and always seemed grateful when food was mentioned. Even though ravenous, he ate with fastidious care. "Nursing my hunger pangs," he observed dryly. He seemed a sensitive person, who had given his situation a lot of thought, even if only superficially. "I don't think anybody should feel sorry for me because I'm a homosexual," he once told me. "In fact,

105

I think everybody should be homosexual. After all, we enjoy both men and women." Like so many of his homosexual type, Hamilton, a sort of blushing "virgin," had never had an actual sexual experience with a woman. "I've thought of it from time to time," he said, "and I like sitting around talking to them, but I've never quite had the push to put it into action. Once, I thought I would, just so I could satisfy my curiosity, but when I got to the point, I decided what was the sense of kidding myself."

When I first met him, he was reciting his own poetry and prose in a coffeehouse in MacDougal Street, in the heart of the Village. He was on the same program as the beatnik poets, from such diverse parts of the country as San Francisco and Jersey City. But alone or sharing the bill, he gave the impression of an almost feline aloofness. He was a great favorite with the uptown tourists who crowded into the place, enjoying the droll, biting wit in which he spared himself least of all. The beatniks didn't like him, because he mocked their bearded pretentiousness as he did everything else that seemed to him phony or bombastic.

He came from a prominent family, and after meeting him, I assured him I would do nothing to indicate his identity. He laughed without seeming to move his lips. "I couldn't care less," he said. "As a matter of fact, I think I would rather like my name being used." His voice was scratchy, rough and uneven, but not effeminately so. "I'm not the least sensitive myself," he explained, "but I'd like to see my family's face. They're so high and mighty." The harshness of his words was softened somewhat by the mildness with which he spoke.

He was a remittance man, drawing a pittance from his family back in Arizona, to remain inconspicuously away from home. He would have fared better, financially, if he hadn't incurred his father's displeasure by courting the public spotlight. "They're all so worried about my publicity," he said, "it's really very flattering. My brother writes me—he's an attorney—and then my father writes. They don't give a hoot about me of course, it's always the sacred family name." He stifled a yawn. "It's such a bore."

He was mostly self-educated. Having finished up at a fashionable prep school in the East, he had not had the interest to go on with college. He had written about many things, including homosexuality, but nothing longer than vignettes in prose or verse, except for an unpublished autobiography, *A Boy in New York*. He was a mordant observer, with a

106

trace of perhaps unconscious bitterness. Like many homosexuals, even his humor appeared self-mocking to the point of being masochistic. Once, in the middle of a poetry reading, before the usual crowd of tourists, he smiled impishly and, breaking his wrist, mimicking a swish, said with an affected lisp. "You know I'm a bisexual myself—I like tall men and short men."

He had not had an easy time in the city, and might have starved had it not been for a hundred-dollar-a-month allowance his father sent him. "Conscience money," Hamilton called it.

"My father's big hope was not only not to see, but not to hear about me. He would correspond, because he blamed himself somehow and was trying to show that he was the interested parent. And besides, he figured that as long as he kept some sort of watch on me, he would have some control."

In New York, Hamilton worked in the public library, toiled as a waiter, painted, and acted. "Not being very good-looking," he said, "I needed money to get somebody I wanted, when I wanted him." He laughed sardonically. "You'd be amazed at the competition here for the eligible males. A good-looking young fellow, who is homosexual, is impossible to get next to, because all the good-looking young men and women are after him, and it's bound to go to his head."

Between bread-and-butter jobs, absorbed in his writing, Hamilton had to appeal for help; and the family thought there might be less chance of trouble if his allowance was increased. Hamilton found the prospect cheering, not because it would increase his standard of living, but because it might permit widening his circle of friends. "It's so stifling," he said, "to be with the same unattractive people all the time." But negotiations came to an impasse. "My wonderful father," he said, "through some lingering feeling of guilt, was going to set up a fund, increasing my income to two hundred and fifty dollars a month, when he heard about my reciting poetry with the beatniks. He told my brother to tell me that unless I cut out reading poetry and hanging around Village places, he'd rescind the fund. I refused, and he refused, and that's where matters stand." He laughed. "But at least this way, I'm independent."

Hamilton had been arrested once on a morals charge and this had already made the family understandably sensitive. When he was haled into court, Hamilton recalled ruefully, his family background had made an imposing stump on which a judge could preach a moral. "There were a couple of Negro boys brought before the judge on a similar morals charge," Hamilton said. "The judge hardly looked at them in passing sentence. But mine was the type of case that social workers could really rub their hand over. My father was a successful businessman, I had come from the upper crust of society, and here I was a degraded person."

The probation officers had been busy. "The judge read a letter from my father in which he declared he was shocked beyond words by my arrest and couldn't understand. And then the judge read me a lecture about how I, so much more fortunate than most that came before him, had made a mockery of my own background and violated the faith of my family."

Hamilton laughed. "Even as I stood there, afraid of what he might say next, it struck me as funny. My comfortable home! The day I was born my father, my wonderful father, left my mother and me. I was thirteen when my mother died, and he and his new wife took in my brother and myself. My wonderful father kept me around for about three months before he sent us packing off to prep school in Connecticut."

He smiled. "At this point," he said, "as I look back, I realize I was very much on the road to homosexuality. I have sometimes thought I was born that way, and have speculated whether I could have had some subconscious knowledge as a baby of my father's rejection of me.

"I think I must have been four or five when these tendencies began to show. I liked to wrestle with other boys, and I enjoyed it when they tied me up and beat me. I was always doing something to encourage this sort of treatment, without realizing of course what I was doing. And then I liked to try on girls' clothing. Prep school didn't help. My aunt sensed my weakness and tried to get me to mix with masculine boys. So I went out for football, for the manager's post, and the second day out the captain of the football team tried to date me."

Hamilton sighed. "What a dunce I was," he said. "All those wonderful boys after me, and I wasn't having any because my aunt's twaddle about morality had frightened me."

His older brother, now respectable, married, and successful, had succumbed at school, but Hamilton held out until he was home on vacation. He was fifteen. "Later," he recalled, "when the problem became known at home, my father was horrified. But he didn't get too violent about it because my aunt, who was his sister, said he couldn't wipe his hands of the responsibility since he hadn't provided his children with the father they needed.

"Anyway, they decided to send me to the psychiatrist. That didn't work because the psychiatrist, a woman, first tried to make me comfortable about what I was and then tried to get me to see that it was wrong. And by this time I actually didn't want to be anything but what I am—and I don't think any other homosexual does either."

I wondered how his brother had worked out his problem.

"Oh," he said with a faint expression of distaste, "I think it would be charitable to say that he compromised. He saw how his bread was buttered, and he took it from there." He laughed shortly. "The only thing I mind is the grand manner. Of course, he doesn't give me any of this morality slop, but keeps telling me to play it cool, and keep in with the old man." He shrugged. "He's all set now. My wonderful father thinks he's great because he's following in his footsteps." He sniffed. "I can do without their advice, but I would like the extra money."

"Then why not play along with your father?" I asked.

"At this stage," he said, "I'm certainly not going to let them tell me how to live." He frowned. "I suppose I could do as they ask, but then I wouldn't be myself and I wouldn't enjoy anything." Being independent seemed to be an obsession with him. He was by nature, he said, a nonconformist.

Like many homosexuals, whose weakness is their promiscuity, Hamilton lives in mortal dread of vice-squad cops who work in plain clothes. He had very good reason. He pointed out that he had been arrested a second time by police and was afraid a third arrest might send him to jail. He insisted he was victimized on both occasions. Once he was picked up in the men's washroom of the Washington Square subway station. "A stranger kept asking if I was a homosexual," he said. "I wasn't attracted but wanted to get rid of him, so I agreed. And then he accused me of making the overture." The next time, he said, a plain-clothes man was again the aggressor, but at least this one was attractive. "After he got talking to me, I became interested—since I didn't know he was a cop—and then he arrested me when I agreed to go with him."

Twice escaping with suspended sentences, he nevertheless maintains a wary eye for cops as he makes his dates on the streets, in bars, or wherever his poetry is best appreciated. In having to be so cautious, he feels he may have missed a lot. "You can generally tell by a look, but not always," he says. Several times movie stars have "given him the message," but only once, he said, did he have the boldness to investigate. "I'm no beauty," he explained, "and I thought I might be imagining."

With time working against him, Hamilton is sadly aware that he is committed to a life of comparative loneliness. "The big trouble, of course," he says, "is that these pickup things never last, so you're nearly always lonely and nearly always looking, maybe it's because I'm unstable myself, or not very strong on looks, but I don't think that's it. I just think there's nothing much to build jointly for, and things fall apart as soon as somebody more attractive or desirable comes along." He smiled sardonically. "There's just no real togetherness, as they say in magazines, and as you get older it gets worse."

As it is to Hamilton, the transitory nature of a relationship is distressing to some homosexual friends who have deluded themselves into believing that they have found a companion with whom they can live in lasting dignity. "One day this friend of mine came over and he was bubbling with elation and good will toward mankind," Hamilton recalled. "He told me about this young fellow he had met, and how they had been together, and how they were going to get married—that is, take vows to be constant with each other. I told him not to take it too seriously. He got angry and said I was jaded and cynical and couldn't understand a true love between men —that all I thought of was in terms of sex and degeneracy. I didn't get angry because I realized he was idealistic and didn't mean to be insulting.

"Anyway, he was going to bring his chum around the next day, so I could meet him and see for myself. Two days passed without Charles, so I went over to his flat to see him. The door was unlocked. As I opened it, the first thing I saw was his body, hanging from the ceiling. There was a note to me. All it said was, 'He never showed up. You'll understand.'"

Hamilton shrugged. "It was a blow," he said, "but if you're a homosexual, you get to expect that sort of thing."

As with many a heterosexual, his work is a blessing. While his writing appears a little fuzzy at times, some excerpts from "thoughts-at-random" suggest what his introverted type gets out of a relationship. "Strong, healthy men," he writes, "don't just stimulate my sexual impulses: they stimulate all sorts of other impulses and hopes. Ninety per cent self-indulge their sensuality, but there are strong, rugged men

110

whose sex life is a necessary expression of their real and vital love and regenerative nature and being. And I give them love, real, hopeful, meaningful for me and them. I give them me, who is something different and vital and expressive and evolving—they create a new child and if they are unprejudiced, they might get an inkling of this."

However, as his moods vary, and there seems nothing more volatile than the homosexual temperament, so does Hamilton's thinking on the spirituality of love. Writing to the magazine *One,* an outlet of homosexual thought, he brushes aside even homosexual objections to relationships with minors. "I can assure you," he asserted, "relations with young people can be very wonderful indeed. And I recall when I was quite young, there was nothing I would have enjoyed more than going to bed with a mature man to my liking.

"Sex is a fine pure wonderful experience when the two parties are in mutual agreement—regardless of age or gender—and whether or not it upsets any ideas some of your writers have on monogamy and so forth."

In his Village forum Hamilton can discuss homosexuality as frankly as he likes. Breaking off from a poetry reading one night, he gave his analysis of the "rough trade," which has been pouring into the Village foraging on obvious homosexuals in the bars and streets. "He has been taught homosexuality is evil," Hamilton said, "but he is so desperate for affection that he allows himself to become hopelessly poor, so he can have the excuse of having to sell himself to others."

Waiting for this thought to sink in, he added, "And after he's through, in order to convince himself he just did it for the money, he may then beat his lover."

The whole passing scene becomes the property of the Village laureate. Once he delivered an open letter to his favorite actor. "Dear Marlon Brando," he extemporized, "stop saving the world, and stick to your art."

Again he advised a roomful of giggling women, "You poor frustrated things, you've had the same husband so long it's coming out of your ears."

Recent efforts by Hollywood and Broadway to treat the homosexual theme sympathetically evoked only his scorn. *Tea and Sympathy,* praised by critics as a courageous treatment of homosexuality in a private school, he saw as not only unrevealing but unrealistic.

"All this junk," he wrote, "about how this guy really wasn't such an awful thing as a homo—they were only making him think so. Well, I got news for the critics. If I had manifested a little more love of my fellow man at my boarding school, I would not have been berated but would have been treated with ten times more kindness."

I saw Hamilton many times. The last time I saw him, I asked, "Have you ever regretted being homosexual?"

He shook his head solemnly. "Not even when I thought I might be going to jail."

He looked so shabby and forlorn, standing there in the street with the cold wind blowing through his worn coat, that I couldn't help but wonder where his next meal was coming from.

"How about a bite to eat?" I asked.

He shook his head. "I'm on my way to a poetry recital."

I looked down and saw the familiar portfolio. "Do you ever compare yourself with your brother, so comfortable and safe back home?"

He smiled. "All the time," he said. "I think he should be homosexual, too."

I turned to leave, and he stopped me. He looked apologetic. "Oh, I was going to call you," he said.

I waited.

"Do you remember my saying you could use my name?"

I nodded.

"Well," he said, "I'd rather you didn't." He looked terribly uncomfortable. "I got to thinking about it," he said. "You see, they might get mad and stop the remittance."

CHAPTER XIII

Police Beat

THE INSPECTOR MADE a wry face.

"It's a medical problem, a social problem," he said, "not a police problem, but since it's on the books, we have to handle it.

"However, if we're going to try to wipe it out, our police force couldn't do anything else but take after homosexuals and they'd keep popping up just as fast as we knocked them down."

When there are complaints of homosexuals overrunning a place and becoming a public nuisance, plain-clothes men from the Police Morals Squad arrive singly or in pairs. They are chosen generally because they are young, attractive, and don't look like cops.

"Our most successful operator," the Inspector said, "is a kid, twenty-two, with a college degree. When we send him into a place we're watching, the chances are that one of these people will make a definite move, a specific invitation to leave the place, and only then can we lock him up."

The backwash of World War II, the Inspector found, had swept the flotsam and jetsam of the deviate world into the huge city. There they could do almost as they pleased without running the same risk of exposure they would in a small town.

To this were added the forays of young delinquents devoid of morality, preying on homosexuals by first submitting to them and then robbing or beating them up. "In the beginning," he said, "these kids are only seeking an outlet for viciousness, and some loose change, but the chances are they'll wind up full-fledged homosexuals before they get through."

Police investigate many homicides among homosexuals, some reflecting important facets of the homosexual personality. "Homosexuals," the Inspector said, "can be very bitchy. They're really sick people and their emotions are rigged to a trigger. Some time ago a big burly kid, eighteen, was killed in a barroom brawl, stomped to death. It developed this kid had been living with a homosexual. We called the homosexual in, and when we told him what had happened, he went to pieces and began blubbering about his great loss.

"However, the next time we saw him, a week later, he didn't even show a sign that he remembered the boy!" The Inspector laughed mirthlessly. "He had a new boy by then."

Homosexual murders often occur as a last resort when the homosexual turns on a blackmailer. Others crop up when the killer claims he was resisting a homosexual advance. But the most common are crimes of passion resulting from jealous rages. Often the investigations run into curious digressions.

"One day," the Inspector said, "a male prostitute was killed in a tizzy by his sweetie. One of his pals was an insurance executive. He wasn't involved, but we found his name in a little black book and we wanted to question him. So we sent a man to his office. He threw up his arms and said he was too busy to discuss the case, knew nothing about it.

"I called this queen up, and he started to give me the

busy routine, too. 'Better get down here,' I told him, 'or we'll send the wagon for you.' He came down in five minutes flat."

In homosexual homicides the victims are often tied up in a way revealing to police. First, the hands are tied behind the back, in Japanese knots, then the legs, and then both hands and legs are tied together. The victim is then gagged. In one of the more recent great unsolved murders, millionaire financier Serge Rubinstein was found mysteriously tied and gagged in his Fifth Avenue mansion. But police insisted the knots were different. Serge, they said, was definitely a ladies' man.

There have been lesser mysteries. "One time," the Inspector recalled, "we were investigating a case where one fag had shot another. When our men arrived, they asked a roommate to give details of the argument leading up to the assault." The Inspector's face screwed up in familiar mimicry. "So this one says, 'I don't know anything about it. I told her not to have anything to do with him. I heard them talking, but I was behind my own curtain. I kept warning her, but she wouldn't listen and that's all I know.'"

The Inspector snorted. "In these cases," he said, "they never know anything."

It is quite common, the Inspector said, for homosexuals to use feminine names, particularly when living together in a casual relationship. "Mabel and Flo are common names for the passive type," he said, "and there are others. Some of these boys—the ones other homosexuals refer to as 'she' and 'her'—try to emulate movie stars like Katharine Hepburn, Bette Davis, and Mae West—stars with a special manner who flounce about the most. Mae is the most popular."

The Inspector, reflecting a traditional police attitude, revealed little sympathy for a group many consider underdogs. "Most of them are arrogant," he said, "they're convinced they have the only way of life. There was a professor of philosophy we picked up, and he spent a half hour trying to convince me that I was wrong and he was right and how much I was missing. I finally booked him for loitering and that ended the philosophy."

Quite often even the police are amazed by the hair-trigger volatility of homosexuals, particularly under pressure.

In the fashionable East Side two plain-clothes men, cruising one night, observed a man hoisting another through the window of a ground-floor apartment. Stopping their car, they got out just as he clambered into the apartment. They grabbed the man on the sidewalk and went into the building. The supposed intruder, hearing their knock, came apprehensively to the door. He paled at the sight of his friend in police custody. Asked to explain what he was up to, he began wringing his hands and suddenly collapsed into tears.

His friend quickly explained that the sensitive young man was a well-known writer and was staying at the apartment as the guest of an even better-known writer. Somehow, he had mislaid the key and, unable to reach his host, had taken this means of gaining entrance. Meanwhile, the writer was inconsolable. "If I could only call my friend," he cried, "he could explain everything and I wouldn't be held like a common criminal."

One cop asked, "Where is your friend?"

"He was going to be at this restaurant for dinner."

"All right," the officer said, "we'll give you one call."

The writer fought back his tears long enough to make the call. The officers saw his face drop. With a quiver in his voice, he said: "He just left."

"Well, you'll have to come along," the officer said, taking the writer by the arm. At this point he fell into a chair, wailing, until his friend pointed out that all it meant was waiting at the station house until the playwright turned up.

Meanwhile, the officers were gazing curiously around the apartment. They had never seen one like it before. In the lofty living room a large cascade of water dropped from the ceiling, watering the greenery planted at one end of an immense room. The foliage was tropical and a scent of ambrosia lay heavy on the room. The ceiling was a mural depicting the moon, stars, and sundry planets, including the Milky Way and certain cherubs.

Fortunately for the window-hopping writer, the policemen's curiosity kept them in the apartment until the scrape of a key was heard in the lock and a man entered in evening dress. It was the host, returning early because he had forgotten something. His guest almost swooned in joy. And then, shuddering exquisitely, he closed his eyes. "Thank God," he sighed. "It has been dreadful, just dreadful."

The playwright quickly clarified the situation. The cops left, gladly, and the writer, for the next hour, related to his host the terrible experience he had just lived through, making it seem, for all his gesticulations, at least the equivalent of the trials of Job.

The hard-boiled police attitude is often no more than a reflection of the usual male disdain for homosexuals, and expresses itself in many ways short of arrest. One evening a detective standing outside a hotel in New York City's Herald Square, just across from Macy's and Gimbel's, was approached by an obvious homosexual, who couldn't have been mistaken anywhere. His eyebrows were plucked, he walked with a mincing gait, his hair was down his neck and blondined. Even his sweater was padded out.

"You seem to be waiting for someone very anxiously," he said with a lisp.

The detective nodded curtly and turned aside.

Unaware that he was flirting with a detective, and sudden arrest, the homosexual persisted.

"I've been watching you," he said, "and I find you most attractive."

The detective had a reputation among his colleagues for a rather rough sense of humor. The least shadow of a smile played about his eyes, and he decided, with a certain grimness, that he would have some fun for himself while he was awaiting a friend.

He eyed the homosexual up and down. "What are you," he said sharply, "one of these queers?"

"How did you ever guess that?" the homosexual asked.

Half-resenting the fact that he had been singled out by a "fairy," half-amused, the detective kept the conversation going. He discovered that the homosexual worked as an orderly at a hospital and lived nearby. "I've made an awful lot of friends at the hospital," the homosexual said. "I'm quite discreet." He looked up and managed what he thought an impish smile. "I'm sure you'll like me," he said.

That decided the cop. "I'm busy now," he said, "but I'll tell you what I'll do. I'll meet you across the street"—he pointed to a store front—"at the same time tomorrow night."

The homosexual's face lit up gratefully. "Thank you, thank you," he said. "You'll never regret it. I promise you that."

The detective looked at him with an enigmatic smile. "I'm sure I won't," he said.

The next morning in the squad room of his precinct he mentioned the incident of the night before to brother officers.

"Why didn't you pull the faggot in?" one of the detectives asked.

"What for?" he shrugged, "and waste my time." He laughed. "I have a much better idea," and he elaborated the plan he had in mind. The others joined in the laughter.

That night, at the appointed hour, a large car drew up in front of a Herald Square store, where a youngish man with blondined hair stood waiting. As the man admiringly studied his reflection in the store window, six burly men piled out of the car. One was the detective. He raised his hand and cried, "Now!" as though giving a signal. At the same time, hearing the commotion, the homosexual turned—and caught a barrage of overripe tomatoes. They spattered his face and hair, dripped over his clothes, and choked his mouth, leaving him gasping for air.

"The last I saw him," the detective recalled, "he was running down the street dodging rotten tomatoes."

Many policemen report unhappy experiences with homosexuals. One day the security head of a famous hotel was sitting in his office when a big, red-faced man burst in importantly and demanded, "What's your job around here?"

Coolly, the head cop replied: "I'm in charge of the police around here, and this is my office. Now, what are you doing here?"

"Fine head of police," the visitor snorted. "I reported my $500 watch missing last night, and that's the end of it."

"We've been doing all we can," the detective said mildly.

The big man gave him a withering look. "Doing all you can," he repeated disdainfully, adding with a ring of utter scorn: "I don't know why I should expect anything; you must make $60 a week." He sneered. "And I make $10,000 a month." Still blustering, he eyed the cop disgustedly. "I don't even know why I'm bothering with you," he said. "What have you got?"

With a bleak smile the cop replied evenly. "I've got something that you haven't got. I've got my manhood."

"What do you mean by that?" the businessman lashed back.

"I mean," the cop said slowly, biting off each word, "that you're nothing but a lousy faggot—and the sooner you get out of the hotel the better."

The businessman's face became threatening. "How are you going to back that up?" he demanded.

The cop smiled without moving his lips. "That's easy," he said. He pointed to the telephone. "Police headquarters called just before you blew in here, and said they had the guy but the watch was smashed." He glanced up at his visitor. "You never gave me a chance to tell you." His voice was cold and lashed out like a whip. "And the guy told them everything, including how you had picked him up in a bar and taken him to your room."

The fight suddenly left the man in front of him. All at

117

once he seemed to look three sizes smaller. His voice changed abruptly. "Please don't tell the insurance company," he pleaded.

The cop's jaws clamped together. "You were ready to tell everybody. Now I'm playing your tune."

The businessman was almost tearful now. "I can't afford to let this get back to Chicago," he stammered.

"I know," the cop said. "You're a big deal back there. But save your breath, they're going to know about you." He stood up quickly. "Now get out of here, while I get the place fumigated."

As the businessman stumbled out the detective reached for the phone and called the claims adjuster at the insurance office in Chicago and told him the story. "You're crazy if you pay him," he concluded.

"We'll have to," came the surprising retort, "even with what you told us. Why, he's one of the biggest wheels in Chicago."

Many policemen acknowledge their personal distaste for homosexuals don't like to appear as witnesses, even when parent indolence on cases of robbery or assault reported by homosexuals. "We just know," a top detective said, "that we can't get anywhere on these types of cases. In a showdown homosexuals don't like to appear as witnesses, even when they aren't themselves directly involved; they have some silly feeling that they should all stick together in an emergency against us outsiders. And then when you do make an arrest it's generally thrown out. Very few juries will convict, once they discover that the victim is queer. They figure he brought it on himself, and it serves him right." He shrugged, "So what do we do, change human nature?"

Many homosexuals become a police problem when they make public exhibitions of themselves. Recently, on the look-out for a stolen car, police turned their flashlight on a vehicle parked at night under the ramp of a bridge. They inadvertently surprised a wealthy businessman with a male prostitute. Instead of retiring to the comfort and security of his nearby apartment, the homosexual had preferred the additional excitement of risking detection. The psychiatrists might have explained that, subconsciously, he was inviting apprehension. The Inspector wasn't convinced. "I've heard all that," he said, "but it sounds like garbage to me. They're perverts, and they act like perverts."

In recent years increasing swarms of male prostitutes, boldly preying on homosexuals, have aggravated the police problem. "Many of these are the 'rough trade,'" the Inspector said, "young toughs, hanging around street corners, wearing leather jackets and showing a great head of hair. That's what some of these homosexuals go for—a great head of hair, like some men attracted by a woman with a pretty face and figure."

The "smooth trade" boys, on the other hand, are well dressed, suave, good conversationalists, and attach themselves to homosexuals in the business or professional world.

The rising prominence of the "rough traders" or "fag workers," as police know these hustlers, is a sign of the easy morality of the times. "These male prostitutes, so often teenagers," the Inspector pointed out, "view the homos contemptuously, take them for whatever they can. But of course they are no better themselves, worse if anything, and are essentially homosexual, even though they don't know it yet."

The "rough trader" is anything but effeminate. No longer are police surprised to pick up young killers and find they have backgrounds as male prostitutes. After a recent senseless killing in Manhattan's Hell's Kitchen, two teen-age slayers, known as the Umbrella Man and the Cape Man, boasted that their gang had been "taking" homosexuals in the nearby Times Square area. "It was almost," a police official said acidly, "as though it were a mark of distinction."

While many homosexuals make elaborate efforts to keep their homosexuality from all but their own circle, they usually reveal their secret to police. "One way or the other," the Inspector said, "they give themselves away, under stress."

Yet few of their families, questioned by police, seemed to know their children were homosexuals, or wouldn't acknowledge it even to themselves. When a young man of twenty-two was beaten and robbed, his father, a wealthy Philadelphia businessman, hurried to a New York hospital to comfort him and then called on police to register a complaint. The Inspector eyed the indignant father quizzically.

"You know," he said, "your son wasn't entirely blameless."

"What do you mean?"

"He kept bad company."

"What kind of company?"

"Homosexuals, characters who prey on homosexuals. They're a bad influence."

"What does my son have to do with people like that?"

The Inspector felt that in this case honesty was the best policy.

"Well, he's a homosexual and lives with one."

The father's jaw dropped. "I don't believe it," he said.

The Inspector shrugged and handed him a statement. "He admits it," he said.

Stunned, the father slumped into a chair and then shook his head slowly. "Maybe I should have known," he said at last. "I can remember now as a boy his lack of interest in dates and dances. And I could never get him to play baseball or football with the other kids."

CHAPTER XIV

Bars and Haunts

THE BARS OF New York are the "country clubs" where the gay boys meet to make friends and influence people. East Side, West Side, all around the town, these gay bars thrive when other bars in the same district go begging for customers. Many bars specializing in the gay trade are so busy during cocktail hours that doors are locked tight and signs ironically announce: "Sorry, but we have reached our legal capacity."

From time to time, due to public outcries, some bars are briefly shuttered while their trade drifts off to other gay bars or straight bars which soon become gay.

To these gay bars throng not only the gay but curiosity seekers and male prostitutes, who prey on the homosexuals and are preyed upon in return. All come and go as they please, and even bars wishing to discourage this lucrative trade can usually do little about it.

Although "offensive" displays are against the law, many homosexuals, tavern owners point out, cannot be readily distinguished from other customers. "How should I know he was a faggot?" a bartender asked police. "He didn't have a sign on him."

Drinking is heavy in these bars, as alcohol loosens inhibitions. The gay boys usually buy their own drinks, though they may stand treat for an occasional queen—so-called for his elegant effeminacy—they are trying to impress. They may also invest a few drinks on a male prostitute, or even a few extra dollars, though they run the risk of being beaten up or blackmailed for their pains.

The bars flourishing on homosexual traffic are often carefully, even ingeniously, run. The sophisticated bars, on the upper East Side, generally hire only straight help—waiters, bartenders, and floormen (actually bouncers) who keep proceedings within propriety and the law.

Bad actors among the homosexuals, or fag workers—male prostitutes—eventually turn up on a blacklist. The names are relayed from one bistro to another, and these homosexuals are excluded from these better-class queer bars.

Before homosexuality was in style, many queer bars were secretly identified by birds names, which provide a clue only for the initiated. There were many innocent exceptions, of course, the most notable, the Stork Club, which not only never catered to this trade but took pains to discourage it.

But with a growing easiness about homosexuality there is no longer reason for a code and the bars have fanned out over the city—along Eighth Street, the main artery of Greenwich Village; in the West Seventies, not far from Central Park; along Lexington, Third, and Second avenues. In scores of these bars are customers packed four or five deep around the polished mahogany with the only woman in the place more often than not a dishwasher or scullery maid. The bars vary widely in décor. However, in all, men are eying other men as men ordinarily study women. In some of these bars, particularly in the West Seventies, all pretense is abandoned. Swishy faggots, with rouged faces, predominate. A few come in drag, female attire, and dance together to the roistering strains of the jukebox.

Though the usual straight owners of the gay bars hold the "faggots" in contempt, they count on their trade. "If the average guy gets in here twice a week, that's a lot," a bartender points out, "but the gay boys apparently don't have any place else to go and they certainly don't worry about what their wives will say."

Many bars find the queer business so profitable that they not only welcome it but hire well-known queens to keep the trade coming. Some bars set special hours aside for specific homosexual groups. The queens, drawing a salary or percentage, serve as greeters and send out cards to announce "meeting nights."

In many bars, of course, particularly in the conservative East Side hotels, homosexuals, no matter how well behaved, are persona non grata. Once they become conspicuous by their numbers, they become a public-relations hazard. One staid old hostelry, beginning to feel its reputation was at stake, engaged a detective agency to clear its bar of homosexuals. Hiring husky bullies to insult and intimidate every suspect, detectives finally discouraged the traffic. It promptly moved uptown to an equally famous hotel, which hired the same detectives to do the job for them.

Even in tolerant Greenwich Village homosexuals are not always wanted. Some have been pitched out into the streets. Others are more subtly discouraged. One restaurant-bar in the Village, catering to politicians, served homosexuals beer in glasses from which the caustic soapsuds hadn't been rinsed. Stricken with diarrhea, many homosexuals concluded the bar was selling green beer and stayed away.

The police, periodically closing homosexual haunts, still realize they are only transferring the traffic to bars which may have to be closed later. "It's like a game of musical chairs," a high police official observed. "We close one place and they pop up somewhere else."

But the gay bars, according to police, have their uses, serving to confine the gay set in areas where they can be watched.

"This way," an official pointed out, "they don't bother anybody but themselves—and we know where to find them when we want them."

For out-of-towners the "Village" is the great mecca. "In the Village," the official observed, "everything flocks together—lesbians, gay boys, and what have you. It's a regular cesspool. We get calls from people disgusted because they saw two boys kissing each other or girls, lesbians, hugging each other with thin hands under each other's blouses. These people went there and saw all this without anybody holding a gun to their heads. Now they want us to do something about it. But there's got to be something a little more overt before we can close a place."

The police official suggested a tour of the bars, either alone or with a friend—"not a girl," he hastily enjoined—to see what went on and to observe how difficult it was to pinpoint an overt move directly leading to homosexuality.

"Just because some pretty boy makes eyes at you," he observed, "gives you no reason for picking him up." I smiled at his unconscious slip. "I mean," he hurriedly amended, "pick him up if you were a cop."

Over the years I had seen homosexuals in many bars, and occasionally I had stepped into a bar which catered to homosexuals. However, I decided to travel with a guide,

122

whom I selected with care. He was a bisexual, a young executive with an advertising agency who had presented himself as an authority on the gay bars. His name was George and I suppose he could be called my date, since I picked up all the tabs. Some of these weren't inconsiderable, with bottled beer a dollar and more in crummy bars that couldn't have commanded twenty-five cents a bottle if it weren't for the "free floor show" put on for and by the customers.

George looked like anything but the popular conception of a homosexual. He cut a manly figure, tall, strongly built, and was neatly but plainly dressed. And while he drank and talked fast, gesticulating a lot, so do hundreds of people I know on Madison Avenue who aren't queer.

His references to homosexuals were in the third person plural, always "they" or "them," never the inclusive "we" or "us." It was as though he were trying to establish a gulf between himself and the others. I recalled a psychiatrist's suggestion that homosexuals frequently express their own feelings of guilt and self-contempt in disapproval of those most like themselves. George snorted. "Those psychiatrists, what do they know? They got problems of their own."

We had met for cocktails at a small restaurant on Sixth Avenue, not far from Rockefeller Center, noted for good food and wine, reasonably priced. Already it was beginning to fill up for dinner. Having heard the place described as a favorite resort for the gay set, I was surprised by the number of young women there with male escorts. "During dinner," my companion explained, "the crowd is pretty well mixed up, but the straights eat and leave and the gay boys flock to the bar where they get acquainted and make their contacts."

Occasionally, a head would nod in our direction and my guide would nod back. "They can't figure me for sure," he grinned. "This isn't one of my pads." He added, "I have to be careful anyway, what with having a wife and kids and a job." George seemed to want to talk about himself. "I've been married five years now," he said, "to a helluva girl. She's great, understanding and all that, and I've got a couple of great kids."

I listened closely but couldn't catch his eye. He seemed to look everywhere but at me and chain smoked between sips of his stinger, lighting one cigaret from the other.

"I'd like to keep the marriage going for the kids," he said. "I adore them. They're three and four, real aggressive kids, all male." He laughed. "The other day we went out with friends, to a dinner spot where they feature a lot of this art jazz. We sat next to one of those Michelangelo-type murals where the girls wear nothing in front and less in back. My kid looks at it a while, and guess what he says. 'Daddy, what happened to Mommy's clothes?' " He looked at me. "I tell you I almost broke up."

His mood changed swiftly, and he frowned into his drink. "I'd miss them like hell," he said.

"What seems the trouble?" I asked.

"It's hard to explain," he said. "We have a good sex life." He looked up almost challengingly. "In fact, it's great. It's one of those deals where everything goes, any time, any place." He shook his head. "That's what makes it so damn confusing."

"What's your wife think about it?" I asked.

"She won't give me a divorce," he said. "She said she'd fight it in Mexico, Florida, Reno, anywhere."

He hesitated, gulped, and said, "Well, I know a guy. He's the only guy. When I'm with him, I'm exhilarated and he digs me. He left his wife and wants me to leave mine. He says we can't have a complete relationship as long as we share it with anybody else."

He looked at me with a wan, half-apologetic smile. "And so that's my problem, Mr. Anthony."

"How do things stand now?"

"Oh, I haven't seen him lately ... keeping away deliberately. He hangs around a couple of spots near his place in the East Fifties, so let's head downtown tonight, if you don't mind."

We stayed for one more drink and headed for the Village, a small tastefully appointed restaurant in Bleecker Street. "This place is like headquarters for the fags," he said. "The drinks and food are good, the price is right, and nobody bothers you."

At the bar they were packed two and three deep, all men. Two young Negroes, who were together, made room for us as we squeezed up to the bar. My friend ordered the third of many stingers that night. "With these in me," he said, "I can stand it better." He looked at me and smiled enigmatically. "You know," he said, "there are men who are homosexuals only under the influence of liquor. I guess it's pretty much like the stenographer who has to get drunk before she can enjoy the office party." Nearly everybody at the tables, beyond the low partition separating the bar from the dining room, was male without being masculine.

The boys, sitting tête-à-tête, needed haircuts, as a rule. The more delicate young men seemed to fancy oversized crew sweaters, which appeared to enhance their delicacy. There were not more than four or five women in the restaurant part and perhaps a hundred men, all neatly groomed.

Just over the partition my eye caught a beautiful girl, with long yellow hair trailing down to her shoulders, a classic profile, and fresh-complexioned face. She looked very much like one of the Valkyrie goddesses. As she smiled, she showed perfect teeth. Everything about her seemed healthy and wholesome.

With her were two young men. The one slouched next to her was in a roomy black sweater. His eyes, dark and brooding, moved constantly across the room. As we looked at him, his wrist broke, limply, and he laughed in a high treble. George seemed amused. "He saw us looking at him," he said, "and he's putting it on now, telling us he's a fag and proud of it."

The other man, similarly dressed, was in rapt conversation with the girl. Occasionally she laughed, as though amused, but he remained intensely serious. He could have been a Greenwich Village poet, or at least a Village version of a poet, reminding one of early pictures of Edgar Allan Poe.

Occasionally, he flounced about in the booth. "Both those queens are really putting it on," George murmured.

"How about the girl?" I asked. "How does she fit in?"

He grimaced. "Oh, any one of a dozen ways. She could be tired of the aggressive male type, disgusted with sex and all that sort of thing, and she's comfortable with these boys. It could be a Village kick, some crazy, romantic feeling that she's giving sustenance to some struggling young artist. Or, it could be a sex kick of some sort."

"She looks terribly clean-cut to me," I said. He smiled almost pityingly. "You don't understand," he said. "There's nothing wrong with all this, so long as you don't think it's wrong. And with most of these cats, anything goes."

The captain, painfully polite, finally led us to a table. There was the least suspicion of a swish in his gait. "Is he?" I asked. "Yes, and so's the waiter. They can't perform here otherwise." He laughed. "Everybody gets into the act."

The food was tasty and well-served. Nobody seemed to be paying us any attention. George laughed, downing his

125

fourth or fifth stinger. "That's what you think. All the while you've been wondering about that blonde dish and her buddies, the boys have been wondering about us." His mood changed. "But nobody'll bother you here. Connections are usually made through introductions or at the bar. It's all very high-class."

He downed another stinger for the road, and we got up. The twosomes on all sides of us were still in animated conversation. Things had slowed up at the blonde's table, however. The young man sitting alongside had taken a position against the partition, his head lolling against an upraised arm, and he seemed to be studying the ceiling. George grinned. "Somebody must have said something to upset Mabel. These cats are terribly sensitive."

As we hit the street, the rain was coming down in a thin, cold trickle. It felt good on my face, and I breathed deeply of the cleansing air. "You've seen the height of respectability," George said, "and now I'll take you to a joint where anything goes."

We walked a couple of blocks and descended rickety steps into a small, smoke-filled room with a few tables snaked around the bar. We bellied up, and my friend ordered another stinger and looked belligerently around the room.

There were no women in the place and the males, none apparently over thirty-five, were dressed for the most part in sweaters and tight chino pants or denims. Some were standing away from the bar near the tables, holding their drinks and boldly staring around the room.

One young husky about twenty-five—in a T shirt, flexing his muscles and rocking back and forth on his toes like Marlon Brando—had placed himself in front of the juke-box which over and over again was playing a popular jazzed-up version of "Mack the Knife." The young man's chinos were so tight they bulged. George surveyed him contemptuously. "That's a real bull," he said. "He's standing there with those tight pants waiting for somebody to make a move in his direction. And when they do, no matter how slight, he'll spot it and he'll be wheeling his meat out of here."

As the Brando imitator continued rocking, elbows akimbo, George again ran his eyes over him and grinned ironically. "You know the old adage, it pays to advertise."

We had barely turned back to our drinks when two young sailors, the down still on their cheeks, sauntered in and tentatively approached the bar. They carried the insignia of Her Majesty's Navy on their hats. Tight Pants looked them over as they rather timidly edged their way forward and ordered a couple of beers.

George scrutinized them carefully and shrugged. "They'll be mincemeat before they finish their second beer," he said. I looked at him inquiringly. "The English Navy is loaded with it," he said. "I don't know why them particularly, since all sailors are pretty much thrown together in close quarters for extended periods."

The sailors kept peering around the room, and Tight Pants kept staring at them. "As soon as one of them catches his eye," he predicted, "Tight Pants will pounce."

With a last look at the two innocents of the Queen's Navy I gulped down my beer and said, "Let's go."

George threw me a curious look. "You better switch to stingers," he said. "That numbs you."

As we hit the street, George said, "There's another spot around the corner ... lesbians ... you shouldn't miss it." His words were beginning to blur, but it was still early and I stifled a desire to quit for the night. This was another walk-down, but visible from the street. At the bar through a haze of blue smoke I could distinguish three females with mannish—butch—haircuts and two boys with permanent waves.

As the lesbians got off the stools, heading for a door opposite the bar, a blond boy barred the way. The bartender, who had a broad lisp, leaned over and advised George confidentially, "We had to close the private room because the heat is on." He peered down the bar at the blond and, busily wiping a glass, said with a grimace, "He's the owner, and it's got him petrified. All this lost business."

"I don't want to appear naïve," I whispered, "but what goes on behind those doors?"

George laughed harshly. "Nothing, really. The lesbians camp it up a bit, dancing and grabbing each other." With one arm he took in the tiny place. "They get everybody here, squares, lezzes, faggots. Even the fairies like to watch the lezzes."

While he was talking, the friendly bartender was starting to serve a heavy-set, red-faced man who had just stumbled in and was pounding the bar. "Move your little behind, you faggot," he shouted, "and get me some whisky." The lesbians glanced up in mild annoyance, while the bartender, abruptly turning his back on the customer, blushed and went back to wiping his glass until the owner gave him a signal.

The newcomer finished the drink off with one gulp, banged his fist on the bar, and began sounding off again.

"I had a fight with my wife tonight," he announced, "and she threw me out." Tauntingly, he approached the young man behind the bar. "What these women want to-day is not a man but some panty-waisted faggot like you." His fist came down resoundingly on the bar. "That's what they want," he bellowed, "somebody they can order around."

The color drained out of the bartender's face. He stood there pale and trembling. For a moment I thought he might hurdle the bar, but then his whole body suddenly sagged, and he poured himself a stiff drink. George, watching with mounting tension, started to move toward the drunk with fire and stingers in his eye. But the wavy-haired blond, with a waiter's help, was coaxing the customer out the door. As he reached the threshold, he lurched against the doorframe for support and shouted: "All you faggots and lesbians know what you can do."

As he finally staggered out, George appeared almost as upset as the bartender. Still shaken, the bartender quivered in his high voice, "I don't know why he keeps coming back."

George said grimly: "Maybe he's looking for a bridge." The remark seemed to lift the bartender's gloom. Suddenly he laughed. "You mean to cross over." "Yeah," said George, "there's lots of them." He turned to me. "Let's get out of here," he said.

In the street he breathed deeply. "I've got to get rid of that taste." He smashed a big fist into his palm. "I'd like to give that punk one on the jaw." He looked at me sharply. "That's the trouble with those pretty little faggots; they stand there and take that stuff instead of bouncing a beer bottle off some guy's noggin."

As we looked for a cab, George said, "One more spot?" We taxied uptown on the East Side, past Fourteenth Street, and stopped off in the Twenties. "In this joint," he laughed, "the fags are the tourists."

There were only a few people at the bar. The bartenders wore tight-fitting trousers and swished around as they made their drinks.

Back of us were a few tables decorated by two or three lovely blondes in dark glasses, though the hour was long after midnight and the lights were low. "Lesbians, the passive type," George said. Two or three girls with butch haircuts, cut close like a man's, were sitting down at the end of the bar, and two men, sitting near, were trying to strike up a conversation.

"You see," George whispered savagely, "there's a couple of straight guys trying to make time with those lezzes, and they talk about homosexuals! What kind of pervert must a guy be to get any satisfaction out of a woman who detests men?"

"Well, how about the women?" I asked.

"That's different," he said almost scornfully, "they're looking for money to finance their relationships with other women."

Down the end of the bar a couple of tired-looking businessmen were huddled worriedly together. "They look like the owners," he said. Beyond them, to the right, was a doorway covered by draperies. "That leads downstairs," he said, "where the girls dance and anything goes." We noticed two or three girls greet the tired businessmen and disappear through the draperies. "Let's try it," George said.

As we started to push aside the drapes, one of the businessmen quickly, but politely, barred our entrance. "I'm sorry," he said, "but the room's closed tonight." It was just as well. It was late and George's wife might be getting worried. "Oh, that," he said. "She thinks I have an appointment with a new account."

I dropped George off at the subway. We were but a block from his station, in the East Fifties, when he suddenly said, "I think I'll make one more stop. I'm going to have one drink for the road."

We said good night. I stopped off in a Third Avenue bar run by a couple of rugged Irishmen to have a nightcap, and see a few familiar reassuring faces.

The next morning, soon after I arrived at my office, my companion of the night called. His voice was bright and cheery. "I just thought of a party you might be interested in," he said. "Tonight, uptown."

"Thanks," I said, "but I'm busy." Something seemed to be bothering him. "You know," he finally said. "I didn't get home at all last night. I only stopped in for a drink, but by the time I got out of the joint, it was five o'clock and there was no point to going home and then turning around and coming back. I freshened up at a friend's apartment and then went into the office at eight." He laughed. "That's one way of getting to work early."

"Sorry I put you to all that trouble," I said.

"Oh, no," he replied, "it was just as well. I met this guy I hadn't seen for a while, and it was like old times."

CHAPTER XV

Against the Law

HOMOSEXUALS LIKE TO tell this story. At the hearing of a homosexual on a morals charge, a nearsighted magistrate saw a young man standing with his arm around the defense attorney. Beckoning to the youth, he said, "Will the defendant please take the stand?" There was a murmur of suppressed laughter in the courtroom, and the young man blushed. An aide whispered in the judge's ear. "Oh," the magistrate exclaimed, *"he's* the cop!"

Homosexuals themselves are bitter over police entrapment methods and argue that men who dress like women or otherwise impersonate homosexuals to make these arrests must be as emotionally involved as they are. "It takes lavender to smell lavender," said one homosexual, referring to the prevailing feeling among homosexuals that "it takes one to know one."

Of the thousands of homosexuals arrested for soliciting, more than half, they charge, were entrapment victims picked up by police who flirted with them in parks, movie houses, subways.

To many homosexuals, liberal groups, and the lawyers who often defend them out of charity, the homosexuals are a persecuted lot, hunted and tracked down, actually, more for nonconformity than crime. "In Holland, Denmark, Sweden, and other continental countries," a defense attorney said indignantly, "they laugh at so-called offenses that result in prison and ruin here. In most of these countries there are no more laws against homosexuality than ordinary love-making. Both are barred publicly, but what happens privately is a person's own affair."

However, despite homosexual agitation, it is seldom that police, busy as they are, arrest anybody for homosexuality practiced in private. "We see enough of them around without breaking down doors to get them," a police officer said.

Though the serious charge of sodomy is often invoked, homosexuals are generally booked on lesser charges of impairing morals, disorderly conduct, loitering to solicit, or breach of the peace. They may get away with a brief sentence or a fine. But, demanding repeal of discriminatory statutes, they protest they are the only minority deliberately induced to break the law. The entrapments are often passive, with plain-clothes men patiently waiting around for the suspect to make an advance. It is no wonder, homosexuals say, that they are so successful. "What do they expect after standing around posturing for a half hour?" a homosexual said. "They should be the ones charged with loitering."

Other homosexuals have charged police often make the first overtures. In some parks and streets, they claim, this is normal procedure. Many homosexuals picked up in Bryant Park, in the center of New York, insist they were relaxing idly, with no thought of recruiting, when they were drawn into incriminating conversations. "One good-looking fellow," a young homosexual reported, "started talking to me so intimately that I couldn't help but get excited, and then when I reached out and touched him, I learned that he was a cop."

However, the magistrate hearing the complaint was singularly unimpressed by charges of entrapment. "What," he asked the accused, "were you doing in the park?"

Many of the controversial entrapments occur in truly intimate areas, such as Turkish baths. In one bath on the lower East Side a young, good-looking officer reported that as he was drying himself a middle-aged man approached, engaged him in conversation, and then invited him to his house nearby for a drink. While the officer was pondering the offer, the stranger leaned forward confidentially and whispered, "And I'll do anything you want me to do."

When the officer asked for clarification, the stranger made his meaning unprintably clear. At this point the policeman made his arrest. More in sorrow than in anger, the stranger, stamping a bare foot, turned on his adversary. "And," he said, "I thought you were my friend!"

Overruling the police, many magistrates often lean backward to give the homosexual the benefit of the doubt. For conviction, though it may mean only a minor sentence, may still wreck the most brilliant career. As it is, even the bare charge is frequently enough to shatter a man's reputation.

Arrested as homosexuals, men from all walks of life have been subjected to gossip and publicity, which often clings long after their vindication in court. Dismissing a morals complaint against a visiting official who had been arrested with a young producer, a city magistrate showed a keen understanding of the injury implicit in homosexual charges. "I hope," he said, "if damage has been done to their reputations, there will be some way to correct it."

The official had been seized with the younger man by plain-clothes men who said they had been watching through a peephole in a subway washroom for a half hour.

From his hide-out in an adjoining chamber, a patrolman reported seeing the official enter the washroom. Through the connecting peephole he said he saw the producer enter twenty-five minutes later. Seeing the two men together in the same booth, he said, he emerged and placed them both under arrest. As political enemies from his home town sat in at the trial, the official protested his innocence, claimed he had been seized by an attack of cramps, and was in the booth when the youth, whom he had never seen before, reached in for a piece of paper to dry his hands. Pending trial, the official was suspended from his job. The magistrate, recognizing a responsible man's future was at stake, took the unusual course of personally visiting the scene. After the official's acquittal he was reinstated in his job and, taking a cue from the judge, brought, and won, a damage suit against the city of New York.

Other judges have thrown out entrapments, arguing the accused were mistakenly booked for breach of the peace or disorderly conduct. In one notable case a determined police officer staked out the pay booth of a men's room in the Long Island bus terminal for forty-five minutes, as the suspect sat behind a closed door. The officer then entered the adjoining booth and sat down himself. After a few minutes the officer observed a naked knee thrust under the dividing partition. A few minutes later a second knee showed up, and then a more intimate portion of the anatomy intruded. The officer immediately rose from the commode, entered the adjoining compartment, and, like the Canadian Mountie, got his man.

Convicted on a charge of breaching the peace, the homosexual appealed to the Appellate Division of the Court of Special Sessions. The court, agreeing the prisoner had loitered for no good, nevertheless felt he had been incorrectly charged. Concurring, another judge pointed out that a locked toilet could hardly be called a public place. The complaint was dismissed and the homosexual's fine remitted.

Dismissing a similar case for insufficient evidence, Magistrate Charles Solomon reflected the prevailing feeling among many jurists. "The law's protection," he said, "is for the despicable as well as for the admirable. And while to some this may be a small case, small cases may carry large issues."

Though homosexuals angrily protest entrapment, police point out such arrests generally take place in areas where there is a good deal of human traffic and opportunity for recruiting.

The subways, because of the millions they carry, are looked upon by some homosexuals, particularly novices, as a happy hunting ground. More than five hundred males of varying ages were arrested in the underground in 1959, and nobody can estimate how many more escaped unnoticed. There are many reasons for the subway's popularity. "They are convenient," a transit official explained "cost only fifteen cents, which is far cheaper than any hotel room or bar, and the washrooms provide easy access for homosexuals, under favorably intimate circumstances."

Of those arrested in the subways only a handful were of the obvious swish type. Nearly all were seemingly respectable, married, living with their families, and shrinking from the terrifying prospect of publicity, once caught. Many of them were apparently latent homosexuals who had been nursing a secret problem for years. And, finally succumbing, they were so unpracticed, a transit policeman said, that they couldn't help but attract attention. "The real swish homosexuals," an official observed, "are too knowledgeable to expose themselves in the subways. They know all the ropes. The inexperienced homosexual, clumsily following his inclinations, not knowing where else to go, is the one who gets into trouble."

Shattered when caught, many men instinctively protest their innocence, often accusing cops of frame-ups. Since frame-ups do occasionally occur, such charges are not dismissed lightly. In one instance even the investigating police, who have seen all types of homosexuals, were impressed by the clean-cut masculine appearance of a youngster who had claimed he was framed. "This kid was such a wholesome-looking specimen, with his shock of yellow hair and square features, that even some of our cops had their doubts about his being homosexual," a transit official said, "and were inclined to believe his story."

Under sharp questioning, with several officers joining in, the boy stuck stubbornly to his charge. With growing concern for the probity of the arresting cop, the transit official finally decided to question the boy alone. "I brought him into my office," he said, "offered him a cigarette, and did everything I could to make him feel at ease. I explained the seriousness of his charge, pointing out it might not only cost this officer his job but his reputation."

As he proceeded, the official could sense the boy stirring uneasily. "What you are accused of is not nearly as serious as what you have accused this officer of," he said. "If you admit it, you may get a suspended sentence, and that will end it. Otherwise, there'll be a big investigation and—unless you are telling the truth—you'll be a lot worse off before it's over."

The boy passed a weary hand over his eyes. "All right," he said finally, "I'll tell you. But I just couldn't admit it before all those people. I was too ashamed." Completely drained emotionally, he buried his head in his hands, sobbing: "I don't know what happened to me. I just don't know. I was in the washroom, and I saw this fellow standing there at the other end. I saw him looking at me, and all of a sudden I felt like I had to go over and talk to him."

The boy shook his head mournfully. "I still don't know why I did it—and I couldn't admit it. I just couldn't." He looked up for a moment, and his lips trembled. "I hope," he said weakly, "you won't have to tell my father."

Many of the busiest subway stations, including Times Square, have their washrooms covered by peepholes, with police checking them regularly. Aware of this trap, members of the homosexual colony nevertheless resent it as an invasion of privacy. "Who else," a homosexual demanded, "is spied on like this?"

But transit police, determined to discourage recruiting in the underground, are especially concerned by the three hundred thousand school children who use the subways twice daily. "There is always the chance that exposing a kid with latent tendencies to homosexuality will make a convert," an official said. "Otherwise, that kid might go through life not even knowing he was homosexually inclined."

Other crimes—blackmail, robbery, even murder—have developed from homosexual pickups in the subways, and transit police feel that in reducing homosexuality, they reduce crime generally. Homosexuals often co-operate with police. Ending one recent blackmail hoax, police smashed a ring headed by

134

a modern Fagin, employing "professional chickens," with the aid of the predominantly homosexual Mattachine Society. Directed by their Fagin, any one of a bevy of boys would approach a subway strap-hanger, preferably one who looked as though he might be "queer," jostle him, and then loudly accuse him of molesting.

The usual phony cop then appeared, and while the rider wavered between outraged innocence and the thought of frightening headlines, the masquerading officer would settle for the customary balm. Since it was essential to catch the crew in the act, Mattachine members, opposed to all who prey on homosexuals, gladly volunteered as subway decoys. After riding a few stations, a Mattachine was accosted by a "chicken," and just as the Fagin pounced down to make the phony arrest, the decoy flashed a signal to the bona fide cops riding the same cars, and a real arrest followed.

While homosexuals bridle bitterly at police "injustices," they resent even more government security regulations which, they charge, make them second-class citizens. "The government," said one homosexual, "treats us as though we were common criminals."

Many still smolder angrily over the fact that hundreds were drummed out of sensitive government jobs, particularly in the State Department, and that known deviates are barred arbitrarily from other government posts. "Joe McCarthy," a homosexual said, referring to the late controversial senator from Wisconsin, "made homosexuality and Communism synonymous in government, with the consequence that homosexuals were looked upon as disloyal. Most homosexuals are Republicans and Democrats, and many died in the armed forces proving their loyalty."

Government investigators, probing job applicants for the homosexual taint, are often confused by the fact that, superficially at least, many homosexuals seem like everybody else. "It is not only difficult to determine if an applicant is homosexual," an agent reported, "but whether that homosexuality, if fleeting, would be a threat to our security."

Some point out that two of the most celebrated traitors of modern times, connected with the British Foreign Office, were homosexuals who capriciously ran off to Russia together; one not only turned his back on his country but also on a wife and children who no longer interested him. "Actually," the investigator said, "it's the personality of the homosexual, his emotional make-up that makes him so risky in

135

vulnerable spots. No matter how brainy, homosexuals can't seem to take pressure and they explode."

Suspected of homosexuality, many government applicants go through lie-detector tests, which are purely voluntary, and are questioned closely on past associations. "Some," an investigator said, "seem to have suffered no serious personality change from casual experiences as kids—but you never know."

Admittedly, the investigative process screens out some of our best young minds. Only recently, an investigator was checking a job applicant, a top student at a major men's college. He was apparently qualified in every respect. Family and social connections were impeccable, academic background flawless. "I thought he had everything," the investigator said, "until I checked with a campus doctor." The doctor mentioned casually that he had advised the student to transfer to another school, coeducational. "But he refused to do anything to help himself."

"Help himself?" the investigator asked.

"Why, from being homosexual," the doctor said. "I thought you knew."

The student, the investigator discovered, was one of two hundred suspected homosexuals at this all-male university. Many, he learned, had been encouraged by faculty members. "They not only favor these boys," the doctor said, "but shield them from discovery."

The boy's background was a familiar one—for homosexuals. An only child of divorced parents, he had been shunted from one boys' school to the next. His father was hardly more than a stranger, his mother smothered him with affection. "As he grew up, older classmates and faculty members were the only males he could identify with," the investigator said, "and if they were homosexual, it was just too bad."

Recognizing the student's potential, the investigator was troubled by the necessity of rejecting him. But beside a possible emotional problem, the blackmail risk, he felt, made the student doubly hazardous. The experience of big business, he said, has shown how risky it can be. "A large concern," he pointed out, "was ready to appoint one of its executives company president when a routine check revealed he was being blackmailed—for homosexuality. He was turned down, for otherwise, in his new job, the blackmailers might have walked off with the company."

Unimpressed by such arguments, homosexuals scornfully demand lists of deviates who have been blackmailed into turning traitor. "There just aren't any," they say. For despite all "propaganda" to the contrary, they feel they are as good citizens as anybody else. "Whenever somebody mentions blackmail," a homosexual said, "I always ask, 'But why should blackmail be possible?'"

CHAPTER XVI

Blackmail

IN THE BEST seller *Advise and Consent* a distinguished senator, blackmailed as a homosexual, kills himself rather than face degradation and ruin. Had this fictional character attended a seminar of homosexuals here in New York recently, the book might have ended differently.

"If all else proves unsuccessful," a noted criminologist advised a homosexual group, "and you feel that suicide or homicide are the only alternatives, my choice would be to kill the blackmailer."

However, other alternatives were preferred by the speaker, Donal E. J. MacNamara, dean of the New York Institute of Criminology. Rather than pay the blackmailer, he urged homosexuals to disarm this leech by confessing all to parents, family, teachers, employers. "They will be more understanding and helpful than you suspect," he said. They were also advised to move out of their neighborhood or city. "Stay away from your usual haunts and activities, your favorite bar, the park or street where you have been making pickups." And before resorting to suicide or murder, they were advised to go to the police or the district attorney.

From long experience with the ways of the blackmailers, MacNamara gave the gathered homosexuals a few tips which would make them less vulnerable to shakedown artists who, so often, are homosexuals themselves. "Pick your companions carefully," he said. "Don't divulge your identity unnecessarily, don't write homosexual love notes or have pictures taken in drag, and don't make an ostentatious display of money, jewels, or other evidences of wealth."

So many homosexuals, he pointed out, are unduly worried. "They fear public disclosure of their sex delinquencies when there is not an editor, columnist, or scandal-sheet writer who would give even their most immoral flaunting of our sex codes a single stick of type."

Despite warnings of criminologists and police, blackmailers of homosexuals do a flourishing business, confident that victims will not retaliate. Even the police are occasionally accused of extortion, but usually offenders are blackmailers only posing as police. Male prostitutes, preying on rich men, are a common garden variety of blackmailer. Some, even without MacNamara's injunction, have been killed by their desperate victims. In one famous case, in which the target was a widely known millionaire, the jury quickly acquitted him of a murder charge.

Panicked by unexpected demands, homosexuals have often yielded their life savings before reason asserted itself. Some have been blackmailed by wives seeking divorces and property settlements. One brilliant editor, rather than face the scandal of the divorce court, killed himself, freeing his wife to marry the successor she had already selected for herself.

Even where there has been no overt attempt at recruiting, homosexuals in their insecurity have frequently paid off rather than risk publicity. It was in recognition of this vulnerability that Uncle Sam purged the security-minded State Department of homosexual employees even though there was no evidence at the time that any had ever dreamed of divulging government secrets.

The increasing spread of male prostitution, particularly among teen-agers, has helped make blackmailers of the young. Careless of their own reputations, these cynical hoodlums soon discover they can capitalize on the fears of their "fag" friends. Many completely amoral boys, preying on homosexuals, have become brazen enough to blackmail even nonhomosexuals. Sometimes in their complacence they underrate their targets. One fourteen-year-old boy, for instance, hitched a ride on the West Side Highway from a man who prided himself on his prowess with the ladies. When the youngster climbed in, the man asked, "How far you going?" The boy hesitated, looked at a sign—they were now at about 150th Street—and said, "Oh, five or six miles. I'll tell you when we get there."

They drove along for a minute, and then the boy said:

"Have you got five dollars?"

"What do you mean, have I got five dollars?"

"Just what I said."

"Look, you must be a silly kid. You better get out of here."

"Not before I get the five dollars."

"You're out of your mind."

The boy was now loosening his trousers.

"You see what I want the five dollars for."

The driver almost exploded as he caught the implication. "Get out of here, or I'll knock your block off."

"If you don't give me the five dollars," the boy said coolly, "I'll tell the cops you propositioned me, and they'll believe me. They always do."

The car braked to a stop. "Get out of here," the man growled, "or I'll break you in two."

One look at the motorist's face, and the youngster, preferring discretion to valor, scooted out of the car.

The fear of blackmail is a constant drain on homosexuals, particularly if they are prominent and are presenting a conventional front. Many homosexuals, moving out of the city, run into additional difficulties in suburbia, where there is less tolerance of sexual irregularity. And they are even more susceptible to blackmail. In one New York suburb two homosexual businessmen lived in great compatibility, content with each other but occasionally looking around for new thrills they could share. One Saturday night following dinner in, they repaired to a local tavern where they picked up a "townie," a young married man who did odd jobs, and brought him back to the luxurious home they had recently bought. He was an obvious "piece of trade," with a local reputation as a ne'er-do-well. After a couple of hours he left with a few dollars and a bottle of whisky they had gratefully given him. Some time later he returned with three husky friends and a moving van, rousing his recent benefactors from slumber and announcing: "We're going to clean this place out."

As the intruders started to remove the twenty-one-inch color television set, the two homosexuals, far from effeminate, stepped forward to resist. In the ensuing encounter, outnumbered as they were, they were beaten, kicked, and left unconscious on their living-room floor as the four huskies leisurely packed the van, carrying off not only costly furnishings, including rugs, curtains, and divans, but expensive jewelry.

The next day the two homemakers, bloody but unbowed, consulted an attorney. Without explaining they were homosexuals, they stressed they wanted to avoid notoriety at any cost. The attorney strongly advised them to bring charges, assuring them there would be little chance of publicity in so small a town. Nervously agreeing, they had the four men arrested. The ringleader, having little status to lose, brought countercharges against the pair, accusing them on a morals count. With hearings in both cases scheduled to come up before a local magistrate, the homosexuals, startled by a brief notice of the proceedings in a local weekly, suddenly realized they may have acted hastily. They hired a new lawyer to arrange an out-of-court settlement. In consideration of the charges against them being withdrawn, they were willing to drop their charges and not press for return of the furnishings, only the jewelry. Attorneys for both sides agreed, and the two friends breathed easier. However, when the case came up, the judge demurred. "I am hearing this case," he said. "Families with children live in this town, and I want to know what is going on." Noticing the reporters and photographers outside the court, the friends panicked. At their request the case was adjourned another week. But it never came to trial. For their lawyer was advised that the hearing, with resulting ruinous publicity to his clients, could be dropped on one condition—that his clients would agree to put their house on the market and immediately leave town. Their promise was given, and they departed.

The vulnerability and wealth of many homosexuals have led to the growth of professional blackmail rings, operating with paid decoys known to police as "chickens," who are expert at setting up a compromising situation. The blackmail coup can occur anywhere; on the beach, in a park, hotel bar, or men's toilet. Sometimes the "chicken" strolls up and down, idly sizing up the victim and waiting for him to make the first move. Invariably, if he is patient, the target's suspicions will be lulled and he will make the overture with confidence. In one instance, a wealthy middle-aged businessman, quietly resting at a beach resort in New Jersey, approached a young man of eighteen, whom he had been eying for days, and invited him back to his hotel for a drink. From the youth's readiness, his smile, and his conversation, he felt sure the youth knew what was expected of him. They were together in the hotel only a short time when there was a thump at the door and two men broke into the room, flashed badges, and announced they were house detectives.

The homosexual, visualizing the headlines back in the city, where he was a well-known businessman, began wringing his hands and reaching for his checkbook all at the same time.

"Aren't you being a little hasty?" he asked. "Maybe we can talk this over among ourselves."

One of the "detectives" looked at the other solemnly, but the latter shook his head. "This is a very serious offense," he said, "impairing the morals of a minor."

The first, who appeared the straight man of the team, frowned and said, "You're right," and then hesitated, "but I hate to see a man's life ruined over a thing like this." He looked at the boy. "It won't do him any good either."

The other nodded sagely. "Yes, but the kid should get something for the harm that's been done him."

The businessman picked up the checkbook and again looked up inquiringly. "Oh, make it two hundred dollars," the "detective" said. "That should be enough." He turned to his partner. "I think so," the other agreed.

As the businessman began to write, one of the "detectives" interrupted. "It would be better all around," he said, "if you made it cash."

The homosexual looked through his wallet and his face fell. "I only have one hundred and fifty dollars," he said. The "detectives" shrugged. "Oh well," said one lightly. "We can't let you go to jail for fifty dollars."

Taking the cash, the two "detectives" left with the young man. Their victim breathed a fervid sigh of relief which, as it developed, was slightly premature. Two weeks later, back in New York, the phone rang in the businessman's apartment. He picked it up only to hear a click. A few minutes later the doorbell buzzed and two burly strangers walked in. They were like the pair back at the beach; if anything, more crisp and businesslike. They announced they were detectives and said they had come to take him back to face charges. "Of course," they said, "you can resist extradition, and then we'll have to book you at a local station and you'll get all that publicity."

At this point the whole problem got too much for the businessman. "Do you mind," he asked weakly, "if I call a friend in the building?"

"What kind of friend?"

"Oh, just somebody I see once in a while."

They nodded together. "No, that's all right."

A few minutes later another middle-aged man, apparently homosexual, walked in and was briefed by his distressed friend. Coldly, the newcomer turned to the two men. "Let's see your badges," he said. As they pulled back their coats, he added, "I want to see the backs." The detectives drew themselves up angrily. "Look," they said, "for two cents we'll pull this guy in."

The businessman almost collapsed in tears. His hands fluttered nervously. "Charles," he said to his friend, "I asked you here to help, not hurt me."

Charles shrugged. "Have it your way, Jim," he said primly, then, turning to the strangers: "Okay, what is the deal?"

The price had gone up appreciably. It was now two thousand dollars, cash. "The boy's father will have to be squared," one of the detectives said. "He heard about how the affair was squelched and he's furious."

Both Charles and Jim blinked, but it was Charles, now suspicious, who encouraged a settlement. "You have no choice, Jim," he said. Jim shrugged hopelessly, nodding, and the group agreed to meet the next morning at ten in front of Jim's bank.

After the visitors left, Charles, reassuring his friend, led him to the nearest police station. "They're phonies," he said, "complete frauds. I knew it when they wouldn't turn their badges." He looked up with an air of triumph. "Real shields are finished off in a special way on the back," he said.

At the station the desk sergeant, trying to mask his distaste, nevertheless agreed the pair had acted wisely. They were told to keep the date and were given an envelope with paper strips cut up inside, representing twenty-dollar bills.

Charles and Jim turned up promptly the next morning with a police escort on the alert, not far distant. However, the blackmailers failed to keep the assignation, though a young man, standing nearby, promptly disappeared after the police joined the two friends in front of the bank.

With perhaps conscious humor, the police advised the wealthy businessman to be more careful hereafter. "You were the target of a professional ring," the sergeant pointed out. "The two hundred was so easy they thought they'd try for the jackpot."

"But how about the boy?" the businessman said naïvely. "He seemed genuine."

The cop laughed. "He may have been genuine all right, but he was working with the ring, a decoy, what we call a 'professional chicken.'"

The credulity of the homosexual, who has been singled out for blackmail, is generally matched only by his fear of exposure. Wandering around Rockefeller Plaza, a twenty-two-year-old youth of good family, who had just inherited a large sum of money, got into conversation with another young man of striking good looks who had been idling near

142

one of the fountains. One word led to another, and pretty soon the pair were on their way to one of the cheap hotels in the vicinity.

They had been upstairs only a few minutes and were partially disrobed when two burly men crashed into the room. "We're detectives," they cried, "and we're placing both of you under arrest."

The two young men appeared to be equally taken aback. The good-looking young man, who was about twenty-seven, sobbed brokenly. "I'll be ruined if it comes out." The collapse of his new-found friend did nothing for the younger man's morale. So vividly reminded of his own situation, he started to sob himself until his partner of a few minutes before comfortingly threw an arm around his shoulders.

The anguish was so intense that even the "detectives" seemed impressed. "I don't like to do this," one stage-whispered to the other. "These kids are really going to have their lives ruined."

"Do you have to?" the older "friend" said, entreatingly, while the younger glanced up with an expression of hope on his woebegone face. "Well," the "detectives" said, "it'll take some doing. There's a lot of people who'll have to be reached."

The young man, clutching at this straw of hope, said between sobs, "I'll give everything I have, everything." He drew out his handkerchief and dabbed at his eyes.

"I'll never be able to face my family. Never."

The officers shook their heads doubtfully. "It'll take a lot of doing," one said. "More money than you've got."

"Oh no," the young man said. "You don't understand, I have my inheritance."

The "detectives" straightened up sharply, but the young man was too absorbed in his own problem to notice.

"Well," one "detective" said with another shake of his head, "it'll take at least fifty thousand dollars."

Even his partner and the accomplice blinked, but the young man only bawled the louder. "Won't they please take less?" he cried, twisting the handkerchief into knots. "All I have is thirty thousand."

Both "detectives" gulped and one said slowly, "Well, it might be all right, if you're sure that's the best you can do."

He looked over to his partner. "What do you think?" he asked. The other managed a shrug. "Yeah," he said, "let's give the kid a break."

The accomplice, the professional "chicken," who seemed

143

to be looking on in awed disbelief, was told he would have to stay around until the money was turned over. The foursome left the hotel, climbed into a cab, and made for the young man's bank.

After a short wait the bank draft for thirty thousand was honored, the money was turned over to the tremulous young man, and he handed it to his benefactors. There was a fond farewell, and the "detectives," accompanied by their "chicken," congratulating themselves over an unlooked-for windfall, quietly got lost in the teeming city.

The young man's family became suspicious when he had to borrow from them to pay bills. Weeks later, brooding over the loss, he confessed the incident to an uncle. The uncle quickly called in the police, descriptions of the swindlers were flashed over the country, and they were picked up months later in New England. However, the money had already gone through their hands and was never recovered. It had been an expensive pickup.

Blackmailing of homosexuals is so profitable a venture that rings of crooks have traveled the country from California to Florida, mulcting the vulnerable of sums ranging from a few hundred dollars to many thousands. One gang of shakedown artists, which operated in many cities across the country, was recently smashed in New York City after it had made a business of preying on out-of-towners.

For good reason, these racketeers were known as the Squeeze Squad by Manhattan District Attorney Frank S. Hogan and his men. They had the blackmail racket down to a fine art. They carried phony police shields and identification cards, establishing their "position," and they didn't pick on just anybody who looked lonely. Their targets were usually the well-dressed and the well-heeled, whom they came upon in parks, bars, and even the "tearooms," as homosexuals sometimes style public washrooms. The phony cops usually worked in pairs, stepping in after their "chicken" had made his pitch to the victim. Then, as a rule, they trailed the two to a hotel room. After waiting a few moments outside the door they would bust in, flash their fake credentials, and make a big show of arresting the "chicken."

Talk of the regrettable publicity was generally enough to make the victim, even the innocent, flinch long enough from imaginary headlines to get up "bail money" for the "chicken," or hush money for himself. The customary payment was $500, but some paid as much as $1500, and one man was frightened enough to pay $10,000.

Even after a victim had returned to his home, and was secretly congratulating himself on his close escape, he was not out of the woods. Other members of the gang, whom he hadn't seen before, would pay a follow-up visit to the victim's home—in Connecticut, New Jersey, or Maine, as the case might be—after first carefully checking his Dun & Bradstreet rating. This time they posed as FBI agents and claimed they were investigating the "illegal bribe" that had been paid in New York. As the victim shook in fear they again showed how understanding "officers of the law" could be—for a price.

Fortunately, the shakedown didn't always work. Sometimes, from innocence or a suspicious nature, victims balked. Ironically, when their targets stood up to them, blackmailers were often content to settle for pocket money, as payment for time wasted.

It wasn't difficult for the crooks to give a convincing performance as cops. Most of them were ex-convicts and could impersonate police by simply drawing on their memories. Quite frequently, they operated with remarkable boldness. On one occasion, virtually walking into the lion's mouth, they piloted a victim right up to the district attorney's door. When he still stood firm they released him, explaining that the assistant D.A. in charge of such cases was out at the moment.

In an effort to get victims to report shakedown attempts the law may grant immunity from homosexual acts to the homosexual who testifies before a grand jury. The homosexual episode behind the blackmail attempt is barely touched upon and sometimes ignored in an effort to protect the individual who has risked exposure to press a complaint.

Sometimes the jurors themselves are puzzled by the deliberate vagueness of the language in which the circumstances of the crime are described. In one recent case an indictment was sought against two men who had been trying to shake down a businessman for five thousand dollars. The victim and one of the alleged blackmailers, the usual young, good-looking "chicken," it developed from the prosecutor's recitation, had met in a bar near mid-town Manhattan.

In the course of conversation the older man invited the younger to his hotel, just around the corner, for a drink. En route, near Grand Central Station, the younger suddenly felt an urge to visit the men's room. The older man joined him. They were standing close together, at adjacent facilities, when a man, describing himself as a detective, suddenly came up and collared the pair. He accused the older man of breaching the peace with an improper proposal and said he would have to take the two of them in. Once on the street, headed for the nearest station house, the "detective" seemed to relent. Not wishing to ruin the older man's life, or break up his home—it developed he had a wife and children—he would see what could be done about the case —for five thousand dollars. Still protesting his innocence, the middle-aged man, shuddering at the headlines conjured up by an overactive imagination, agreed with alacrity to buy himself off. Later, rehashing the situation with friends, he was encouraged to go to the police instead. The arrest followed.

As the details unfolded before the grand jury, many of the jurors, looking solemnly wise, were nonetheless obviously confused as to exactly why the victim had been so fearful. "I could sense," one knowledgeable juror observed, "that many jurors didn't know what it was all about." Not once did the prosecutor mention the word "homosexuality." The only indication came from correlating the invitation for a drink with the scene in the men's room. "I managed to get the drift because I knew of a similar case in actual life," the juror recalled. "But I'm sure some of the jurors just decided that anybody who would try to hold up somebody for five thousand dollars was automatically guilty of something."

Homosexual promiscuity often leads to robbery bordering on blackmail. The thief, so often a male prostitute, capitalizes on the homosexual's reluctance to reveal himself and the police refusal to get excited about such crimes.

Unfortunately, few homosexuals observe criminologist MacNamara's injunction to choose their company carefully. Sauntering out of a Third Avenue bar one night, in the fertile pickup area in the East Fifties, a wealthy professional man caught the eye of a well-dressed Negro about thirty, strolling about outside. After a few words they adjourned to the professional man's flat in nearby Sutton Place, a walk-up, since he deliberately avoided an elevator apartment with attendants. There wasn't a discordant note until the men were putting on their clothes. Then the younger, huskier guest pulled out an ugly-looking switchblade, casually strolled over to a window, cut down the ropes holding the venetian blinds, and proceeded, under threat of stabbing him, to expertly tie up his partner in love, doubling him back Japanese-style and knotting wrists and ankles together.

146

Then he rolled him into the bathroom, gagging him, pushed him into the tub, and calmly began to loot the place, taking virtually everything that wasn't monogrammed or nailed down. He filled four large suitcases with suits, shirts, linen, rifled the gem box of gold stickpins and cuff links, bade his victim a cheery good-by, and vanished.

The victim worked his way out of the bathroom and slithered across the floor till he got to the phone, knocked off the receiver, and dialed "operator." The operator called the police, who came running because the city's richest and most influential people lived in this area. But after they had talked to him, their attitude changed—noticeably. "Aren't you even making a list of the missing articles?" he asked.

"Oh, we'll remember them," he was told. "You'll be hearing from us in a few days."

Months later he still hadn't heard from the police but was curiously philosophical about the whole incident. "At least," he told a homosexual friend wryly, "he didn't rob me first."

CHAPTER XVII

The College Boy

THE GREEN SPORTS car drew up before my office, and a dark, handsome young chap reached out and called cheerfully:

"Are you the reporter?"

I was mildly surprised. Although used by now to homosexuals who neither swished, swayed, nor sashayed, I had not expected a facsimile of the typical American college boy. His face looked out alertly, a slight smile playing on sensitive lips. His hair was crew-cut, his eyes clear, and though it was a cold, snappy day, he wore only a jacket and his collar was open.

He had been described to me as a homosexual who was not yet so involved with homosexuality that he did not appreciate the heterosexual point of view. And there was hope he might even reform.

But as we settled down in a nearby restaurant, Frank soon dispelled notions of any serious internal conflict or change-over. With a smile, he said, "There must be some

147

mistake. I'm quite happy about being a homosexual. I don't want to be anything else."

He seemed amused. "You remind me of my father," he said. "My father tells me to stay away from queers and go out with girls, and everything will be fine."

I pointed out that I had understood he actually was not a confirmed homosexual, and could go either way. "You certainly don't look the part," I said.

"You mean," he said almost mockingly, "I have a chance."

He seemed to be enjoying himself. "If instead of trying to help us, people would just leave us alone, there would be no problem. It is the outer world, with its hypocrisy about sex, which creates the problem for me."

"If everybody felt like you," I said, "it might be the end of the human race."

"And what would be so horrible about that?" he asked with an engaging grin. "After all, if everything we read is true, we're on the verge of destruction any day, anyway."

"But don't you feel there's a certain morality involved?"

"I don't see how I'm being immoral by being with somebody who wants to be with me. There is no force or coercion, and I am not picking on small children." He laughed, as though struck by a sudden thought. "I have seen younger boys, high school kids I thought attractive, but that's no worse than a college senior dating a teen-age girl."

"Don't you ever wonder whether you're kidding yourself?" I asked.

His eyes went blank. "I don't understand."

"Actually, haven't you chosen a way of life which is wrong, for purely selfish reasons, and are now trying to justify it philosophically?"

He smiled almost pityingly. "Why should I have to justify it at all? How much adultery is there today, and yet how many men or women are ever charged with adultery?"

His remarks had a familiar ring. "You realize, of course," I said, "that this is all common jargon among homosexuals."

"That doesn't make it any less true." His brow furrowed, and his eyes became serious. "Why," he asked, "am I expected to be more moral as a homosexual than as a so-called normal person? I can have an affair with my sister's girl friend, who I don't care about, and nobody, including my sister, would think anything of it. But if I'm really interested in a young man who's interested in me, I suddenly become a pervert in the eyes of the world."

He shrugged. "And, even then, the world really doesn't care," he added bitterly, "unless you get caught."

"I should think," I said, "from only a selfish view, you would be concerned about your future."

He smiled. "You sound more and more like my father," he said.

"I have a son almost your age," I said.

He seemed momentarily embarrassed, avoiding my face, but quickly recovered. "It wasn't until recently," he said, "after my arrest, that I realized how little the so-called normal world had to offer me."

This was the first I had heard of an arrest, but I felt he would get around to the details in his own time.

His appearance still intrigued me. I couldn't detect the least trace of homosexuality in voice, gesture, or dress. Even while discussing homosexuality, he appeared more masculine than many people whom I knew to be straight.

"Looking the way you do," I said, "you must be constantly exposed to the influences of the normal world—work, girls, family, and the rest."

"Oh, I see a girl now and then, a friend of my sister's or somebody like that, but I don't go around thinking of girls." He glanced up from his food a moment. "What people don't understand," he said, "is that the whole romantic image is different for homosexuals."

I didn't understand.

"When I visualize anybody," he explained, "I don't see the female form. I don't carry pictures of Marilyn Monroe or Ava Gardner in my brain. I see the male body. That is the only image that sticks with me." There was a new gleam of interest in his eye as he warmed up to his subject. "I first noticed it in high school, in gym class. I kept picking out the kids with the best bodies, and I would enjoy thinking of them later. Men are built so much better than woman, anyway." He grinned. "Since I wasn't particularly athletic, everybody was surprised that I never missed a gym class."

That brought me to the inevitable question. "When did you first realize you were a homosexual?"

He answered impatiently. "I never thought of myself as a homosexual until my homosexuality became a problem to others and, therefore, to myself. It was never a problem before that and I didn't think of it as such, nor did I think of myself as queer, or anything like that."

149

"All right then, when did you experience your first act of homosexuality?"

"Oh, about the time I was going through the gym-class routine. I would get these desires to go out for walks at night, just around the house. I'd usually find myself over by the park. I ran into this older man one evening—he was about twenty-six or so—and that was it. I never saw him again, though I went back a number of times."

He seemed lost in thought. "Did it bother you later?" I asked.

"Oh no, I only worried about somebody finding out. I was afraid my mother and dad could tell by looking at me. But they acted like always, and I began to feel confident and secure once more."

His sister was the first to suspect. "We'd always been close," he recalled, "and she seemed a little curious about me at times. I went out with girls from time to time, including her classmates, but I didn't show an enthusiasm I didn't feel."

"How did your sister happen to sense it?" I inquired.

He laughed. "She had been suspicious for some time. I suppose from talks with her girl friends, and then one day when I was on vacation from college, I surprised her reading a letter from my roommate. There was an odd look on her face and without excusing herself, she said, 'Say, what goes with you?' "

He had answered evasively. "You don't have to be afraid," she said, "I won't say anything to the family." And so he had admitted it.

He had looked at me almost impishly as he mentioned his roommate.

"I guess," he grinned, "you would call it love at first sight. We met in class, and our eyes kept meeting, too. Later I invited him to my room." They had to be careful at first because they had other roommates at the time, but the following semester they managed to bunk together.

Everything had been fine until his arrest, brought on by his own carelessness and overconfidence. The incident leading up to it had occurred not far from his suburban home during the holidays. He had noticed a young fellow in a lunch cart late one night, given him a searching look, and thought he returned it. As the youth left, he followed, accosting him on the street. "If I hadn't been drinking," he recalled, "I probably wouldn't have gone after him, but drinking made me careless."

He had invited the stranger for a ride, motioning to his car. When the young man shook his head and quietly walked away, he thought that was the end of it. But a few days later the police turned up at his house and took him to headquarters to book him. The young man had taken his license-plate number and gone to the police with it.

The case was heard in chambers. Afterwards, the young man who had brought charges explained that he had brooded a long time before coming to a decision. "I had to do it," he explained. He had once participated in a homosexual episode himself and in an agony of remorse had been trying to live down that mistake. "Realizing how wrong it was," he told Frank, "I couldn't let you go on converting others."

The argument had left Frank singularly unimpressed. "Actually," he said, "the boy was still fighting it, and I had to suffer because he felt himself threatened." He laughed. "At least his admission showed that my antenna hadn't been off completely."

Frank was put on his good behavior. Suspending sentence on a disorderly-conduct charge, the judge warned that with one more slip-up Frank would go to jail. In this suburban community, in New Jersey, there was a prevailing view that homosexuals were a threat to the children. Frank became the subject of a major reclamation project. He was referred to a local minister for spiritual guidance. They were soon at loggerheads. The clergyman, with many other demands on him, had little patience with a young man who seemed to flout all the teachings of a good home. He saw the youth as a "pleasure-loving psychopath, interested in nobody but himself." And Frank retaliated by complaining that the minister had more interest in his newborn twins. "They make a problem out of me," he confided bitterly to a friend, "and then they don't pay any attention to me."

As the problem of Frank's return to his southern university came up, a social worker suggested a fresh start at a New England university where it was hoped that puritanical tradition would have a beneficial effect.

Privately he resented being separated from his old roommate, but felt he had no alternative. However, before the semester was over, he had dropped out of school.

Why had he quit?

He became vague. "Oh, somebody must have told them about me, because they gave me a hard time." He was equally vague when his parents questioned him. He preferred not to discuss his problem with his father, a sales

151

executive, whom he flippantly referred to as the hero of
Death of a Salesman.

"He refused to regard my homosexuality as anything
more than a boyish prank," Frank remarked, "saying a lot
of kids went through this stage. He told me to stay away
from psychiatrists, ministers, and homosexuals. What it really
amounted to was that he and Mother didn't want to ask
themselves whose fault it was."

Right now he was being careful, and it suited his humor
to be dating a young girl. "My shill," he said with a pleased
grin. She was a young model, also a commuter, whom
he saw two or three nights a week around home. "When
the other mood comes," he said, "I go to New York. I
don't like to think of going to jail."

At the girl's suggestion they had formed an alliance, airing their problems over their beers. "She had just been
through one of those boring things with a married man."
He laughed. "I have no illusions about her. Sooner or later,
probably at my sister's urgings, she's going to try to make
a man out of me."

He spoke impersonally about women, even his sister, as
though they were inanimate objects, worthy of only casual
mention.

"To some of these girls, a homosexual, who isn't too obviously one, is a challenge," he pointed out. "The more
disinterested he seems, the more eager they get. They practically wage a campaign, calling on all their subtle charms,
to get a reaction out of a fellow."

"And did you react?" I asked.

"No," he said smiling, "that would have spoiled the fun.
Now I can keep her as a confidante, discussing the men I
like, and she can keep her illusions."

What did he mean by that?

He shrugged. "Oh, I don't think a closer relationship
would have been very satisfactory either to her or me."

He made frequent sorties into the city, taking an hour
or so for the drive. "I generally go to the upper West Side,
the West Seventies," he said. "The bars are a lot gayer than
in the Village, and they get a better class."

There were other advantages. "Some of them have dancing, and it's much easier to see what the boys look like,
dancing, than it is to stand at a bar where you have to keep
craning your neck."

My face must have registered surprise. "Don't tell me,"
he said banteringly, "that it shocks you to think of two

men dancing in each other's arms." He grinned. "It's really fun, camping it up once in a while. You ought to try it."

Was it any trouble meeting new friends?

Frank was his usual modest self. "Being young and good-looking," he said, "there's never any problem that way at all."

In the average barroom serving homosexuals there are invariably two or three with whom he hit it off at once. "I'm rather fussy," he said, "but there are so many homosexuals there's really no problem. I like the hard-to-recognize type, like myself."

There were other questions, but I had had enough for the day. He agreed, pleasantly enough, to another meeting, promising to call me the next day. Two weeks went by and I hadn't heard from him. It seemed the exception, rather than the rule, for "my" homosexuals to keep appointments.

Finally, I contacted the social worker who had arranged the initial meeting.

He laughed good-naturedly. "By this time," he said, "you should know most of these people are oncers—you meet them once and that's it."

"He looks so normal," I said, "I get the feeling he should respond normally."

"There's nothing I can do unless he comes in," he said. "His family resent my calling, and if I gave you his phone number, I would never hear from him again." He paused, tentatively. "But maybe I can help you."

I hesitated, "Oh, there were a few things I needed to round out the picture."

"Like what, for instance?"

"Well," I said, "I never quite understood why he left that New England college. I just don't see how anybody, without having been told, could have suspected Frank was a homosexual."

The worker's laugh came over the phone in rising waves. "I'll tell you how they suspected," he said. "He was going after the town constable's son, of all people, and when I heard of it, I pulled him out of there before he got us all in a jam."

"But why," I asked, "would he jeopardize his whole future and embarrass you in the bargain?"

Again he laughed. "Did he tell you what the minister said?"

"What minister?"

"The one who called him a pleasure-loving fool who thought only of himself."

"Psychopath was the word."

The worker grunted. "Well, that's a little strong, but the other fits most of them with one slight revision."

"What's that?"

"They're not thinking of themselves but only of their own selfish whims, and they realize this all too late."

Something still bothered me. "Originally," I said, "I had the impression that our young man was torn between heterosexuality and homosexuality."

"And wasn't he?"

"The heterosexuals," I said, "came off a poor second."

He chuckled. "You had him on one of his bragging days."

"How's that?" I asked.

"Well, he has one story for the reformers, and another for you." He laughed. "You should feel flattered—you got the truth." He laughed again. "Either that, or he didn't care what you thought."

CHAPTER XVIII

The Mattachine

THE MATTACHINE SOCIETY, a nationwide organization whose members are predominantly homosexual, asks "sexual equality for everybody" and "full civil and social rights for the world's most oppressed minority group."

To help raise "the curtain of silence," to which members strenuously object, I arranged to meet the leaders of the New York branch of the Mattachine Society in their small office not far from Madison Square Park. Nobody in the building seemed to know anything about the Society. The elevator man who brought me up, without understanding what they stood for, thought them "a nice quiet bunch of boys." Secrecy prevailed even inside the office. Two or three mentioned they were using pseudonyms. Others, disdaining this subterfuge, felt that their two worlds—homosexual and heterosexual—were so separated there was no danger of their overlapping. One officer, listed by name in the masthead of *The Mattachine Review*, a group publication, shrugged, "The people I meet from nine to five wouldn't even begin to know there was such a publication, and wouldn't believe it was me if they did see my name."

The group, originally launched in 1950 as a secret society, dedicated to gaining a fair hearing for the so-called third sex, has chapters in many states. Anyone twenty-one or over is eligible for membership, without regard to "race, creed, color, or sexual inclination."

The New York chapter is only one of seven scattered around the country. Headquartered in San Francisco, with a charter from the state of California, the group has other flourishing chapters in Boston, Detroit, Denver, Chicago, and Los Angeles. And the group, once shunning all publicity, makes no secret now of its aim of sexual equality for all. Realizing that secrecy often defeats its originally stated purpose of winning acceptance for homosexuality—and homosexuals—the Society has been meeting openly for six years, sponsoring publications which even find their way onto the newsstands. In New York they meet regularly in a midtown office building, in the heart of Manhattan, listening to such widely divergent non homosexuals as novelist Fannie Hurst, former Magistrate Morris Ploscowe, the Reverend C. Edward Egan, and Dr. Wardell Pomeroy of the Kinsey Institute for Sex Research.

About seventy-five to one hundred persons usually attend the lectures, which are generally announced through group periodicals. As an experiment, however, testing popular interest, the New York chapter publicized one meeting with posters in cafés, stores, subways, and an overflow crowd of three hundred turned up, including the police vice squad. The police, apparently bored by the proceedings, took no action.

At closed sessions, which are almost seminars held at individual homes, smaller groups discuss such intimate topics as: "Transvestitism," "The Homosexual and His Family," "The Homosexual and His Job," "Homosexuality and Religion," and "A Personal Code of Ethics."

While Mattachine publications, including a monthly review, have a circulation of five thousand, only a few hundred take the social risks involved in belonging to such a group. Contrary to one popular conception of homosexuals as a privileged class of wealthy dilettantes, most members are in moderate circumstances and often have trouble getting the office rent together.

Instead of holding down glamorous jobs, as is commonly supposed to be the lot of all homosexuals, Mattachine mem-

155

bers were clerks, chemists, students, salesmen, laboratory assistants, truck drivers, waiters, and pants pressers. "There is not a single prominent homosexual in our group," an officer told me. Not a playwright, actor, choreographer, designer, or decorator. Once, looking for support, the Mattachine approached several successful personalities in the entertainment world and received a frosty reception. "They felt," the officer said, "that they couldn't be identified with us because they would suffer professionally, and most of them wouldn't even talk about it."

Intent on establishing that they are no different from anybody else, the Mattachines deny homosexuals are unduly drawn to the artistic fields and claim there are as many, proportionately, in less glamorous walks of life. "In every section of the city, Brooklyn, Jamaica, Bronx, Staten Island," one said, "there are bars that cater to homosexuals who live in the neighborhood, many with families of their own, who form their contacts in that neighborhood. And some of these homosexuals do nothing more interesting for a living than drive a bus or sell ladies' lingerie."

The Mattachine have no criticism of homosexuals, whatever their occupation, who keep their social contacts quietly close to home. "It's not a bad thing, really," another put in, "because such contacts provide a safety valve while permitting them to keep marriages together and have children if they like."

Like many other organizations, the Society has inspired its feminine counterpart, the Daughters of Bilitis, comprising a handful of lesbians who derive their name from the heroine, Bilitis, in Pierre Louys' *Songs of Bilitis*. The name Mattachine has a prouder origin, stemming from the medieval court jesters. It indicates perhaps what members think of their own place in society. "These fools were in reality wise men," states a Society brochure, "and although they lived under the thumb of tyrants, they did not fear to speak the truth."

Although the Society desires publicity in its bid for social equality for an aggrieved minority, members are still skittish about talking for publication. There were four leaders, aged twenty-one to forty-five, in the Mattachine rooms the night I arrived for the interview. They greeted me noncommittally, appraising me carefully without being rude, and speaking guardedly. One was the Society president, another the editor of the group's newsletter. They were chemist, clerk, accountant, and writer. There was nothing about them to suggest they were homosexuals, and yet in this case, just by receiving

156

a reporter, they openly acknowledged they were sexual deviates. Before they would listen to any questions they demanded reassurance. They were primarily concerned about the type of book I proposed doing. Who was the publisher? How did I happen to be writing it, and what was I trying to prove? Was it to be an exposé, apologia, or a straight job of reporting?

"Of all the people who have come here to write something," the accountant said, "only one, a newspaperman, did a factual account. Everybody else seems intent on dramatizing or fictionalizing the information to suit their own purpose." The reporter, it developed, was a personal friend, and this helped my interview along.

Even so, they had found his visit amusing. "He came here with a young lady," an officer observed with a chuckle. "I guess he felt he needed a chaperone."

Once they were satisfied their views would be accurately reported, they frankly discussed the most vexing personal problems.

One of their pet peeves was the homosexual himself. They were opposed to the stereotyped faggot who brought the third sex contempt and derision. Consequently, they urged homosexuals everywhere "to adopt a behavior code which would be beyond criticism and would eliminate most, if not all, of the barriers to integration"—meaning integration with heterosexuals. They were against communism, sexual relations with minors, and the use of coercion in homosexual relations. Above all, they were striving to rid the public of its "misconceptions." "A lot of people," said one with an ironic laugh, "see the homosexual as a pinko who sneaks around picking on kids."

Although they had good jobs and were veterans, all resented the homosexual's precarious place in society. "We can be dishonorably discharged from the armed services," said one, "even though our service record is satisfactory."

They deplored the fact that the public automatically associated homosexuality with vice, lewdness, and violence, and that a homosexual crime often results in a police crack-down on all homosexuals. "Just like any other unpopular minority," said the chemist, "we pay for it every time any homosexual makes a public spectacle of himself or breaks the law." Even among themselves, there were differences. One officer felt the homosexual's civil liberties were threatened by the New York City statute prohibiting men from masquerading as women in public places, others felt the homosexual should restrain himself publicly for the common good. "If that is how he gets kicks," the chemist said, "let him stay home and wear all the dresses he wants." But, alas, they acknowledged they had but little luck persuading the obvious deviate to conform to their standards of propriety. "They just won't work with us," one said ruefully.

While all went along with a current theory by psychologists that homosexuals are made, not born, they vehemently rejected psychiatrist claims of cures. "All we hope for," the chemist said, "is an adjustment on our part, and the public's so that we can live with society in mutual respect and dignity."

The Mattachine leaders were in themselves a representative group. There were as many variations among them as among normal men. They were tall, short, stout, and lean, but all had in common, it appeared to me, an eagerness to explain they were really very little different from other men, except for their sexual idiosyncrasy. And they blamed the society which made it impossible, or at least unwise, for them to reveal their affections openly.

Nevertheless, they had little difficulty getting their personal messages across, though some caution was necessary. "We can usually tell one another within a few minutes; they let us know by a look, a word, a gesture," one officer said, "but we don't dare express ourselves spontaneously." The need for secrecy enhances the quality of a relationship. "It is wonderful to touch hands in the street, or put arms around one another in a dark movie," he continued. "But, of course, we have to be more careful than other people." He laughed mockingly. "This is where the lesbians have a great advantage. Nobody thinks it particularly odd if two girls walk down the street arm in arm, or embrace or kiss on meeting. But just let a man do that and see what happens."

Nearly all homosexuals have wondered at some time what made them that way. "I was nine when I knew," said another. "I kept wanting to wear my sister's dresses."

Said still another, nodding, "I was twenty-two. All I knew until then was that relationships with girls left me dissatisfied." Discussing this feeling of dissatisfaction with a college roommate, he discovered that he, too, discontented with female dates, would unceremoniously leave them and wander the streets peering at men's faces, strangely a-thrill, without even realizing what he was searching for.

Eventually, walking the streets, the roommate had encountered a young man whose piercing gaze stopped him in his tracks. And he knew then, with a sudden quickening of his heartbeat, what was so lacking in his life. The experience of his roommate proved terribly and suddenly revealing to the future Mattachine. All at once he realized what his problem was.

In more than one way marriage was a problem. All had thought of it for family pressures, if no other reason. "It was a great relief to me," the accountant said, "when my younger brother married and my father finally stopped worrying about my marrying and perpetuating the family name." They had only sympathy for homosexuals who had married, for one reason or another, and then discovered they couldn't confine themselves exclusively to a wife. They pointed out that other married men had extramarital affairs with other women almost as a matter of course. And they saw no incongruity in homosexuals who had married having affairs with men on the side. "We have the same aspirations as other men," said the young salesman. "We fall in love the same way. It may only last a week, a month, six months, or a year, just as it does between the two sexes. We cheat the same way and we make our home together the same way, either one or both doing the housework or cooking. We are really little different, but we are stigmatized because we don't produce children; it's as simple as that." There were many nods as he went on:

"Children aren't necessary to a good relationship, and many good marriages don't result in them." Having lived with two men, at various times, he felt he could authoritatively deny that the relationship of homosexuals is primarily sexual. "My roommate was ill for two and a half years. He was a semi-invalid, and the physical aspect of our relationship stopped. But I nursed him, cooked for him, and kept the house without our relationship deteriorating, or my once thinking of getting another roommate."

"That was quite a period of abstinence," I observed.

He laughed. "Oh, nothing like that. There were other men, and my roommate knew about it and approved. After all, I'm not a saint. And I imagine most normally married men would do the same in similar circumstances."

One of the others cut in bitterly. "They do the same all the time." He looked at me glumly. "People keep saying we're promiscuous because we may have a number of friends, even though we're living with somebody else. Well, you find that in married men all the time. And as for old men and young boys, how about old men and young girls? El Morocco and the other night spots are full of them."

Oddly, one of their greatest problems was their dealings with women. Since it would be disastrous to their position—socially and job-wise—to allow it to be generally known they were homosexuals, it was also essential for the same reason to keep their secret from women.

"In my job," explained the accountant, "it is necessary from time to time to go out with girls, generally with other executives who have their wives or mistresses. And the first thing you know, some of these girls are trying to build something out of the relationship, either marriage or something else. Naturally, I can't explain that I am completely satisfied with my roommate with whom I have lived for a number of years."

In his position he couldn't afford to take any chances, and exposure might mean more than loss of a job. "We have never caused any trouble around the apartment building," he said, "and have been very careful as regards parties. But we would probably get tossed out if it got known, since we live in a good, wholesome area where there are lots of married folks and children."

Homosexuals, the Mattachine insist, are no more of a threat to children than anyone else. And they are as much opposed to perversion as anybody. "The few homosexuals who prey on children," an officer pointed out, "are no more representative of our group than the occasional sex offender who seeks out little girls is representative of heterosexuals. Generally, they are perverts who don't care much whether their victim is male or female, so long as it is a child. They are pedophiliacs—child-lovers—not homosexuals."

I wondered how much progress the Mattachine were making in their announced goals and how they measured that progress.

"We feel that if we can reach a point of acceptance where we can sit down with other people, like yourself, and discuss the problems of homosexuality, we have accomplished our immediate mission," the chemist said.

And I also wondered about something else. "Some homosexuals told me that you probably met just to form new contacts," I said.

They smiled. "It is not necessary to make friends like that," one said, "but what people do after the meetings is entirely up to them, just as it would be after a concert, recital, dance, or any other function they attended. But we are definitely not after recruits. On the contrary, on the basis of our own experience—the embarrassment, shame, and humiliation so many of us have known—we would definitely advise anybody who has not yet become an active homosexual, but has only misgivings about himself, to go the other way if he can."

Accordingly, one of their great problems is the matter of advice to teen-age boys or young men with latent homosexual tendencies. "We don't know whether, morally, we should invite them to join or discourage them knowing they would be unhappy normally, and eventually slip away," the accountant said. "This business of giving advice can be a terrible responsibility. This boy came to me and said he had never been satisfied with a girl and wanted counsel. I felt that I knew what he wanted, but I didn't feel I should be the instrument to change him, and then perhaps have him unbraid me later. I told him I would talk it over with him, on the proviso that nothing personal would come of it between us. I discussed my own problem and how I had arrived at my own decision. He kept nodding his head as though our problems coincided. And after we got through talking, he said he wanted to go ahead. I only saw him a few times. I didn't find him particularly interesting myself. But whenever I have encountered him, he has always expressed his gratitude, telling me how much happier he is and that he doesn't bother with girls any more."

He looked up. "But I can say in all honesty, he made his mind up for himself." The others nodded approvingly, and the chemist said, "That's right. Every man has to choose his own way—and then he can't blame anybody else later."

CHAPTER XIX

Among Friends

THOUGH MEETING QUIETLY in a Denver hotel, where they made no effort to cultivate the press, the Mattachine Society's annual convention still wound up on the front pages of the San Francisco dailies—much to the surprise and dismay of members.

An innocent-seeming resolution, which members later felt was planted, was at the root of the trouble.

"I suppose we were rather naïve," a New York delegate said, "but when somebody proposed a routine resolution praising San Francisco authorities for being so enlightened, we thought it only gracious to approve."

The resolution was adopted unanimously, as a tribute to the predominantly homosexual Society's picturesque birthplace. Carried back to San Francisco, which was then having a hot election campaign, the resolution became political ammunition. Trying to turn out the incumbent Mayor Christopher, his rival candidate for City Hall, one Russell Wolden, pointed out that even faint praise from homosexuals was damning. And then while the press and radio blared the news, he went on to charge that grand old San Francisco had become national headquarters for dens of dangerous sexual deviates. With election day rapidly approaching, candidate Wolden's forces made a hasty survey of Frisco's downtown area. And what did they discover? Why, of course, a city swarming with homosexuals.

Checking a hundred public places in San Francisco's downtown area, the candidate reported more than twenty catering almost exclusively to homosexuals. These were not only bars and restaurants, but hotels and Turkish baths. "All of them," he declared, "operate as male pickup spots. Crowds of young men, conducting themselves in a repulsive manner, move from place to place, accosting normal young men and boys in the streets."

Wolden's charges were soon echoed in letters-to-the-editor columns. Flayed by some for flinging a taboo topic into the family home, Wolden was praised by others for his candor. "The most moronic slug," wrote one observer, "knows that San Francisco is the deliriously delightful paradise of the degenerate and deviate." Others deplored the shrill cry of males calling fondly to each other in the main avenues. Still others attacked community apathy to a homosexual threat.

"Such males are well-organized," observed an outraged female, "and real men do not trouble about them. Women prefer to play an ostrich game or else accept such eccentricities as cute. And the columnists—well—you know yourself how every single day one of the twerps is being drooled over and a story given out about his bogus romance with some glamorous girl."

Mindless of the charges—and the homosexuals—San Francisco's sophisticated voters gave Mayor Christopher a thumping vote of confidence at the polls. And the Mattachine, feeling themselves vindicated by this reassurance of municipal "enlightenment," went ahead with plans for future conventions in San Francisco.

As tempers cooled, a million-dollar Mattachine suit for damages was withdrawn, but members were nevertheless concerned at being labeled a homosexual organization. For although predominantly homosexual, the group insists it is not confined to deviates. Indeed, some five per cent are heterosexuals—parents, interested observers, or just friends of an oppressed minority. "As long as the group has no homosexual label," an officer explained, "it is possible for any member, even a homosexual, to be a member without being automatically branded a homosexual."

The sessions together seem to be helpful, as well as informative. Actually, officers explain, get-togethers are a form of group therapy. "Our meetings, lectures, and conventions," the official said, "bring together homosexuals who for the first time can express themselves freely with others and still feel comfortable."

In attracting conservative elements in the homosexual fraternity, discouraging swishes, members manage to raise their own self-esteem as they develop a corresponding respect for the homosexuals they fraternize with. "Our members can hardly be distinguished from any heterosexual group, so long, of course, as they don't reveal they are homosexuals," the official pointed out. "They have good educations, for the most part, useful jobs, and a place in society."

While the Mattachine hold meetings regularly in many cities, including New York, very few sessions receive the attention accorded the Denver convention. Nevertheless, lectures are often controversial—and illuminating—and members bravely choose speakers, knowing they might hear something unpleasant. On one occasion Dr. Herman Goodman, of New York City's health department, sharply upbraided homosexuals for promiscuity and pointed out that a result was the dangerously rising venereal-disease rate. The members listened respectfully.

Then, more tolerant of criticism than many, the Mattachine made the doctor's address available at a dollar a copy, the proceeds going into the club treasury. Another speaker, who made the point that only homosexuals foraged for romance along the waterfront and in public washrooms, was defended by Society members. They agreed that the statement was, by necessity, only too true.

By invitation, I turned up for one of these lectures which, actually, were open to the public. The speaker was a young

Methodist minister, and his subject: "Morality and Homosexuality." Like my colleague, who had taken a girl with him to a Mattachine interview, I was accompanied by a young woman, a writer, who had expressed some interest in the group. While obviously amused by my choice of a companion, the club president's only comment was a dry smile.

As I walked in with my date, I took a quick look around the Freedom House lecture room, in the heart of New York. Some seventy-five or eighty men and women of various ages were present. Some were well-dressed, others poorly clad, none obvious homosexuals. Each new arrival was mildly inspected by the audience, which had only one eye on the speaker. He was a young, earnest man of the cloth whose voice droned along monotonously. His attempts at humor were weak and ineffective and struck me as out of place. He digressed and was slow coming to the point. Almost at the outset he stressed that though he was a pastor with a congregation, he was speaking only as an individual, from his observations as a onetime chaplain and as a counselor to the young.

When he finally got around to his subject, audience interest manifestly quickened. Heads perked up, men and women ceased fanning themselves in the stuffy room, and all now glued their eyes on the speaker.

One of his first statements came as a bit of a bombshell. "Every relationship between two people stands on its own," he said, "and if there is truth and integrity in the relationship, then it is justified."

Others were also struck by his remark. "Does this mean that homosexuality is moral in some circumstances?" somebody asked.

"If there is love and integrity in the relationship," he virtually repeated, "it is a moral relationship."

His questioner persisted. "Then where homosexuals have truth, love, integrity, they have a moral relationship?"

Pressed hard, the minister finally nodded. "Yes," he agreed, "it could be put that way."

Many of the men in the room, enjoying the colloquy, echoed their agreement. One pointed out, "After all, there are places where homosexuality is not considered illegal—or immoral. If something is truly immoral, it should be universally so."

Another elaborated on this point. "How can it be immoral here when there are a number of countries in Europe—I

164

think Holland, Sweden, etc.,—where there are no laws against it so long as people behave in public?"

The minister could only clarify his own views, and throw in a little religion. "It is the basic Protestant principle," he said, "that a man's behavior is up to him and his conscience. Each case of morality, or immorality, has to be judged in its own context, in respect to the individual involved."

How had he become interested in the homosexual problem?

As a chaplain overseas he had been on a troopship whose sailing was held up for the court-martial of a serviceman accused of homosexuality. He was disturbed by the injustice of stigmatizing a man before his fellows for something he may not have done, or, even if true, was certainly not so grievous an offense as to bring about his ruin. In a sense, he pointed out, the sailor was a victim of the times.

"Yesterday's heresy," he quoted, "is often today's commonplace and tomorrow's orthodoxy." This little homily stirred an amused ripple in the audience.

He found the attitude of the younger generation—the teen-agers—toward homosexuals particularly disturbing, deploring a youthful cynicism and callousness which revealed a startling indifference to any code of morality. "Once while driving," he related, "I picked up a fourteen-year-old hitchhiker. Apparently trying to impress me, he boasted how he had recently made believe he was a 'queer' with two sailors and had robbed them when they weren't looking."

The minister took off his glasses and frowned. "I tried to point out the error of his ways, and how stealing was wrong no matter what the circumstances."

At these words, so earnestly delivered, there was a burst of laughter in the audience and the minister looked up questioningly.

One of the Mattachine, a youth in his late twenties, explained, "We just thought it amusing that you seemed more concerned that the boy was a thief than a homosexual."

As the minister cheerfully joined in the general merriment over his unwitting slip, another member broke in pleasantly. "That's right, for that's what that boy was, whether he liked it or not—a homosexual."

After the minister had finished, a young man sitting nearby commended the speaker's tolerance to a neighbor. "And he is not one of us, either," he whispered. "He has a wife and children and is perfectly content with them."

An open forum followed. But many of the questions seemed more statements of opinions than questions. And what answers there were, were in reply to a man who wasn't even there. His name was Dr. Bergler, and he was a psychiatrist who held that homosexuals were sick personalities.

A middle-aged man with a round, expressionless face was saying, "Well, Dr. Bergler implies that immorality is involved, since he argues homosexuals can help themselves if they want to."

That started it.

There were good-natured boos and catcalls as the Mattachine vehemently expressed long-standing objections to claims of psychiatrist Edmund Bergler, a well-known writer on homosexuality, that homosexuals were neurotics who could be cured if they wanted to.

As the discussion rambled on, a Mattachine officer silently handed me a copy of the Mattachine newsletter describing a recent appearance by Dr. Bergler at a symposium on homosexuality at the New York Academy of Science. The Mattachine had assigned one of its group to cover the meeting. In his review he made no effort to hide his disapproval of the doctor. "Dr. Edmund Bergler," I read from the newsletter, "expounded his well-known theory that 'not sex, but psychic masochism is the cause of homosexualism.' He stated that he had 'cured' one hundred and eight out of nine hundred cases of 'homosexualism' after eight months of treatment (at, we have been reliably informed, fifty dollars an hour). He said if you can overcome masochistic tendencies, homosexuality disappears, but specified that the individual must want to be cured."

The Mattachine editor had added the footnote: "It would be interesting," he observed, "to know more about the motivations of Dr. Bergler's patients. If they went to him against their will, one 'cure' out of nine appears impressive, but if they 'wanted' to be 'cured,' the same one-to-nine ratio speaks poorly of the therapist."

On the floor, reflecting the general sensitivity, they were still discussing Dr. Bergler.

A new speaker, a young man, got up and said, "We should know more about this than Dr. Bergler or any other doctor. We have to live with it." Amid cheers, he continued. "We disagree with Dr. Bergler, we feel that it is a social problem and that it is not the homosexual but hostile society which creates this problem. [*Mild applause.*] Essentially, it is our feeling, Dr. Bergler to the contrary [*jeers*], that we are no different mentally or emotionally than anyone else, except that we like men instead of women."

Amid cheers of approbation the speaker sat down, apparently well-pleased with himself. The serious portion of the meeting concluded with an expression of thanks to the pastor, who had followed the discussion with interest. However, as with many other clubs, there was still some small routine business to be transacted. Officers discussed plans for group outings, and there was an urgent call for donations, with all present urged to purchase some of the leaflets and literature on sale at the door.

The session ended with a special announcement. Members of a friendly Philadelphia group, who had no connection with the Mattachine, were to join the Society for a festive outing and picnic at the lush summer paradise of Fire Island. "A good time," an officer announced, "should be had by all."

Afterward, I discussed the extent of homosexuality with some of the audience. "We have friends in many big cities," one said, "and they tell us the same thing—the percentage in most of these places is just about the same as it is in New York." He shrugged. "The bigger the city, of course, the more open it is—that's the main difference."

Another nodded. "I don't know if it's one out of six, one out of ten, or one out of two, but I do know that a lot more people would be admitting it if they dared, and even more would be experimenting if they thought they wouldn't be caught or rebuffed. Believe me, the title of your book shouldn't be *The Fifth Man,* or *The Sixth Man,* but *The Sea Around Us."*

CHAPTER XX

Happy Honeymoon

MANY HOMOSEXUALS LIVING together speak of themselves as married, occasionally referring to their partners as "my husband" or "my wife." And while the majority of homosexual relationships are fleeting affairs, some relationships are as enduring as heterosexual unions, and the principals seem as devoted. Some, either through devotion, or ostentation, have shown an increasing tendency to take private vows, as a few friends look on. Others have merged in formal ceremonies, with all the trimmings of a big wedding.

The trimmings vary. But usually they include a bridal party, "minister," and a rousing reception, with everybody kissing the "bride," and the guests tossing rice, traditional symbol of fertility, at the happy couple.

Many of these weddings have justifiably become the talk of the homosexual community. One of the liveliest was held recently in a large New York apartment borrowed for the occasion. More than one hundred guests, half of them male homosexuals, the others lesbians, received engraved invitations to the affair. They were sent out by the couple themselves, two office workers of twenty-five or twenty-six.

After living together a year they had decided they would like religious sanction of their relationship, since both had been raised in a church and felt something was lacking. Although the minister was not of their faith, they were pleased as any couple could be when they were pronounced man and wife.

A gala assembly turned out for the affair—decorators, clerks, engineers, truck drivers, masseurs, salesgirls, masseuses, models, actors, and hairdressers. Notably absent were the parents of the pair, who were not among the invited.

The ceremony was as formal as any could have wished. While the bridegroom wore the traditional tails, the "bride" was a vision in shimmering white, a circumstance which inspired mingled reactions of merriment, admiration, and embarrassment.

Scorning the ceremony as "faggotty" ostentation, some onlookers felt themselves much more married than the participants, even without the benefit of clergy. Others, who did not object to the marriage in principle, thought the execution in bad taste. A middle-aged businessman, himself "married" for fifteen years, was distressed over the fact that the "bride" came in drag. "If both had been dressed as men," he said testily, "it would have been all right. But my feeling, shared by many, was that they robbed the occasion of its dignity by their masquerade. They should have been married as two men should—like men."

The ceremony itself was performed by a young man of severe features in a gray habit, with a clerical collar, and a solemn way of intoning his words. Obviously, he took his job seriously and had a sharp, reproving glance for any who tittered or otherwise indicated they did not take a grave view of the proceedings. The pastor's denomination was vague. Most guests had gained the impression he was associated with a splinter sect or cult, but he claimed marrying privileges for normal couples, too.

168

There were, however, a few minor deviations in the ritual for deviates. "The ceremony," an eyewitness reported, "was similar to most ordinary weddings, except that the word 'spouse' was substituted for both husband and wife, and the 'lawful' was deleted from the traditional marital question."

After the nuptial knot was tied, the guests took turns kissing the "bride," who blushed becomingly. Then the champagne bottles began to pop. The wedding reception rolled on merrily for hours, long after the radiant couple finally scrambled for their waiting car—and a two-week honeymoon —with a hail of rice beating down on their gaily retreating figures.

The ceremony itself won few recruits for formality. "In my case," one onlooker said, "we cut our veins and let our blood flow together." He sniffed. "I'm sure it's just as legal."

Many veteran couples, who have roomed together compatibly for as many as thirty or thirty-five years, see little reason for taking time out to get married. "Unless it's done right," a conservative broker said, "it's bound to make you look ridiculous."

But for a goodly minority the ceremony, with all the time-honoured appurtenances of the traditional wedding, provides a twisted link with the normal world whose approval they secretly covet. Still others feel that it will confer a greater sense of mutual belonging and serve as a "Keep Off" marker to cruising homosexuals. "There are so many faggots," an older homosexual observed, "who are constantly trying to filch a man's partner from him."

Like some freebooting males, many homosexuals believe that no ceremony, however seriously undertaken, will preserve a relationship when either partner wants to end it. "If you want to stay together," said a marital veteran of twenty-five years, "you make adjustments as you go along."

These adjustments include a tolerant attitude toward the partner's outside activities or peccadilloes. "Sometimes, to keep the harmony," the homosexual, a male type, continued, "you have to close your eyes or look the other way—and sometimes you expect your wife to do the same. From time to time, in my own marriage, each of us has had our extra-curricular relationships, but we haven't allowed them to affect the investment we have in each other."

Their first crisis developed years before when another homosexual had approached him and casually announced, "You may as well know it, Ed, I'm going to take Harry away from you." Though inwardly startled, Ed had responded

169

coolly, "I don't think you can, but if you do, you're welcome to him." He said nothing to his roommate and tried to conceal his concern.

"I was determined," he said, "not to be the nagging husband."

Some time after that the homosexual Lothario accosted him again and said with a sly smile, "Do you know where your Harry was last night?" Ed shrugged indifferently. "Most certainly I do. He was with you." He smiled condescendingly. "We have no secrets from each other." The other's face dropped, and Ed followed up his advantage. "Harry," he said carelessly, "gets over these camping bits quickly."

It was a confidence he did not feel. But over the years Ed had become philosophical about such things and so had his partner. "This goes on all the time," he said, "and you have to expect it if you're living with anybody that's at all attractive."

It was dangerous to show concern or become a scold. "Just start fretting or nagging a bit, and you'll soon see your partner crawling into a shell and getting distant," Ed said.

"As I told this faggot, who was trying to take Harry away from me, I had been through it all before, and I would again. But I knew that as long as I did nothing to jar the home atmosphere, and it remained the same comfortable retreat for both of us, where we could sit around and laugh and talk things over—including things like this—there was no danger of our splitting up."

In the last analysis, Ed insisted, his relationship with Harry was deeply rooted. They had similar appreciation of the same things—art, theater, the ballet, books, and the beach. They had a sense of humor, which made the same things amusing and permitted them to enjoy their private little jokes together in a crowd. And, through living with each other for so long, they had built up a certain easiness together around the house.

But still, with it all, Ed always found himself a little disturbed when Harry was even mildly involved with somebody else. "I keep telling myself it's nothing," he said, "just as it's nothing with me, but I still get a funny feeling in my stomach, until I can look up at Harry one morning and discover it's over."

And how could he tell?

"Oh, all his tension leaves him; he's not cross or irritable, not snapping at me because he can't find things, or a chair or lamp isn't in just the right place. He's smiling and good-natured and relaxed, and invariably he looks up and says, 'What's new?' with that big grin of his. Then, I know it's the same old Harry."

With many homosexuals, married or not, ego is the spur that drives them to prove themselves in brief stands in bars, hotel rooms, subway, and bus stations. "There was a time," said the still handsome Ed, "when I could have walked into any gay bar in town and walked out an hour later with any nine out of ten men at the bar. Even now, as a matter of vanity, frankly, I still occasionally like to establish for my own satisfaction that I can still grab off somebody I like from under some other chap's nose."

In living together many homosexuals have fixed on a comfortable design for living. While they may occasionally stray, there is always the stability they require in the background. "We all need somebody to go home to," Ed observed seriously.

While too sophisticated to "get married" themselves, they had their own set code, as binding as any homosexual marriage they had ever witnessed. "Neither of us," said Ed, "ever brought anybody else back to the flat. Some of our friends have done this without their partners being upset, but we just had a feeling that there was something we wanted to keep for ourselves. Even when Harry was in the hospital, and wouldn't have known, I kept everything—and everybody—outside where it belonged."

Some homosexuals, including those who have sworn marital vows, are not always as fussy. By mutual arrangement, some set apart certain nights for brief interludes with pickups, as their mate conveniently disappears for the evening. Still others, in a togetherness alien to the heterosexual world, blithely bring home and share new friends. "This," one homosexual agreed, "is hard for nonhomosexuals to understand, but any homosexual will quickly recognize that it is quite a camp, bringing the couple a common experience, which helps to enrich their relationship."

Still, homosexuals insist their record for fidelity compares favorably with the average heterosexual. "As a matter of fact," another pointed out, "there is no infidelity, when deception isn't involved."

Even among lesbians, the female homosexuals for whom male homosexuals often have a strange antagonistic attraction, "religious" marriages are not uncommon. But they are frequently more of a "camp" than the male ceremonies.

171

One of the more notable of these weddings took place at a resort area in the upstate Catskills, in a luxurious motel-restaurant which had long been a happy hunting ground for the gay set and their women's auxiliary.

The wedding scene itself was described as a veritable "Mad-Hatter's tea party" by an innocent bystander, who had wandered into the restaurant quite by mistake. It was one ceremony that he will never forget. Long before the bride or groom turned up, the bridal party, featuring lesbians dressed as men and homosexuals dressed as women, did a gay twirling dance to a stepped-up version of the "Wedding March." It was played, rather fitfully, by a bewildered straight man who had been dragooned into service at the piano and who was rapidly drinking himself to the point where he could barely hold the stool.

Besides the scores of invited guests, there were many others, including counselors from nearby boys' camps, straggling in after a few drinks. They were obviously very much at home.

But nobody could steal the spotlight from the bridal pair. The bride was a picture all by herself. A shapely ex-strip-teaser in her early thirties, she went through a series of bumps and grinds for the edification of her guests as her groom, a deep-voiced lesbian machinist, ten years her junior, beamed proudly—and the pianist kept pounding away.

But the amenities had to be served. Quieting down for the ceremony, the former strip-teaser pulled down her slip, re-arranged her billowy white gown, brought down her veil, and stepped up to a makeshift altar attended by both a matron of honor and a flower girl. As usual, no members of the family were present. So she was given away by a homosexual friend who unashamedly wept tears of joy throughout the ceremony. The groom, a butch-type lesbian in top hat and tails, looking more male than many men, solemnly exchanged rings with "his" bride.

"It was disconcerting," a startled spectator reported, "to see the bride blushing behind her flimsy veil and the groom tittering nervously, just as though it was a real marriage."

But to the clergyman, a young solemn preacher in gray habit and white collar, no marriage could have been more sacred. The ceremony was correct in every detail.

But immediately after saying "I do," the bride launched into a strip tease with a bottle of beer in one hand and a clump of ferns in the other. "Look, no hands," she cried.

The "minister" frowned and left.

Meanwhile, the proceedings kept getting gayer and gayer, with the "bridegroom" explaining why they had gotten married after living together for months. "The biggest Hollywood stars do it," she said. "Why can't we?"

However, even the best marriages sometimes spoil the best friendships. Only a few minutes after the bride had completed her dance, the happy couple were quarreling furiously. It was a case of simple jealousy. "The groom got jealous," a guest explained, "because the bride was making eyes at my sister."

As the party progressed, with liquor adding its bit to the festivities, the two principals began pulling each other's hair and had to be pried apart. Then, staggering, they were helped to the bridal chamber, slapping out at one another whenever they lurched out of control. Meanwhile, the party roared on for hours, until the last of the guests finally scurried for cover. While the wedding was acclaimed a great success, some thought it had its drawbacks. "I must admit," one onlooker said, "that I have enjoyed homosexual weddings more; the gay boys can be very charming at times, while the lesbians seem to combine the worst features of both men and women."

Sincerely and quietly, some legitimate clergymen support religious marriages for homosexuals who can show a desire for a lasting relationship built on love and loyalty. The Reverend Robert W. Wood, thirty-five-year-old Congregationalist pastor in suburban Spring Valley, some thirty-five miles from New York, does not see how the church of Christ can charitably turn away from those whose problem is already complicated by rejection.

The young cleric, and army veteran, who has counseled many homosexuals on emotional problems, asserts that the morality of "marriage" between homosexuals is largely a matter of individual conscience. "Depending on the circumstances," he says, "a marriage between homosexuals can be as moral as that between heterosexuals." Because of his makeup, he points out, the homosexual can generally find a true, enduring love only in a relationship that is not heterosexual. "There are many pathways," the minister asserts, "to finding God."

But it is not easy to qualify for a "sacramental" marriage. Although the youthful pastor has counseled more than a thousand homosexuals, he has not yet found one couple whom he felt ready for "holy" union. "It is perhaps significant," he says, "that in the majority of cases they are merely infatuated, and are repeating the business of falling in and out of love to which so many are subject." Actually, but one couple asked to be married, and he did not take their request seriously; their relationship obviously followed a transitory pattern.

Theoretically, the minister sees some justification for legalized homosexual marriages because of what might be accomplished. "Given the right people," he said, "it should add dignity to the relationship and gave it a better chance of succeeding. As it is, so many of these relationships break up the first time some problem comes along." Morality, too, would be improved, he hopes. "Self-expression and the element of choice are factors," he pointed out, "in any real morality."

Feeling the liberal Protestant church, not to mention other religious groups, had failed to give due attention to the homosexual problem, the Reverend Wood prepared a report for the consideration of the Social Action Committee of the New York City Association of Congregational Christian Churches. In this report the committee was urged to weigh carefully their religious obligations to the homosexual.

The pastor's views were later elaborated in a recent book, *Christ and the Homosexual.* But in his message to his church, the minister earnestly touched upon the doctrine that love is to be encouraged in all its best forms. "Can we say homosexual love is right or wrong?" he asked. "The ultimate standard for Christian morals is God's will for us. Whatever we do to thwart or frustrate that divine will is wrong. But there is a compulsion to love, and no one can love *in vacuo.*"

Marriage without the possibility of children, he said, did not violate the liberal thinking in some churches today. "If we concur with our leading Protestant marriage counselors," he said, "that the most valid single reason for wanting to marry is that two people are in love and wish to spend the rest of their lives in the closest possible relationship, then is this not equally valid whether the two people be of the same sex or the opposite?"

He had witnessed but one "religious" marriage himself. This, he said, was performed by a chaplain in England during the war. Subsequently, the Reverend Wood was impressed by the lasting nature of the relationship sanctified by "holy" ritual. It continued devotedly until the principals were parted by death.

Both "bride" and "groom" had been members of the American armed forces. The dominant partner was the groom. He was an older man, a Mexican, well-known south of the border. His mate, whom he met during the war, was of Scandinavian extraction. Opposites apparently formed a magnetic attraction.

They hit it off from the start. A twenty-five-year age difference only seemed to strengthen the blind devotion felt by the younger man. After the war the two lived contentedly together in Mexico for several years, the "marriage" lasting until the older man's recent heart attack.

In his grief the young "widow" was consoled by the chaplain who had married them. With no ties in Mexico, he then repaired to New York City, where he had once lived before the war.

There he found work, and forgetfulness, in an association with a young man nearer his own age. Soon they were sharing an apartment, but the bereaved youth would never marry again. One broken heart was enough.

Even though churches may never sanction marriage between men, the Reverend Wood does have hopes for an increasingly liberal attitude on the part of the ministry. Such leniency, he feels, would have an over-all beneficial effect on society. In greater permissiveness toward homosexuality, for instance, he sees one of the solutions of the global over-population problem. Only recently, the pastor took cognizance of this possibility in a regular sermon in his First Congregational Church.

"If artificial birth control fails to check the explosive demographic increase, the other alternatives are not pleasant. These are state control of birth, including infanticide; sterilization; prohibition of marriage; or a greater permissiveness of homosexuality."

His statement was carried on the front pages of the local newspaper. However, there was no mention of homosexual marriages. "I didn't think," the serious young pastor said, "that my congregation was ready to listen to anything like that yet."

CHAPTER XXI

Man and Wife

UNTIL THAT TIME when the homosexual dreams of equality—or superiority—come true, homosexuals will probably differ sharply over the best way of living comfortably in a heterosexual world. Some believe a homosexual can find contentment in a hostile society only if he makes the social gesture of marrying and having children, using this as a convenient cover for the male relationships he actually prefers. Others, scorning this sop to society, feel that a stable relationship between males of like interests is the simplest route to happiness, but concede that even this relationship, disguised in deference to prevailing customs, is fraught with emotional pitfalls.

There are homosexuals like the one I was now studying —and who was as closely studying me—who have experienced both types of relationships and have made a serious effort to avoid the promiscuity for which so many homosexuals have forfeited stability and peace of mind. And yet the man scrutinizing me across the table did not appear to have come to terms with himself.

He was young, in his late twenties, with a dark, saturnine countenance, looking very much like a youthful Edgar Allan Poe. Until he moved, there was nothing about him to suggest he was homosexual. He sat upright as he dabbled with his dinner, occasionally swishing his hips around as he deliberated a question. Making a point, he would purse his lips and lean forward, his hands together prayerfully. He spoke calmly, almost primly.

"My friend said you were interested in doing a story which would show the hypocrisy with which homosexuality is treated in this country."

I nodded.

"I see nothing wrong in loving another man," he said. "My church forbids it, so I have left my church. My wife forbade it, and I have left her. My family could never accept it, though they tried, and I'm no longer close to them. All my sentimental and emotional ties are with homosexuals, and yet I cannot proclaim them without risking rejection or arrest. And to hide the fact that I'm homosexual I must live the life of a hypocrite in a hypocritical world which will not tolerate me otherwise."

Erect and taut, he sat there studying me, then continued with a trace of annoyance. "Nobody but a homosexual can understand what a homosexual goes through. Can you imagine having to watch what you say and how you say it—how you stand, lean, walk, or run?" At times, rebelling at the hypocrisy of it all, he felt like wearing a sign which said: "I am a homosexual."

Now divorced, Steve had met his wife while both were

with the armed forces during the Korean War. He had entered into the marriage with misgivings but thought Lorraine would be understanding because she herself had confessed to an early experience with another girl. "But in her case," he explained, "it was mostly curiosity." The marriage, yielding two children, ended in divorce after five years. He returned to his native New York to find a job and continue his education begun in a midwestern school. He now shared quarters with another young man from the same college and appeared quite happy with the arrangement, meanwhile tending bar in the Village while studying for his master's degree.

Before entering college together Steve and his wife had lived briefly on her family's farm. "Farm life was dull, almost unbearable," he said, "but once on the campus, I met congenial young people who felt as I did."

I was mildly surprised. "A midwestern college hardly seems the place for that."

He permitted himself a mirthless smile. "Oh," he said, "it's not difficult to find congenial males in almost any college."

I had thought that homosexuality was generally confined to the cities. "I just can't visualize pink-cheeked, tow-headed corn-huskers as homosexuals." He laughed, almost exuberantly. "Well, that's just how my lover looks—he's from the country. We've been living together now for three years." There had been other "lovers." "Ever since I can remember," he said, "I had always felt a yearning for other boys, but had tried suppressing my feelings."

While still in his teens he fell in love with a young man. "And still," he said, "though this love was pure, I had to conspire like a criminal to keep it from my family and friends."

"What do you mean by pure love?"

He frowned. "Exactly what you would mean; the physical is incidental to the over-all glow you get from just being with someone you love."

"Would you say that you had that kind of love for your wife?"

He shuddered, and a faint expression of distaste crept over his face. "That," he said, "was the big mistake of my life."

"Why did you get married?" I asked.

"There were a number of reasons," he said, "but as I look back I think fear was uppermost: I was constantly afraid of detection. I was attached to the hospital corps during the for examination. I was always afraid someone would give me away. Lorraine wanted to get married, and I thought I would be safe since people have a tendency to dismiss such reports about married men." He looked up blandly. "There were other reasons. I suppose I wanted to prove I was as much a man as anybody else, and I liked children." I saw the first faint trace of a real smile. "Most people don't understand that about homosexuals—their genuine fondness for children. I'm not speaking now of the faggot whom we all find a little intolerable, but of the homosexual who is normal except for his preference for men." He laughed as though he had suddenly said something amusing. "There," he said, "you got me doing it."

"Doing what?" I asked.

"Oh, that word 'normal.' What's normal? Are half the things men and women do to each other normal? The more we know about sex, the more we realize there is very little we can classify as normal. So it's really meaningless to say a man is normal sexually, because he most likely wouldn't be if we knew the truth about him."

"Don't you think you're splitting hairs?" I said.

"Not really," he said, "not when the majority, the heterosexual like yourself, can almost subconsciously make me slip into their erroneous way of thinking."

I went back to the marriage, which intrigued me.

"It never had a chance," he said. "It was based on a false premise." He paused as though thinking back. "Before our marriage my wife led me to believe she understood my problem and it would never come between us." He laughed harshly. "Twenty-four hours after our marriage she announced there would be no men in the future." Rather than face unpleasant scenes, Steve decided to continue his relations with males surreptitiously. Shortly thereafter there was a showdown and he promised to behave. "She had a very good weapon," he said quietly.

"What was that?"

"Blackmail."

"Blackmail? What kind of blackmail?"

He began twisting his collar. "She knew I lived in dread of exposure, and she said if I gave her the slightest reason to suspect me, she would report me to my service superiors."

"But didn't you have a similar weapon?"

"No, there was nothing really wrong with her. Her experience, if she actually ever had one, had occurred back home and there was no proof of it."

"Were you in love with her?"

An expression of distaste again crossed his face. "Not really," he said, "as a matter of fact, after that incident I detested her." He smiled thinly. "Like a lot of women, she thought that she could cure homosexuality by offering her lily-white body on the sacrificial altar."

"What made your marriage last as long as it did?"

"What makes so many bad marriages last—the children." His face lit up in its second smile as he spoke of his boy and girl. "I love my little daughter—nothing psychological, I'm sure. It's just that I had more time with the girl. We broke up soon after my son was born."

"Do you see them at all?"

He shook his head.

"I suppose you write regularly."

Again he shook his head, his dark face revealing no emotion. Almost dully he remarked, "I write them once a year—that's all I'm permitted—once a year at Christmas."

"How is that?"

He was toying with a cube of sugar. "Oh, the same old tactic—blackmail. She doesn't want me communicating with the children, complicating their lives. She said if I persisted in writing or trying to see them"—his voice wavered—"that as they grew up, as soon as they were able to understand, she would tell them their father was a homosexual."

"What does their stepfather say about it?"

He looked up scornfully. "Nothing," he said tartly, "he's only a stud. I'm sure their marriage is no more normal than ours. But as long as neither person is homosexual, or nobody thinks they are, it seems to be perfectly all right."

Suddenly Steve looked down at his watch and gasped. "Sorry," he said, "but we're having a meeting tonight."

"Who's we?" I asked.

"Oh, some of the boys I met recently. They've got a club and talk over homosexual problems."

"May I come along?"

He laughed. "I asked if I could bring you and they panicked."

"How many will be there?" I asked.

"Oh, five or six boys at one of the apartments." He smiled, as though reading my mind. "I suppose one or two will be there to make new friends, but my only interest is curiosity. I'm quite satisfied with Jerry."

179

"Jerry?"

"Jerry, my roommate," he said quickly. "Now I really do have to run." As he went out the door, he called back. "Come up and have a drink with us sometime."

It was three weeks before I caught up with Steve again. After three or four calls I wondered if he was ducking me. "Not really," he said. He hesitated. "You know, you never did make clear the kind of book you were doing."

"I thought I had."

"Well, Jerry couldn't see why I should get involved, and" —I could see his lips pursing over the phone—"and he doesn't want to get involved."

"But I had the impression you were interested in clearing up a lot of misconceptions about homosexuals."

"That's right," he said. "Most people think all homosexuals are a pack of screaming faggots, interested in anything in pants. They keep saying homosexuals can't have a permanent relationship, but Jerry and I have been together three years—and we'll always be together."

I found this statement interesting.

"The more I continue my investigations," I said, "the more I discover there are as many different types of homosexuals as heterosexuals."

With this remark the walls of Jericho came tumbling down. The reserve instantly left Steve's voice and he invited me to his apartment. When I arrived the following afternoon at five, he apologized for the place being a shambles. The apartment consisted of one large room, Pullman kitchen, and bath. The day bed was unmade and the floor littered with cigarette butts, socks, shorts, even ties. As I plopped into a chair, which he had just cleared off, I felt a gentle nudge and, looking down, saw a small dachshund with one eye. "That's the Monster," Steve said. "That's Jerry's name for him."

"Where's Jerry?" I asked.

"He had to go off to work. He runs a restaurant in the Village—a straight place." His eye traveled to a profile photograph of a curly-haired blond young man in a Caesar Augustus pose.

"That's Jerry," he said. "Good-looking, isn't he?"

I nodded. He continued his haphazard tidying up. My eye fell on some half-empty bottles. "Sorry," he said. "Would you like a drink? We had a little party last night, that's the reason for the mess." He seemed swishier now than he had in the restaurant.

180

I shook my head. "Do you always do the cleaning?"

"Most always. And before you ask, I do the cooking. Not so much because I have the feminine role, but that I just happen to be a better cook. Jerry helps with the cleaning"—he laughed—"but he'd rather not."

"Almost like a married couple," I said.

"Somewhat," he said with a sly smile, "except that I think there's a little more understanding on both sides." He looked up and said, "Jerry understands me better than my wife ever did."

The phone rang and he said hell in a noncommittal voice. "No, he isn't in," he said blankly, "but I'll leave word if you like . . . No, I don't know when he'll be back, Leslie," he added with a trace of impatience. "Oh, yes, he'll be back. He always is."

Carefully he put down the receiver and said primly: "You'd never guess that I detested that person, would you?"

"I got the impression," I said, "that you don't approve of this man's interest in Jerry."

He snorted. "Leslie is a woman—a girl—if you like." A shadow fell over his face. "You'd think some of these girls would give up after a while. But that's one of Jerry's weaknesses—he likes to fancy himself the ladies' man." He shrugged. "We all have our foibles and that's Jerry's—that he can do anything that any man can. He doesn't mind the idea of being homosexual, so long as he doesn't think he has to be—an illusion perhaps, but one that he finds reassuring."

I tried phrasing the next question as delicately as possible. "Since Jerry sees other people, isn't there always the chance he may move out someday?"

He moved across the room to adjust the television set which had been on without either of us noticing. As he turned back to me, I caught the nervous flutter of an eyelid. "You are assuming, of course," he said blandly, "that I am more devoted than Jerry, and I suppose you are right. But I don't think there is any danger—not any more. We understand each other too well. As in any marriage, it isn't so much a question of love as of need—and we need each other."

"In what way?" I asked.

"There is no specific way, just as another man couldn't tell you what there was about his wife that made her so necessary to him. Yet he would be lost without her."

He poured himself a drink, a stiff one.

"But what is there to keep Jerry from walking out?" I persisted.

Steve shook his head slowly. "I hadn't wanted to go into that," he said, "but it was that very thing that eventually helped us reach a mature understanding." He drained his drink and proceeded. "It was my fault, not Jerry's. I behaved like a real faggot. I never gave him any peace. Because I was insecure. I was insanely jealous and was over him all the time, like a mother hen. I practically drove him away by making such demands on him, nagging every time he even spoke to another man. And then as I felt him drawing away from me, I felt helpless and desperate."

As I waited to hear how it was resolved, he suddenly took new interest in his cleaning and in Monster, stroking the animal affectionately and talking to him as though the dog understood every word.

"And how was it finally settled?" I asked.

"Oh, I got an assist from the psychiatrist," he said sourly, then laughed mockingly. "You can't get away from the old head-shrinker." More solemnly he added, "But he was a big help. He made me understand how truly devoted Jerry was, and he made me accept things as they really were. Jerry was wonderful through it all, giving up his job to take care of me, even after what I had done to him."

I was genuinely puzzled. "I don't quite understand," I said. "What did you do to him?"

He grimaced. "It's not the sort of thing I like to talk about. But one night we had a particularly violent quarrel. Jerry seemed so cold and indifferent that it maddened me. As he turned away from me, saying he was through, I must have lost my head and picked up the first thing that came to hand."

"What did you pick up?"

He shrugged. "A knife—isn't that the usual thing?"

"And how did it happen?" I asked.

Without a sign of emotion he said: "I caught him in the back, wounding him in the shoulder as he twisted around—and then I stabbed myself."

He was speaking as casually as though he were giving me traffic directions. Both lost a good deal of blood. Steve, ironically, was the more seriously injured and Jerry, giving up his job, slowly nursed him back to health.

After the "crisis" the pair lived in new harmony. "The psychiatrist showed me," Steve said, "that if Jerry had not been devoted, he wouldn't have seen me through. I also saw how my jealousy had brought on the problem. So it was really my fault, not Jerry's."

"But suppose Jerry should leave," I insisted, "suppose he should get married?"

"He won't. He needs me as much as I do him, though differently. I found that out during our crisis. A woman could never do anything for him emotionally."

"Nor another man?"

"That's always a possibility, of course, but we have a lot invested in each other emotionally, and we have learned to live together."

There was a flat, almost hollow note in Steve's voice as he added: "Of course, a permanent relationship is what most homosexuals like myself hope for, but not many get their wish. Most relationships last a few days or weeks, though I do know one couple who have been together thirty-three years, and I get encouragement from that." He laughed sardonically. "When they first started living together, homosexuality wasn't as accepted as it is now, and they separated because they felt people were becoming suspicious. But they kept seeing each other and years later, when things changed, they went back into light housekeeping."

As he looked up, I asked if he had met many men who interested him. "Straight people," he said, "have the idea that the homosexual is interested in any kind of guy. I have found so much satisfaction with Jerry because he's one of the few men who ever attracted me. I could go weeks without seeing a man I found attractive." He wrinkled his nose. "It really gets me when some dirty old bum comes into a gay bar and screams he'll hit the first fairy who comes near him." A look of ineffable disgust came over the saturnine face. He shuddered. "I couldn't bear the thought of touching somebody like that."

Unlike Jerry, Steve was not the least interested in anybody else at the moment. However, he made it clear that it was not through lack of opportunity.

He ran a large orange comb through his thick, dark hair and darted a quick side glance at a mirror. "Without being silly or boastful," he said, putting down the comb, "I know that I've been considered quite a queen by some, and I've known a few celebrated stars myself."

I mentioned the name of an actor appearing recently in a film with homosexual overtones. "Oh, I knew him well," he said, "but it ended badly."

"How long ago was that?"

"Oh, seven years—I was twenty-one then—just before I married."

Now he was smoothing down his hair. "He was a wonderful man. But he was always having trouble with women, and never quite knew which way he should go." He pointed a finger to his temple and said with a toss of his head: "Sick, sick, sick."

"Have you seen him lately?"

"No, just before he started this last picture, his bookie called me and asked me to go with him to a health camp and help him get in shape."

I wasn't sure I had heard correctly. "His bookie?" I asked. "Do you mean a fellow who books bets?"

"What's so odd about that?" he asked. "The bookie introduced us in the first place."

Thinking of bookies as rough, unlettered characters out of Damon Runyon, I found it hard to visualize one with a homosexual. "Well, he wasn't homosexual, was he?"

A challenging note crept into Steve's voice. "Why should you find that so amazing?" he said. "Is there any reason why homosexuals can't be bookies?"

"I just thought it a little incongruous," I said, "since they are such roughnecks as a rule.... You said earlier that it had ended badly."

He hesitated only a moment. "For me, that is. Not many people knew he was a homosexual, and then a straight friend of his discovered our relationship. The friend was so upset that I had to be blamed for forcing the relationship." He snickered. "On the surface, this was an absurdity, but the actor saved face and I went my way." He shrugged. "Naturally, now, I wouldn't leave Jerry for him or anybody else."

I wondered why he had talked to me so freely.

For the first time his impassivity deserted him. "I think it is important that people realize we are not all kooks and freaks. And I think it important that homosexuals, trying to live quiet lives, should realize there are many homosexuals like themselves and that the time is approaching when they will not have to hide the fact that they are homosexual."

"Do you think that time will ever come?" I asked.

He nodded vigorously. "There is more acceptance all the time. Look at the disgrace that overtook Oscar Wilde some fifty years ago when he was convicted of homosexuality. He couldn't show his face anywhere. Well, Sir John Gielgud, who's as famous an actor as Wilde was a writer, was convicted and he is still welcomed, socially and professionally. And in this country a famous crooner was convicted on a morals charge, and had no trouble getting work."

He looked up at me sharply. "Someday," he said, "homosexual relationships will have the sanctity of other relations—and why not?" He stared off into space with dark, brooding eyes. "Certainly," he said, "I've had more of a marriage with Jerry than I ever had with my wife."

CHAPTER XXII

Women in Their Lives

FOR NEARLY EVERY homosexual there is a woman who thinks she can change him. This illusion has led to many unhappy alliances, including holy matrimony. It has helped swell the national divorce rate, contributing to juvenile delinquency and further homosexuality when children have resulted. It has also left perfectly normal women with sadly deflated egos, wondering ruefully about their own sex appeal. In some instances, especially in theatrical circles, where women are more than ordinarily aggressive, desiring an admiring audience even at home, such matches of convenience have occasionally lasted, though infidelity is not uncommon on both sides.

No longer is a man's marriage an automatic refutation of homosexuality. Quite the contrary, some homosexuals have married many times, with unvarying and quite understandable lack of success. And the world is slowly beginning to understand that status-minded homosexuals frequently have more motivation than the average male to marry and have children.

However, the uninitiated woman, apprised of a man's homosexuality, still turns incredulously and gasps, "But he's married."

And the sophisticated, well-versed in the ways of the modern homosexual, have so often sardonically replied, "But, dear, *they're* always married."

Sometimes, it seems that about everybody but the bride knows that the husband is homosexual. On one occasion, a well-known young actress, infatuated with an older actor, was warned by her studio against marrying him. She asked studio officials why they objected, and they blushed without giving her a satisfactory answer. Thinking they might be opposed because he was already married and had children, she said:

"But the marriage failed a long time ago, and they're getting a divorce anyway."

They still silently shook their heads. That wasn't the reason.

The actress finally went ahead with the marriage. Several months later, she knew at last what they were trying to tell her. Now, she, too, is divorced, and when friends ask her why, she becomes as mysterious as the studio officials. "I will never tell anybody," she says, "what the problem was."

In still another example of mismating, a beautiful actress-model, more definitely forewarned, married a young writer whose name had been prominently linked with a publisher overseas. This time the rumors which had been circulating came to the attention of the brilliant young beauty and she dismissed them contemptuously. She was still dismissing them when the marriage broke up, and blamed the misalliance on the universal frailties of the male animal. "I'm through with marriage," she said, "and with men."

To which observation a girl friend, who knew the situation, perhaps more astutely observed: "She's through with men, and she's never known one."

Without close observation, and some careful analysis, many of these marriages would seem to have no rhyme and reason. However, even the oddest marriage combinations can somehow be accounted for, once the backgrounds are known and the facts are in.

There are many odd marriages between various homosexual combinations. The oddest perhaps occurs between males and females with a strong homosexual streak and an almost equally strong need for social approval, frequently causing them to take the plunge against their better judgment. Some of these marriages have lasted, others have been violently brief and disastrous. In one such contretemps, a young editor, thirsting for a life of normalcy after brooding about an isolated homosexual contact in his youth, decided to take a chance and get married after first consulting a psychiatrist. Unfortunately, he chose as a bride a young editorial aide who had not consulted the same psychiatrist. Both had private misgivings about themselves. The young lady, who fancied male haircuts and a piping British accent, had quietly left an eastern women's college amid dark whispers of a dormitory scandal. Neither knew about the other but, working closely together in the same office, became good chums, admiring each other's wit and efficiency. With a common yearning for respectability, it seemed likely they could hit it off.

The marriage didn't last a night, and for the next two or three years the luckless bridegroom, who has never again attempted matrimony, tried to drown his memories in drink. According to an unsympathetic friend, who heard both sides, the problem was elementary: "They couldn't decide who was the queen."

A similar but more drastic case involved a young artist who had thought himself independently homosexual until his ardor was stirred by a rather emaciated fashion model with the neck of a swan and the breast of a chicken. He was thoroughly confused by this experience, which ended with him completely unstrung when the lady acknowledged she had only been tantalizing "a poor miserable faggot." On recovering from this venture, he thought it possible that he might fall for a woman again. He thus hoped to gain the approval of heterosexual friends and of his family, particularly his father, who had ridiculed his effeminate ways since childhood.

Thinking it worth another try, he managed to woo and win a young model who had posed for him intermittently. They were as opposite as a pair could be. The groom was short and dark and Latin, quick, sensitive, volatile; the bride, tall, and fair and Anglo-Saxon, phlegmatic to the point of being bovine. There were also religious differences. Within a few weeks the husband, who had been doing his best to appear masculine, was complaining that his dearly beloved was flirting, petting, and otherwise encouraging intimacies with chance acquaintances at bars. "She doesn't even mind that I'm watching," he moaned to friends.

Eventually, prodded by pride, he forced her out of his East Side town house. She, instead of considering a bad bargain well ended, threatened a separation action which would publicly brand him a homosexual, disgracing him and his family unless he handed over practically everything he owned. Stricken with fear and apprehension, he was ready to yield when a heterosexual friend asked if he had retained a private investigator.

"What for?" he inquired.

"To have her watched, of course," the practical heterosexual replied. "I've done that with all my wives."

The unhappy bridegroom was still mystified.

His friend patiently explained. "She's blackjacking you, so you blackjack right back, and she's the one who'll be worrying about publicity, not you."

It seemed like a good idea. The friend made the necessary arrangements. One night, after the estranged bride and her playmate, a Broadway agent, had been under surveillance for some time, a raiding party, including the righteous husband, surprised the pair in a compromising situation. The detective had gained entrance by posing as a messenger boy.

As the raiding party burst in, with a photographer's incriminating flash bulbs highlighting the scene, the bride's lover, spotting the smiling bridegroom, attempted to maim his adversary. He was restrained by detectives. The bride also concentrated her fury on her mate, who was now grinning broadly. Angrily unconscious of her singular lack of attire, but standing in pristine splendor, a fitting model for any artist, she spat at him venomously, "You're nothing but a Catholic faggot."

And he, no whit daunted, replied with a smile. "And you, my dear, are a Protestant lesbian."

Most marriages of homosexuals are far less bizarre. Generally, they marry all too normal girls, who are soon blaming themselves for the misadventure. The more innocent the girl, the more likely she is to condemn herself in her confusion and inexperience. Often young women have been wed for years, even divorced, before realizing through more normal relationships that the husband they could not reach was abnormal, not they.

Many of these girls have developed all manner of inferiority complexes, rushing off to psychiatrists and shying from new marriages because of damage to their egos. To most, marriage was a nightmare in which, without their awareness, their femininity was constantly under attack. Sometimes the bridegroom, a latent homosexual, was not aware himself of why he found his wife unattractive or the sex act unappealing, preferring in his restlessness to saddle her with the responsibility.

Married to latent or concealed homosexuals, many attractive women who would gratify the ordinary male have suffered for years without a compliment from their males, without the simplest tokens of affection that make a marriage warm and enduring. Many soon reached a stage where they looked desperately for reassurance that they were not ugly and ill-formed. In nine years of matrimonial infelicity a beauty of twenty-seven, married as a virgin, reported that her husband had not once had an approving word for her appearance. He constantly criticized her dress, hairdo, make-up, and general façade. And yet, following a marital breakup, this young woman, beginning to think of herself as an ugly duckling, was able to prosper as a commercial model because of her beauty. This was not all. The sex relationship had left her feeling miserably aware of her own incompleteness. In a second marriage the great awakening occurred. "I had wasted all those years," she recalled bitterly, "trying to please a man whom no woman could please."

In a world where women play so aggressive a role, it is perhaps not surprising that so many young girls have married homosexuals in the confident hope of "reforming" them. "They think," one homosexual said, with a toss of his head, "they can do it with one act of love."

Even when quickly disillusioned, they have persisted out of stubbornness or devotion. Some, marrying blindly, have tried keeping the marriage together because of children, pushing from their minds the disconcerting realization that their most dangerous rival was a man.

The truth doesn't always strike at once. A virginal eighteen-year-old debutante, daughter of a wealthy industrialist, married the twenty-one-year-old son of a prominent publisher over the protests of her family. The objections had been so vague—"We just don't think he's right for you" or "You're both too young"—that she finally threatened to elope, and they yielded. Apparently they sensed something that their daughter, in her innocence, could not have begun to suspect. Yet they couldn't be sure.

The wedding was a splendid affair, with the pick of society in attendance. But the wedding night was a harrowing experience for a sensitive, inexperienced bride who waited expectantly, blushingly for her groom to make the overtures that would seal their marriage.

"Instead," she recalled, "he sat up in bed, reading the congratulatory telegrams. There must have been hundreds of them."

Fretfully, the bride finally turned off the light and tossed fitfully through the night while her relaxed partner snored serenely by her side.

The next night was even worse. He read aloud from comic books with appreciative laughter, while she curled up beside him in the negligee he didn't even notice.

The bridegroom's abstinence, so different from his ardor

while courting, soon made the bride nervous and unsure. After two weeks she began scanning herself in a full-length mirror, wondering what could possibly be wrong with her. Pride prevented her from discussing the situation with her parents, modesty kept her from discussing it with her husband.

Finally, in a mood of black despair, she said to her bridegroom, "If you don't find me pleasing, why did you marry me?"

He looked up, surprised, and then blushed, as he caught her meaning.

He threw his arms around her and drew her close to him and said with the old tenderness, "I didn't want to rush things, that was all."

Consummation of the marriage brought the bride little satisfaction. "Somehow," she said, "the love-making seemed so different from what I had imagined. It almost seemed make-believe."

Because of his indifference, she felt that she was at fault. She consulted a psychiatrist. Soon, with the aid of psychotherapy, she recognized that it was her husband who had a problem, and some doubts of her own femininity were relieved.

She began to observe little things she had never noticed before. Her husband's lingering handshake with many of his cronies, the way he carelessly threw his arm around male friends with whom he was conversing. More disturbing were the late phone calls, rousing him from sleep and sending him out of the house at one and two in the morning. "At first," she said, "I thought it was just a carry-over from bachelor days, a restless desire to knock about old haunts. But I discovered that he didn't go anywhere but to some old friend's house."

After six months the marriage fell apart in mutual recriminations and she went tearfully home to mother. "Even then," she said, "I wasn't sure. It seemed too fantastic. He'd always been so strong with the girls. But I kept hearing things."

Not for years, however, did she accept the complete truth. "What a relief finally to realize it wasn't me but any girl. Now, for the first time, I was able to think of marrying again."

Shortly after her remarriage her ex-husband married again, too, sending her an invitation to the wedding. "Only recently," she said with a shrug, "I got an announcement they were having a baby."

Many women seem to have a failing for attracting men not 100 per cent male. "I suppose it's the challenge," observed Ethel, an unusually attractive girl in her early thirties, a college graduate who worked for a well-known magazine. "I had known him most of his life and thought I understood what was bothering him," she said. "We'd sit around and he'd cry on my shoulder and I'd feel so tender and womanly inside, as though I wanted to just reach out and embrace him. I guess it was the mother in me."

She laughed harshly. "I could see it all, or I thought I could. Here was a boy whose father had left the family when he was a kid of six. He grew up resenting Dad, and resenting his mother, too, because she had become the mistress of a prominent man with a family of his own. As a boy, Howard called him 'uncle.' As he grew older, understanding the relationship, he felt offended by the humiliating role in which he saw himself, living off a man who was having an unsavory relationship with his mother.

"As Howard talked about those days, I felt warm and tender toward him and I could feel myself wanting to comfort him. No wonder, I thought, the poor boy was so confused."

They were intimate before he told her of his relationships with other young men. It was a shock, but since she had felt from her own experience that he was basically masculine, she was confident marriage would straighten him out in short order.

"In fact," she related, "I thought confession good for his soul. And so we were married, and all his male friends were there tittering in the background." She grimaced. "And I was thinking to myself, 'I'll fix you harpies.'"

Her self-confidence was sadly misplaced. "I guess I had been married about a week when I came home unexpectedly one afternoon and surprised Howard in the bedroom with a crony. Instead of being embarrassed or ashamed, both of them started aping the love embrace for my edification as they got to their feet.

"I thought of leaving but decided I should give him another chance. After all, he's been this way for a few years. Maybe expecting reform overnight was just too much." She sighed. "The marriage was over then, of course, though I didn't realize it at the time. However, it took another six months for me to recognize that reform was the last thing he wanted."

As time went on, Howard became more open about his friends. Encouraged by him, they seemed to take delight in

191

making her the butt of inside jokes she found silly and inane.

"When his friends came over they would sit around and mock me, anything to belittle my intelligence, appearance, or demeanor," she said. "They'd sit on the floor, hunching their knees, and one would say, 'What's Dr. Schweitzer's first name?' and I'd say, 'Oh, that's easy, Albert Schweitzer,' and then they'd laugh like I was a bloody moron and say, 'Albert Schweitzer—she thinks it's Albert Schweitzer.' And then, 'It's Robert Schweitzer—Albert invented Swiss cheese.' "

When Ethel threatened to leave unless Howard got rid of his cronies, he started to cry. "His need for social approval was so strong that he actually fooled himself that he wanted me," she recalled. "Of course, all he wanted was a front, but it took me a while to see it. If there was ever any talk about him in his office, people would say, 'That's ridiculous —he's married.' "

One night there was a country-club party. Howard had a few cocktails before they left the house and a few more at the club, during dinner. "When the lights went down and the band began playing," she related, "one of his pals cut in just as we were getting ready to dance. Playfully, he called out, 'C'mon, Howard, we'll show Ethel how it's done.' And so they danced cheek to cheek around the table while everybody clapped hands and laughed, thinking it a joke.

"That finished me. It's hard enough to cope with another woman, particularly if she's young, pretty, and involves no responsibility, but I discovered I just had no understanding of the other thing at all."

More recently, Ethel was courted by another young man who admitted to having become a homosexual when he was thirteen. A photographer, he may have been the only college student to earn his way through school as a male prostitute. "I saw him a few times. Like my husband, he was bright, scintillating, and an object of sympathy. I found myself thinking about him, caressingly, as I would a sick puppy. We discussed marriage, and I told him I had made that mistake once and would never repeat it."

Meanwhile, Ethel began to wonder what there was about her that was a magnet for the sexually confused. "Of course," she said, "working in publishing, in the heart of a homosexual bastion, I knew that many women dated homosexuals because they felt they could let their guards down and relax. But I didn't think I was that type."

Ethel has not remarried and sees no likelihood of it for a

while. "I don't know," she says. "I may have to go back to the Middle West where I came from to find a real man. But"—she threw up her hands—"that's where my husband came from."

After empty marriages some wives have separated from husbands with only the suspicion their mate was homosexual.

One woman of thirty, married to a doctor, wondered about him because he was always arranging double-dates with another couple, friends from South America. "At first," she recalled, "I was jealous, thinking that he was interested in Jorge's wife, who was a pretty blonde with liquid dark eyes. I watched closely but never saw anything more than perfunctory attention being directed at her, either over the dinner table or on the dance floor. In fact, his only animation came when the husband, who was one of the handsomest men I have ever seen, entered into the conversation. With a choked feeling in my throat, I realized that it was the husband he was interested in. But men, I told myself, could be great friends without being homosexually attracted to one another.

"I couldn't ask about it and I couldn't be sure. One day, finally, Jorge was called back to his own country. And we all went out for a last time. As we were saying a final good-by, I accidentally intercepted a glance between my husband and Jorge. There was a world of sadness and desolation in his look. He felt bereaved and alone, and I, his wife, sensed all this at once. And a curious feeling of understanding and sympathy came over me. For the first time, perhaps, I realized his problem and felt perhaps I could fill the gap. But there wasn't a chance."

Eventually they were divorced, the grounds—mental cruelty. Not once were her suspicions voiced. "All I knew," she said, "was that I couldn't help him—and he could do nothing for me."

Earlier there had been other telltale signals which had made her uneasy, without seeming significant. Several weeks after the marriage her husband had casually suggested twin beds. For some reason, though his work kept him uptown, he preferred dining in Greenwich Village in restaurants frequented by homosexuals. And during the summer, though an apparent conservative in a conservative profession, he would propose weekends near the homosexual colony in Fire Island, watching with evident amusement Saturday nights as the gay boys danced and capered in a carnival of bad taste.

"I should have suspected," the wife said, "when we kept going back. It was amusing the first time, and thereafter disgusting, but he was fascinated."

The motivations for marriage with a homosexual are not always clear-cut. Some girls, perhaps, driven by destructive impulses, have chosen abnormal mates out of spite, with often disastrous results. Despising her father, whom she thought an old satyr, a young heiress malevolently decided to steal his boy friend, a valet who was actually little more than a paid male prostitute. Behind her father's back she flirted recklessly with the good-looking young man.

Flattered by her interest, the young man, who was bisexual, found himself reluctantly falling in love. This interest, bolstering his self-esteem, led him to a dream of a life with marriage, children, and a place of his own. The girl encouraged his dreams. Finally, she announced to her father that she and his young man were to be married. He was angry, stunned, hurt, and outraged that she would bring a nobody, whom he contemptuously regarded as no better than a prostitute, into the family. There was a furious quarrel, the daughter holding the upper hand because of her control, at twenty-one, of the family fortune.

"You must be out of your mind," the father stormed.

The daughter looked at him coldly. "If he's good enough for you," she said, "he's good enough for me."

The wedding, splitting the family, was not much of a ceremony, but the bride eventually paid dearly for it. Soon bored, wearying of the mismatch, she began seeing other men, meanwhile taunting her husband with his lack of manhood until one night he killed her in a jealous rage.

Other relationships, without benefit of clergy, have ended as badly. There was the young actress who found herself in love with a brilliant writer who made no pretense of his preference for men. Besides being impressed by his wit and charm, she considered him a challenge. Warned by friends, she plunged headlong into the romance, anyway. She not only hoped for marriage, but for a new career in the theater. The writer, though emotionally detached, was flattered that any young attractive woman, particularly one so prominent, should throw herself at his head. "She was not bringing out his manhood," a friend said, "just his ego."

For the actress the relationship was a ruinous one. A reformed alcoholic, she had not touched liquor for three years until she was prodded by her homosexual "admirer." "Let's live it up," he would say. "Send for the champagne."

Over her doctor's objections, her drinking continued. One morning she was found in her flat, with whiskey and barbiturate bottles strewn all over the floor. As friends gathered for the last rites, the homosexual writer delivered the epitaph. "I guess," he said, "my baby didn't love me enough."

CHAPTER XXIII

A Woman's Life

I HAD KNOWN her for years, though I didn't know much about her private life, except that she was apparently comfortably married. She always wore a wedding ring. Occasionally, I saw her at lunch or cocktails with other men, but I never wondered too much about it. She was a fresh-looking blonde from the Middle West who had retained her freshness, while adding a certain big-city sophistication and articulateness. She was one of the most attractive women in a city of beautiful women. She modeled a bit, acted a little, appeared on television from time to time, but somehow I had gained the impression she was not terribly caught up in a career. It was something to do, a concession perhaps to her own beauty.

Our conversation, on one occasion, had touched on homosexuality quite by chance. I had mentioned I was doing a book on the subject, and she evinced immediate interest. "There are all kinds of homosexuals, you know," she said. I nodded, wondering a little at her reaction.

"Some," she went on, "are as masculine as any male, except in that one area." She had leaned forward across a small table, and was leisurely smoking her cigarette.

"And in this one area, though they may derive no great satisfaction themselves, they are able to fulfill the woman they care for. I know of one man, homosexual in this one regard, who is more man than anybody I have ever met. He has more courage and nerve in a crisis than most of these he-men who go about flexing their muscles and running with girls. He is a fashion photographer and works with other homosexuals, who are positively 'flying' when the least upset occurs. But not he." They had been on location near Southampton shooting beach pictures when they saw a boy, fishing offshore, accidentally hook another boy in

195

the eye. There were several other men in the group, including an advertising account executive and the client. As the boy screamed, the blood pouring from his eye, they became panicky and fluttered about helplessly. The only two men to keep presence of mind were the photographer and his assistant, another homosexual. Moving calmly and swiftly and with the help of his assistant, the photographer soothed the suffering boy, meanwhile removing the fishhook by a nimble twist of his fingers.

She looked up at me to see how closely I was following her story. "Never," she said, "have I witnessed anything which filled me with so much admiration for a man."

While I thought the man's conduct highly laudable, I felt the praise a trifle strong.

"How do you think you, or most of your friends, would have acted?" she asked.

I shrugged. "I don't know. I might have run for the nearest doctor, or fainted dead away."

She laughed. "I can see you're not impressed."

"Well, I should think there's more to maleness than nerve and courage. As we all know, some of the bravest people, and certainly the most enduring, are women." I paused. "How would this man be with children, particularly a son?"

"That's no problem," she said. "He loves children, wants a family of his own, can hardly wait, in fact. And he is good with them. I have noticed him with the children of friends; kind, patient, understanding."

Suddenly her mood changed. "Oh, you newspapermen make me sick," she said. "You're suspicious of everything."

"Not really," I said. "I was just trying to visualize this paragon."

"You should see him in business. He is all-male—aggressive, decisive, firm, yet courteous at all times. I have watched him decide deals involving thousands over the telephone."

"He sounds so little like a homosexual," I said, "that nobody probably takes him for one."

"Well, there is no sense of advertising it," she observed, "but he is not ashamed of it. As I said, he is no different from any other real male, except for that one thing."

She took out another cigarette and lit it as I fumbled for a match. She smiled good-naturedly. "He would have had the match out before I found my cigarette." For a moment her fair brow furrowed in a frown. "You have no idea of the delicacy and sensitivity of these men. There is no pretense or clumsiness about their regard for women they like.

"He would never swear or think of using indelicate language in front of a lady. I have never heard him tell a dirty story. As a matter of fact, he has left a room when they were being told. At a party you would never see him drinking beer in the kitchen in his shirt sleeves. It would offend his sense of fitness."

"I don't see anything horrible about drinking beer in shirt sleeves."

"Perhaps not," she said, "but to a woman, dressed for a party, it is demeaning, and he is male enough to appreciate this."

I didn't quite see what she was driving at. "That still doesn't make him a real man or good husband material," I said.

She laughed. "What would a man know about that?" She seemed to be looking off into space. "Most men, real men, as you put it, don't know what it is to be tender. They put so much emphasis on one thing. They are kind and considerate when they are after a woman, and then when she returns their love, they become cold and indifferent." A note of derision crept into her voice. "They call that the conquest. But what does it make the woman—not a partner with equal dignity, but a slave fearful of her master's whim."

"We all have unfortunate experiences," I said rather sententiously, "but the next experience could be the happy one."

"When you are hurt once like that," she said slowly, "you never quite put back all the pieces."

"But why turn to a homosexual?" I asked. "There are other men, heterosexuals, who might be kinder, gentler, considerate enough to make the most sensitive woman forget a bad experience."

She pondered a while. "Perhaps, but when a child has singed his fingers, all fires look pretty much the same after that." She laughed rather harshly. "That is, if he or she had learned his lesson."

"But can it work out?" I insisted. "It seems a little like pairing oranges and lemons."

"There are any number of successful marriages," she replied, "where the woman is married to a known homosexual. There's one well-known case on Broadway where a celebrated star has been happily married for years, and even has children. She has the perfect mate. He reads script

197

for her, manages her personal affairs, escorts her to and from the theater, and keeps her from wearing herself out with people she doesn't want to see." She smiled. "That is only one of many."

That was all very nice, but suppose the husband should suddenly become involved with another male?

She still smiled. "How about the husband who becomes involved with another woman?" She closed her eyes and thought a while. "Competition from other men is really less disturbing, since there's less chance of it interfering with a marriage."

When I looked puzzled, she explained. "When a married man falls in love with another woman, the chances are that he'll either leave his wife or give up the woman." Again she smiled. "Homosexuals usually aren't as demanding."

"But," I said, "it must be difficult to be a woman and love somebody and know a man is your rival."

She sighed. "In all marriages people must sometimes turn their heads. Like most men," she added, "you overrate sex in marriage. As long as it isn't completely negative, it isn't terribly vital."

I marveled that a woman of such obvious appeal should minimize the importance of an adult sex relationship.

"As you get older," she said, "you realize it is far more important to have a good roommate, somebody who picks up after himself, brings you breakfast in bed, or prepares dinner when you are tired or busy. All this is more conducive to a happy marriage than having a husband who is a bull." Again that enigmatic smile. "Perfect understanding," she said, "is the priceless ingredient for any successful marriage."

Somewhere I recalled a psychiatrist's saying that, without being lesbians, many women have enough of the masculine in them to feel threatened and insecure in intimate association with a real male.

She laughed uproariously. "Oh, *they* have an explanation for everything," she said, "and it generally revolves around sex. Don't they realize that when people reach a certain age, when the first flush of youth is gone, they want above all to be comfortable and secure, to know where they stand? That is what's important, not being madly, wildly, painfully in love, up one day and down the next, sitting around like a teen-ager for the phone to ring, afraid to answer it for fear it isn't he. Counting the minutes until you see him or hear his voice again." She sighed and ran a languid hand through her tawny hair. "Any woman whose stomach ever turned over when a man frowned knows what I mean."

We seemed to be getting away from my newspaper interview, which concerned career girls on Broadway. I attempted to swing the conversation back to its original track. "Let's not talk about my career," she said. "I'm more interested in your book."

There was no mistaking this. I observed that she was the first actress I had ever known to dismiss an opportunity to talk about herself. "Well," she said with a flash of the warmth I had noticed at cocktail parties, "I may never get another chance to discuss this subject for publication."

She blew a faint wisp of smoke across the table and watched as it climbed to the ceiling.

"Has it ever occurred to you," she said, "what a male homosexual must go through every day of his life?"

"Don't you think it's a question of living with one's self?"

She snorted. "What does that mean? Nobody lives by himself. How can a sensitive man be insensitive to injustice, especially when it involves himself?" She looked at me almost in anger. "How would you feel," she asked, "if you were made to feel you were less than nothing simply because you did not like to make love like most men?"

I could think of nothing to say and again tried to get back to the interview. She brushed me aside. "One day," she went on with emotion, "I dropped by Bill's studio unexpectedly. He was on the telephone and I had never seen him so upset. His face was pale and taut, and he was bellowing into the telephone. 'Yes, I am a homosexual. What has that got to do with it?' he was saying."

After he hung up, he stood there for a few minutes, trembling, speechless, unable even to say hello. "What is it?" she asked.

He turned away and then finally said, "I'd rather not talk about it just yet."

She pleaded. "You'll feel better getting rid of it."

With a visible effort he pulled himself together. "It was the police," he said slowly. "Something had been stolen from the studio and I called them. They came over, looked around, and left. I didn't hear from them again, and I called the precinct and asked how the investigation was coming." He passed a hand wearily across his forehead. "You heard the rest. They were more interested in my homosexuality than the robbery."

Neither could find anything to say just then. She threw her arms around him comfortingly and he drew away. For the first time there was a gulf she couldn't bridge.

"My heart bled for him," she said, "but I didn't know how to reach him. I was afraid that whatever I said would be wrong." She felt a surging anger against the cop who had stripped him of his dignity. But she knew that to display it would only point up the slight.

She bent to kiss him, and he drew away. Refusing to be rebuffed, she pressed his arm affectionately and said, "I'll be back." She felt he needed time to compose himself, and she was right. It was a week before he was his old self and had apparently recovered from the incident.

I wondered a little at her earnestness, until she explained, after some hesitation, that Bill was the photographer she had admired so much that day at the beach. They had become quite close.

She leaned across the table in her intentness. "That cop," she said, "would never have dared talk like that to Bill's face."

That hardly seemed the point. "How," I asked, "did they know he was a homosexual? From what you have said, he was masculine enough to fool anybody."

She bridled at the "fool" which I had used without thinking and again showed hesitation.

"You don't have to answer that," I said.

"Why not?" she shrugged. "I've told you about everything else."

She grimaced. "Bill wasn't always careful about his friends. One or two were always around, male models or younger boys he was helping out. He was always an easy mark." She sighed. "I mentioned it a number of times, but he would only laugh and say I couldn't expect him to go back on people like himself." Again she sighed. "But they really weren't his own kind. These were real swishy, even though most of the men he saw were as male as he."

A silence fell between us as I wondered how male that was. She was immersed in thought, and it looked like a good time to leave. "I'm afraid I haven't helped you much," she said. "But I'll be looking forward to your book."

"How about your story?" I laughed. "Aren't you interested in that?"

She shrugged. "What's another story?"

I was to see her again before work on the book was completed. It was at a cocktail party, attended by theater people and the usual collection of café society personalities. Her escort was a rugged-looking, heavy-shouldered young man whose name I didn't quite catch. He stood nearby, possessively, as we chatted.

Though I had never met her husband, and didn't even know his name, I was pleased to note that she was still wearing her wedding ring. "Is that your husband?" I whispered, pointing to the young man.

"No," she whispered back, with a smile. "Bill doesn't like these parties."

"Who?" I asked.

"Bill," she repeated. "My husband, the photographer! Don't you remember? We were talking about him the last time we met."

CHAPTER XXIV

Old and Gay

IN GREENWICH VILLAGE gay boys laughingly pass around cards which read: "Nobody loves you when you're old and gay."

To many, including the homosexual colony, the aging homosexual is an object of scorn and derision. Though his loneliness is often abject, he seldom arouses sympathy or interest, unless he has money or influence.

When they have the means, older homosexuals may keep a boy or "master," just as some rich men keep mistresses, with the young men frequently passing as a favorite kinsman. Still other wealthy homosexuals, with less taste and discrimination, turn to the growing crop of male prostitutes.

For the aging homosexual—without means, no longer attractive enough to capitalize on homosexuality's easy promiscuity—the support of male prostitution becomes almost a necessity. Some, with irregular incomes, keep a small cash reserve around their flats against the time of greatest need. "They become panicky," a top police official told me, "at the thought of not being able to afford entertainment when they want it, and guard their hoard with their lives, even concealing it under mattresses for a rainy day."

The salad years for most homosexuals, as with pretty girls

of no particular character or attainments, appear to be the carefree twenties, when they are sought after for their youthful freshness and good looks. Thereafter, unless their work has given them a sheen of glamour, as they grow older they are of diminishing interest to other homosexuals.

And nobody grows older faster.

Ordinarily, with the conspicuous exception of the acting fraternity, the aging process begins as they approach thirty. Recently addressing a scientific group, Dr. Alfred A. Gross, executive secretary of the George Henry Foundation noted: "The homosexual's world is a young person's one. Among men without special gifts, a man is middle-aged at thirty, elderly at forty, and unless he has unusual endowments of talent or wealth, by the time a homosexual reaches fifty, he is obliged to buy companionship."

And in the "golden" years, when other men gain dignity, he is often only a target of ridicule. "To the younger members of the group, a man who tries at the age of sixty to keep up with the social procession, and who makes a business of going abroad in homosexual society to seek objects for his affectionate attention, is a sorry spectacle," Dr. Gross pointed out. "If he undertakes to dress and act as his younger brethren, he is called by all manner of unflattering epithets, not the least unkind of these being 'Old Auntie.' "

Without money, the aging homosexual may wind up in the Bowery, seeking oblivion in handouts and cheap wine, or, "losing confidence in his ability to attract a suitable sex object, he may seek satisfaction where the threat seems less." He may even regress to a point where he preys on small children, but then his problem is often more senility than homosexuality.

For the most part, though, the aging homosexual is usually his own worst problem, so desperately lonely and frightened at times that he frantically beats the walls in his anguish.

The homosexual does not appear to live as long, generally, as heterosexuals. Some hold that a benevolent nature comes to the aid of the aging deviate, shortening his term of life. Others reason that nature moves him along faster because, as a rule, he has no basic reproductive function to fulfill. But still others contend that an apparent decrease in elderly homosexuals is illusory, stemming from the fact that as they grow older, they become less active. "Unable to compete, many just take themselves out of circulation," one sociologist observed.

Doing things to "keep young" is all-important. For the

homosexual who still retains a semblance of his old looks, there are many lingering pleasures before the shattering realization that he must pay for what he wants. Through the homosexual underground the aging but well-preserved homosexual learns of haunts where he will be welcomed by others of his own stripe. These are usually little offbeat bars. To the cognoscenti, one is known as the "Mustache Bar," where full-blooded, middle-aged men of apparent robust natures meet over drafts of heavy ale. Then there is a "Wrinkle Bar," where the truly older set get together, and a "White Haired" bar which attracts not only distinguished-looking older men but some younger homosexuals with a father complex.

Many young men are only attracted by older men; some with beards, others with glasses, some with white hair—all the hallmarks of age—but these are personal idiosyncrasies, fetishes almost, and have relatively little impact on the over-all aging problem.

And it is nearly always a problem. Even where homosexual "couples" stay together for better or worse, differences in years become socially significant as one partner reaches the "age of descent" before the other. As in the heterosexual world, the jealousy and insecurity of the self-consciously older partner often complicates these uneasy unions.

Two successful businessmen, for instance, had lived together for twenty years with great compatibility. But one day the junior partner, in his prime at thirty-five, suddenly realized he was tied down to a house companion of fifty-five, an Old Auntie with whom he could no longer enjoy things. Though content, out of loyalty, to continue the relationship, he felt a need for younger companionship. But the Old Auntie, as though aware he was slipping, refused to grant the younger man a moment to himself.

The junior partner became desperate, harried to account for every move he made. "Finally," a homosexual friend related, "Ed began using phony business excuses for getting out of town weekends." But his conscience bothered him, for when he was away, Old Auntie would break down and cry and otherwise carry on, making him feel terribly guilty. Yet he was angry that he should feel this way when he was only trying to have a little fun.

Though he was becoming unhappy about the situation, there was little thought of a breakup. The home in which they lived, a costly East Side town house, was jointly theirs, as were the furnishings and many of their investments. They were really together for better or worse. And Ed didn't ask much. "If only Joe would give me a couple of nights off a week," Ed sighed to friends, "I'd love him till the day he died."

As they get older, many homosexuals experience spasms of self-pity and mourn the children and grandchildren they never wanted anyway. Others coldly take steps to avoid an "unloved" old age.

Reaching the age of thirty-two, one security-minded homosexual, who was concerned about his future, got to brooding over his celibacy. He decided to have a family of his own before it was too late. Abruptly breaking off from a homosexual friend with whom he had lived for years, he began searching around for a female mate. Six months later he was married, and duly thereafter the children started arriving. "It gave me the position I wanted," he explained to another homosexual, "and it still didn't bar me from other things, so long as I was careful about it."

Even when they can indulge their fancy for youth, aging homosexuals still have the problem of putting on the conventional front demanded by their wealth and position—a problem that must be carefully considered.

The elderly owner of a large business, traveling in Europe, returned from his sojourn heavily loaded down with additional baggage and a nineteen-year-old youth whom he installed in his suburban home. The newcomer had been there several weeks without incident. Then one night, after a dinner party, one of the guests took advantage of a long friendship to speak confidentially to his host. "Unless you get rid of that boy," he said, "people will start talking. This is suburbia, not the big city, and once the tongues start wagging, you're in trouble. If you want to keep him, you've got to justify him somehow."

The host was grateful to his old friend and, as the pillar of the local country club, somewhat concerned. He discussed the situation with his young protégé at some length. The youth, naturally reluctant to give up his comfortable berth, agreed that convention must be served. In deference to American custom, he suggested bringing a distant kinswoman, a young, attractive girl from his home in Central Europe, to supervise the household and act as a blind.

"Why not marry her?" the young "master" grinned. "Everybody will then be sure she is marrying you for your money, and nobody will think a thing about it."

The wedding was one of the big social events of the suburban season. The bride, palmed off as the young man's sister, charmed everybody but the groom. And with wagging tongues silenced, her young kinsman assumed an unquestioned and favored place in the household as the dearly beloved brother—and brother-in-law. Inside the house the recent ceremony caused little change in living habits. "Everybody was happy," observed the friend who had counseled caution. "The girl was happy with her new clothes, the parties, the car, and the swimming pool; she had never known anything but poverty before. Moreover, she was genuinely fond of her kinsman and happy to show her gratitude for all he had done for her."

Meanwhile, the merchant was richly enjoying the situation, laughing with friends at the warm reception his marriage had received in the community. "Nobody," he said dryly, "seemed to think it odd *she* was so young. Marrying for money, as they thought, was something all could understand, and accept."

There are all kinds of accommodations for the aging homosexual. Some considerate heterosexuals, alert for any kind of a dollar, have even organized male prostitution rings to serve a growing clientele. There are many similarities to the more common call-girl operation. Instead of being called "madams," the chief procurers, usually older straight males, are ironically dubbed "misters." They do most of their business over the phone. Often boys are summoned, sight unseen, the customer depending on the mister for appreciation of his likes and dislikes.

There is often haggling about price. The market for young men is not as active as for young women, since the amateur competition is much keener, with the bars and streets filled with homosexuals trying to give themselves away.

However, resorting to well-screened lists of youths is a convenient way, some homosexuals feel, of avoiding exposure to arrest, blackmail, or even attachments that may become embarrassing.

And money is generally not too much of a problem for homosexuals sufficiently endowed to get on the misters' lists. And things can always be worked out, when the customer is a valued one of long standing. On one occasion, for instance, a middle-aged homosexual of some economic position called a mister and asked for a certain young man. He was out of the country, but the mister suggested an alternate, a newcomer.

The customer was only mildly interested.

"How much?" he asked.

"Twenty dollars," the mister replied.

The customer was incredulous. "Twenty dollars for untried rough trade!"

Eventually, a compromise was reached—ten dollars. When the young male prostitute, just out of his teens arrived, he was greeted with a drink. They sat around a while and then retired. Later the customer offered the youth the ten dollars. He declined with thanks, indicating he was still on probation.

"Oh no," he said. "I can't take it. I'm new and I'm not trusted with money yet. The mister will be around later and pick it up, and then he'll pay me."

The client shrugged. "As you please," he said.

Three days later the mister turned up. He pulled out a black book with a long list of names. And then he took the ten dollars from the customer, crossed out his name with a pencil, smiled, and asked whether everything had been all right. The customer nodded and the procurer seemed pleased.

"He's an honest boy," he said. "I hope he works out."

Some misters have connections in other large cities, such as Chicago, Los Angeles, and San Francisco. And for their traveling clientele they are able to phone or write ahead, securing customers hotel "accommodations" soon after their arrival.

Through fear of police wire taps, negotiations for call boys are sometimes liberally sprinkled with code words.

The references are rather obvious to those in the know. "Usually," a homosexual related, "the mister will call and say: 'We have a package for you—when can we deliver it?' "

"What is the vintage?" you ask.

"Oh," he says, "it's a fine ten-dollar champagne, about twenty years old."

What could be more obvious?

Or, as one client pointed out, if the commodity was something special, fair and fresh and young, it might be more elegantly described perhaps as "an extremely light scotch, bottled, twenty-four years, and priced especially for you at twenty dollars."

Not all who drift into male prostitution do so for money or excitement. The desperate need for companionship momentarily drives many young men into a loss of integrity from which they may never recover. One twenty-year-old disclosed he had become an overt homosexual as easily as he might have become a motorist or a swimmer—so naturally that he didn't even think about it while it was happening.

One evening, not knowing a soul in the city, this good-looking, corn-fed product of the Middle West stumbled into a bar seeking to slake his loneliness by even rubbing elbows with strangers, and listening to their talk and perhaps joining in, given the opening wedge.

By chance, this night he had stepped into a gay bar catering to older men. For a few minutes, as in other bars, nobody paid him any attention. Then one of the gray-haired men, standing near, cordially smiled as Jack darkly studied his drink. They began talking, small talk about jobs, plays, books, weekends. The young man was thrilled, stimulated. He felt he had found a kindred spirit. When he left the bar that night, saying good night, he no longer felt his familiar emptiness. He came back night after night, engaging in conversation with the same man and getting to know his friends. All complimented him on his fresh-faced good looks and charm. "For the first time in years," he said, "I finally felt I belonged." And he either didn't know they were homosexuals or, knowing it, didn't want to face up to it.

But he soon could no longer avoid realization of the truth.

One night as he left the bar with his friend and was having a late snack at a corner cafeteria, the friend invited him to his room. "I wasn't shocked, surprised, indignant, or anything," he recalled. "I was just grateful for his taking me out of my loneliness, and wanted to please him." And he was also afraid, he acknowledged, of losing the only friend he had.

He soon discovered homosexuals have fleeting interests. "After a week or so my friend didn't seem pleased to see me, and I sensed a change in the others, too. The old conviviality and friendliness was no longer there. They now talked down to me in a patronizing way, with a slight sneer. I wasn't one of them, but I belonged to them—that seemed to sum it up."

Desperate for acceptance, he took up with a succession of gay partners. Yet soon he was ridiculed or ignored whenever he came into the bar. But while Jack was hopelessly confused, the bartender who observed it all seemed to have no trouble understanding. "He was a queen," he philosophized, "who let himself become a punk."

207

Soon he was making the rounds of other homosexual bars, looking for new friends. When I met him, he was at a public health clinic, being treated for venereal disease, picked up through homosexual contact. Jack was not unique.

Thousands of homosexuals eventually wind up at the health clinic, being treated for venereal disease, picked up ing treatment. The promiscuity staggers the imagination. One male prostitute produced a little black book revealing relationships with one hundred and twenty-five men and thirteen women within the year. Dates, fees, and other incidentals were duly noted.

Another young man, a secretary, had joined a club whose members were pledged to the practice of homosexuality. He had turned up at the clinic with a case of syphilis. He felt he had got it from one of his fellow members but couldn't be sure, since he also had numbers of older friends who found him attractive.

All of his eighteen brother members were examined. Eight were found in a highly infectious stage of syphilis. "These men and their comrades," said Dr. Herman Goodman, veteran health official, "admitted homosexual practices, active and passive, despite the fact homosexuals generally insist each practices only one phase of the act." The truth, as Dr. Goodman found, was that the active partner in one situation, may be the passive partner in another.

"Promiscuity and change are features of homosexual relationships," he observed. Intimacies with women were not unusual, either. One of the patients had exposed himself to every member of the club, and had a girl friend besides.

Even homosexuals are hard-pressed to defend such promiscuity. Nevertheless, it is very much a part of the homosexual pattern. The homosexual world, as Dr. Gross pointed out, is "a hedonistic one" with dignity going before a fall. With his scrabbling about for male prostitutes, and his lack of a decent home life, the aging homosexual is truly a pathetic figure. And even lasting long enough to become old and lonely seems a problem. Some time ago a random study of several thousand homosexuals brought out one revealing item— out of all those homosexuals only ten per cent were over forty years of age. Less than a handful were over sixty. "The homosexual," Dr. Gross concludes, "lives in a world devoted to the worship of youth. In such a world there is no room for old people."

CHAPTER XXV

Parental Problems

FEW TRAGEDIES LEAVE parents with a greater sense of helplessness than the revelation that a son or daughter is homosexual. It not only saddens some, almost as much as the actual loss of a child, but embarrasses virtually all and fills many with secret pangs of guilt.

Many of these parents, wondering where they have failed, have sorrowingly given up fond hopes of children marrying. Some, particularly mothers, whom modern-day psychology blames for much of the rampant homosexuality among the rising generation of males, manage gradually to reconcile themselves to their disappointment. Others never get over it. Usually, the father seems harder hit, often unable to continue a comfortable relationship with a son he has suddenly discovered is not all male.

With notable exceptions, as in the case of a well-known writer whose socially prominent mother could never quite excuse him, mother seems to adjust easier, untouched by her husband's traditionally masculine contempt for "fairies." And she also recognizes, in many instances, that she has acquired a solicitous, considerate companion for her declining years—her homosexual son.

In trying to cope with a son's homosexuality, parents have usually failed abjectly. One father thought his college son could cure himself if he stayed home after classes, barricading himself in his room until "the madness" left him. Another father, ridiculing attempts to give his son psychiatric help, ordered him to go out with girls and "keep away from bad company."

In their confusion some parents have appealed for help to trained individuals or organizations. One troubled mother, who turned to the George Henry Foundation, was the typical parent in need of skilled guidance. In some way she had discovered that drinking brought out her son's homosexual tendencies, and she tried ultimatums with indifferent success, repeatedly telling her wayward son, "Don't keep coming home drunk and expect to stay here." Whenever he staggered in, she could, with justification, suspect the worst.

209

After contacting the Foundation she developed a new approach. "I realize now how woefully ignorant I was of how to proceed and now content myself with trying to express such kindness as I am capable of, issuing as few orders as possible," she gratefully wrote Foundation directors. The Foundation, she said, had kept him from liquor for six months, thus curbing desires encouraged by drink. "Each visit with you, particularly in the evening, his roughest time, sent him home with improved morale," she wrote. "For it was then he missed most his former associates—drinking and night prowling."

Before consulting the Foundation her son had suffered long periods of despair, intensified by his discharge from the armed forces. "Now, his face lights up," the mother said, "as he tells me how understanding you are, expressing none of the contempt he met with after asking for help in the services. Now, for the first time, he feels optimistic."

Homosexual children are even more embarrassed than their parents by revelations of their homosexuality, and find it easier to discuss the problem with almost anybody but their parents. Nothing short of a calamity could induce most homosexuals to tell parents something which, they feel, could only disturb or alienate them, without accomplishing anything.

The problem is frequently debated by homosexual groups which discount the seed-parent theory of more objective authorities, for one of free choice. At one such homosexual forum, a young man observed blandly:

"I just don't see what purpose it would serve. As a matter of fact, I live with Mother, and I would do anything to keep her from finding out."

"Why is that?" somebody asked.

"Frankly," he said, "she wouldn't understand in a million years, and I would rather let her think I was a mama's boy and let it go at that."

"How can you be sure she won't understand?"

He laughed. "I just know. My mother is of rigid New England stock. She was raised with a moral concept that wouldn't permit her to accept such weakness. The knowledge would only hurt her, without doing me any particular good." He looked around the room and said without the least trace of a smile, "How much better for both of us to encourage the idea that I prefer her to any other woman in the world." He laughed. "As a matter of fact, that wouldn't be too far from the truth."

He shrugged. "As it is, we're both content with our relationship now. Why spoil it all with a maudlin confession?"

There were understanding nods. As another pink-cheeked young man in his late twenties added his assent, the others listened with noticeable respect. He was a college man with a master's degree, well on his way to a doctorate in philosophy. He seemed extremely sure of himself. "I don't even know what there is to discuss," he said. "We all know most parents suspect it, but why rub their noses in it?"

There were grunts of agreement on all sides. "After all," he went on, "parents aren't stupid. But, like a lot of us, they'd rather not face up against something unpleasant."

He smiled broadly. "The old girl," he said, "isn't so dumb that she doesn't know who's emptying out her mascara bottle." There was general laughter, and he said with a wink: "I'm speaking figuratively, of course."

Still more laughter.

He thought parents should relax and not blame themselves for something their children didn't blame them for. "Parents these days," he said, "are mentally conditioned to think that anything considered failure on the part of their children is due to their failure as parents. Well, we all know that's a lot of hogwash."

He looked around again confidently. "We've all had as good parents as anybody else, so why make them feel they haven't done their job well?"

Most of these young men had been raised in homes that were apparently normal. There had been no great traumatic experiences which had made soul-searchers of them at any early age. They didn't look different from any comparable group of young men anywhere, though they frequently laughed at allusions that might not have tickled the risibilities of nonhomosexuals. Now they were listening to another young man. He couldn't have been more than twenty-two or twenty-three. Sitting on the edge of his chair, obviously more nervous than the others who had preceded him, he mentioned that he, too, was living at home with his mother, his father having died a short time before. His problem was a little more acute than the others. "You see," he said, "I think my mother suspects, and I don't know what to do about it."

"Why should she suspect?" somebody asked.

He hesitated, then laughed nervously. "Well, there was an unpleasant incident at home once. It was while my father was alive. It was some years ago. I was sixteen or so and

211

didn't know quite what I was then. A friend of mine had come over to the house, and we were in my room. It was warm, and I had taken most of my clothes off and he did the same. We were alone, with the door closed, but we really didn't do anything except"—and here he smiled, to be met with understanding smiles—"except that we engaged in a little exploratory research."

When the young visitor left, the boy walked him to the door, arm in arm, clad only in his shorts. He was spotted from the living room by his father and mother.

After the visitor left, the father went to his son's room. There was a stormy scene. "He accused me of being queer and said that no queer would live under his roof and he was throwing me out of the house if I didn't get out."

The boy's mother interceded, attempting to placate her husband, and pointed out that the boy hadn't done anything except, perhaps, commit a small error in judgment. "Dad didn't swallow it, but I guess he didn't want to hurt Mom. And, anyway, I've always suspected that after he quieted down, he preferred not to have to accept the fact that his son was queer. It was a matter of pride with him."

Many times, thereafter, the boy would look up to surprise his mother studying him. She never discussed his marrying or commented on how rarely, if ever, he saw a girl. Around the house, following the incident with his father, he was careful not to do anything to arouse any more suspicions.

After his father died, even though he no longer had him to fear, he was even more cautious at home.

There were no more visitors, and he spent more time with his mother. She may have guessed by now, but he gave her no new reason to speculate about it. "I went out occasionally with the fellows," he said, "but she never questioned me. Somehow I got the impression, without her mentioning it, that she was beginning to get used to the idea I might never leave home."

There were understanding nods all around. "We all know," said a middle-aged man, who evoked instant attention, "that a lot of mothers, even without realizing it, bring up their boys with the secret wish they will never marry. Subconsciously they see every young girl as a potential rival."

"I don't think that was the case here," the first speaker said. "I think my mother was more resigned than receptive."

Disclosures were sometimes dictated by special circumstances. "It wasn't a matter of just hashing things over with them," a young man said. "I just felt I had to tell somebody at the time and they were elected." He had been living with another young man for about a year, in what his family considered a normal situation, when there was a quarrel and the friend walked out. "I was shattered," he said. "I thought ours was a relationship that was different." Emotionally upset, he slashed his wrists and was in the hospital when his parents finally saw him. In his own loneliness and confusion he suddenly felt an overpowering urge to reach out for understanding.

"I could see they didn't understand," he said, "but it was some comfort to know they were trying to accept what I had told them and trying, somehow, to help me."

After his "confession" he felt immeasurably better. Even the pangs of his broken "love" began to fade, and he started to take interest in getting well. After his aborted suicide he realized for the first time his own emotional vulnerability. He would have to put up more guards in the future.

Even without full understanding he found it reassuring to bask in the radiating warmth of parental love, mustered for the emergency. He was especially grateful to his father for not expressing doubts, the bewilderment, the distaste he must have instantly felt. For his mother, the shock may not have been so great. "A woman," he said, expressing the prevailing homosexual view, "whether she's mother, sister, or wife, never really understands the sex reactions of any male, so it would be just another confusing situation for her."

When he finished, a brooding silence fell over the room as each sat alone with his thoughts. At last a red-faced youth, with a faint European accent, broke the spell.

As he rose to his feet, he expressed the view that each case, of course, stood on its own. "In my own case," he said, "I left my parents and homeland before I knew what I was myself."

In this country he had confided in a younger sister, but she could hardly have missed knowing anyway. "She came over to live with me since I was responsible for her here, and I was already living with somebody else." Nobody seemed to question who or what that "somebody" might be.

"Was she surprised at your situation?" an older man asked.

"Not really," he replied. "In Europe they are broadminded about these things, and, anyway, I think sisters, who are nearer your own age have a way of sensing it."

"She could hardly have missed it," a younger man said

with a smile, "since you and your 'somebody' were presumably sharing the same room."

"Yes," the European agreed, "but it wasn't necessary to tell her, and she didn't care when I did." He shrugged. "Besides, she had a room to herself."

It was a rather unique design for living. The sister's boy friends, calling at the apartment, were received in the living room by brother and his friend, as she got herself ready. Nobody apparently thought anything of it. "They just figured we were putting her up, which," he laughed, "we were."

Sister helped with the meals, tidied the small flat, and generally made sure her "roommates" were comfortable. Neither looked forward to the day she would marry and move away.

"What kind of men did she date?" an older man asked.

The brother laughed. "My sister is very normal. There was little chance of additional complications. She preferred the kind of men who preferred girls."

There was a ripple of appreciative laughter.

Very few outsiders understand the attachment between some parents and homosexual children. These relationships rarely have to contend with the distractions of a normal man's own married life, since relatively fewer marry, or work at marriage seriously. And they provide many homosexuals with a reassuring sense of stability.

In clinging to parental ties, emotionally, at least, many homosexuals retain some semblance of normalcy in their abnormal lives. One middle-aged man, who had been following the discussion closely, rose to observe that he had been the sole support of his father for the last ten years. The father had been in a nursing home since the death of the mother, but only because he preferred it there. "I wanted Dad with me," the son said, "but he thought he would be more comfortable where he is."

Even before his mother passed away, the speaker had shared an apartment with an older man. But he didn't think his parents had suspected anything. He was very cautious.

He had several brothers and sisters, all married, and he spoke disdainfully of them because they had been no help to his father. "For once in their lives," he said, "they were grateful for little old me."

He never saw them, and thought they might have suspected because of the questions they had once asked him.

But he couldn't care less what *they* thought. "There's little danger of their giving me away," he said. "Somebody might wonder if it ran in the family."

One young man had to tell his parents he was moving out to live with a friend. Even though they didn't suspect a homosexual relationship, they were devastated, felt they had failed as homemakers and parents. To relieve this sense of failure, he decided to tell them the truth. He told how his friendship developed in the Army. At first they were incredulous, but after the shock had worn off, they were satisfied, at least, that there was no loss of affection for them on their son's part.

Now, instead of losing a son, they have gained one. "We see them all the time," the young office worker said, "and they're crazy about John." He laughed. "They're particularly mad about his cooking."

"Have you ever regretted telling your parents?" an older man asked.

"No," the young man said, "because they would have been unhappy otherwise."

Curious eyes appraised the next young man. This was his first appearance at a get-together of this particular homosexual group. In his early twenties, with deep-set eyes and a thick shock of dark hair, he was a dramatically attractive figure.

He had been discharged from the armed forces as an undesirable but wasn't sure he was a homosexual. He had committed only one act of homosexuality, he said, and been caught at it. When he couldn't get a job because of his discharge, he felt he had better explain to somebody in the family. He finally told his sister, and she broke it to the mother.

Without quite understanding, the poor woman was vaguely troubled by her son's problem. But she was also vaguely sympathetic, without knowing quite what to do or say. However, she was sufficiently knowledgeable to warn him from saying anything to his father, who was critical enough of him as it was.

He was still looking for a job, and that, he said, was his major problem. "And," he said, with a shrug and a smile, "I really don't even know if I'm a homosexual or not."

He had the instant sympathy of the group. There was a chorus of hearty agreement as somebody cried, "It's a shame you should be hounded like that."

After a few similar remarks the group therapy had its

salutary effect. The young man brightened visibly, and he soon was beaming.

Some asked how he had wandered into the meeting room, and he explained. Wanting to know more about homosexuality, so he might resolve a few of his own doubts, he had tried to buy a copy of the homosexual publication. *One*. The dealer had been sold out but suggested another pamphlet. The address in the masthead had told him the rest.

After the young man sat down, a group leader got up and said he was glad to greet the newcomer and hoped the group could be of some benefit, either in helping him find a job or in clearing up his doubts. "However," he said, "we want to make clear this is not a recruiting station. We don't encourage anybody to become homosexual. We only suggest they choose the course that makes them happiest. That is something each must find out for himself. Ask all the questions you want, come back as often as you want, read what you want."

After listening to another young man, whose parents had become so reconciled to his homosexuality that they gave house parties for his gay friends, the group came up with some advice for all homosexuals.

It was contained in the following resolution:

"There is really no necessity for children to tell parents unless a special problem exists. Then parents will probably accept and stick by the child. However, parents are human, and there is no reason to tell them what would be sure to hurt them."

CHAPTER XXVI

The Outlook

LONG BEFORE Oscar Wilde went to jail for "the love that dared not speak its name," the Anglo-Saxon world was embarrassed by even the mention of homosexuality. The judge who pronounced sentence on the English writer at the turn of the century looked away from him in loathing. And as he imposed the maximum sentence of two years, he expressed only regret that the law would not allow him to make it more.

Two generations have passed since the names of Wilde

and Lord Alfred Douglas were linked together. Homosexuality is now much more open in many social areas, and it certainly has more acceptance.

In England, the hostile homeland from which the broken writer fled in ignominy and shame, there has been a recent disposition to view the homosexual more sympathetically. Representatives of both the Church of England and the Roman Catholic hierarchy supported the Wolfenden Report, the official government paper which recommended that homosexual acts between privately consenting adults be stricken from the statute books as a punishable offense. While Parliament refused its sanction, many homosexuals still cling to the dream that an Anglo-Saxon society will eventually give homosexuals the same sexual freedom enjoyed by other men and women.

Even so, unless the homosexual should become a majority, as he sometimes visualizes, the problem is still essentially that of harmoniously living with himself and with society. Even considering the increasing homosexuality a social malady, reflecting the decadence of the times, many think it becomes all the more urgent for society that the homosexual be helped. And the fact that such help is being offered— both in England and this country—shows this growing awareness that society as a whole has a strong stake in the matter. "There is a pressing need to help those who desire it," observes the authoritative Dr. George Henry. And he distinguishes significantly between the help for homosexuals quietly wrestling with their problem and those who seem to glory in flaunting their homosexuality in society's face. "There will, of course," he points out, "be those who are seemingly satisfied with their lot, and for such only the bitter lessons of experience might possibly be of some avail. For the psychopath, the individual unable to profit from experience, stern measures of social control must always be in readiness."

In some cities, and sections of the country, much has already been done to establish "help centers" for the homosexual. Many psychologists, sociologists, clergymen, and social workers have specialized in the field and have become sufficiently expert to form a bridge over which the homosexual can find his way back into society. With the right help, at the right time, many men, desperate with despair, have been rescued from jail, blackmail, destitution, alcoholism, and even suicide.

Tormented by the fear of being homosexual, some have learned that their fears were actually groundless; they were

217

just overly shy with women, a common and completely normal phenomenon. Others have discovered, gratefully, that a rare incident of homosexuality, either from curiosity or social pressure, does not necessarily make them confirmed homosexuals.

Often when homosexuals have been shattered by discovery or exposure, the big task is one of restoring self-respect and confidence, encouraging them to pick up the broken threads of their lives. In this way many have been restored to jobs, friends, and family. "Studies of men convicted of homosexual offense," one authority says, "indicate that those who are able to get help stand a much better chance of keeping out of trouble."

Those helped by the George Henry Foundation come from virtually every strata of society, and every walk of life. They were doctors and lawyers, teachers and students, clerks and business executives. They came from off the Bowery and Park Avenue. They have arrived here penniless immigrants, and they have been descendants of the Mayflower elite. And their problems, while related to homosexuality, are quite varied.

There was the young, married bisexual, a society figure, whose marriage to an actress had foundered after a return to the homosexual activities which had ceased after he left prep school. A marriage counselor was recommended. The diagnosis was immaturity. The prognosis: "He has to be taught that he is a little bit elderly to play the role of a charming adolescent and that, once having taken the responsibility of becoming a husband, he cannot shake off these responsibilities because they turned out to be a little more than he cared to cope with."

There was the fat and ugly teen-age homosexual who had been arrested in a subway washroom and placed on probation. He didn't like men so much as he was embarrassed in the presence of women. With psychiatric aid he was able to abstain from overt homosexuality, but became tense and irritable, like an alcoholic deprived of drink. However, improvement was noted with time. He seemed to mature, become more confident. He went through college, got himself a good job, and traveled. As his confidence built up, he began thinking of himself as perhaps acceptable to women. On a holiday jaunt, out of the country, he finally mustered up enough courage to embark on his first heterosexual relationship. With male friends he visited a house of prostitution. In jubilation he sent a one-word telegram back to his mentors. It read: "Eureka." Soon he became bold enough, and sure enough of himself, to contemplate more selective feminine relationships. And eventually he picked out a girl, married, and had children. He now regards himself as cured of homosexuality. "And as long as he thinks so," a trained observer pointed out, "so long will that cure be permanent."

Government workers, discharged in the State Department purges some years back, have applied for help at the George Henry Foundation. One disgraced diplomat, his career tumbling down on him in ruins, was referred to the Foundation by government officials. He responded reluctantly, taking two days to make an appointment. As became a career diplomat, his background was socially impeccable. He had attended a "correct" preparatory school and an Ivy League college. After graduation he married a girl from his own social set. They had two children.

He had been introduced to homosexuality at college. But through fear of exposure he seldom had relations with men of his own station, skulking around the poorer and darker sections of the city in his search for male prostitutes. After he married and entered the government service, he cut down on his activities. He had to keep his secret from his wife, and he liked his job too much to run too many risks. Once he flirted with disaster, when a young man began blackmailing him. But a transfer to another country saved him. After more than ten years in the service, his future seemed assured, and then the government purge focused the spotlight on homosexuality. Reports of an indiscretion in a European capital resulted in his being returned to this country. He was questioned by security officers and discharged. As soon as his wife learned of the reasons behind his dismissal, she left him, taking their children with her.

He was in a rather hopeless state of mind when he turned up at the Foundation offices in New York's lower East Side. A clergyman, schooled in homosexual problems, was assigned him. For days the pastor did nothing but bear the brunt of the homosexual's hostilities. During these discussions some of the diplomat's hopelessness and hostility began to diminish. Soon he showed signs of wanting to do something worth-while to vindicate himself with his wife and children.

But what could he do—and where? There had been no publicity about his separation from the government service. His name had not been mentioned. Outside of Washington few knew about his case. His advisers didn't want him to go back to Washington, where there could only be painful reminders, or remain in New York, where he had no interests. He needed warmth, kindness, and, above all, acceptance to finish the job of restoring his faith in himself. They thought it might be a good idea for him to go back to his old home town, where he had family ties and could count on a warm reception. A plausible story was invented to account for his leaving the service. Contact was made with a home-town minister, who was taken into the secret and agreed to help. Arrangements were also made for him to see a local psychiatrist regularly. He got a job and became interested in making money and helping his wife and children. Advisers encouraged him to look to the time when they would all be rejoined. Two years later he felt sufficiently redeemed in his own eyes to ask to see his wife again. Before the meeting took place, she was approached by the friendly minister. He expressed the feeling that her husband had surmounted his problem. Husband and wife then met, and the reunion resulted. At last report, four years later, there has been no recurrence of homosexual activity. As one observer put it: "He had not only learned to live with his homosexuality—but without it."

In many parts of the country there is growing realization that homosexuality is not just a police problem or something to be swept under the rug. Many cities have homosexual problems, but unfortunately they are recognized only when a scandal breaks out, shocking citizens out of their complacency. Even then, however, it is not too late for something to be accomplished—if adequate social forces can be mustered.

In one southern city, whose name is not revealed for fear of opening old sores, most of the population of about 100,000 would have been scandalized if anybody had dared link some of the town's leading figures to so monstrous a thing as homosexuality.

Yet there had been ugly whisperings in the community for some time. And then one day a minister got up in his pulpit, damned the sinners in their midst, and demanded that the police act immediately.

Not many days passed before some of the offenders were hunted down and brought to justice. In all, about twenty men were arrested, many of them socially prominent. They were proud names that had once graced only the society pages.

It was only the beginning.

Heads hanging, some of the men went off to prison in disgrace. Their families were equally shamed. Rather than face the notoriety of a public trial, one leading citizen, a prominent physician, committed suicide. Still others fled the city where they had lived all their lives, fugitives from justice. Some families were broken up, with disillusioned wives leaving their husbands. Spared jail terms as minors, many teenagers were still hopelessly labeled for the rest of their lives.

The crime of all was homosexuality.

For a while the community became panicky. Men even wondered about their neighbors. As the arrests continued, so did the homosexuality. "Those who hadn't been caught," an observer noted, "became more cautious or moved away."

There was much soul-searching in the community. Civic leaders decided, belatedly, that nothing was to be served by wrecking all these lives and possibly many more. Who knew who would be the next to be arrested? It had become obvious, too, that the principal unfortunates were not the homosexuals, but their families, who, innocent though they were, found it hard to hold up their heads in public.

Painfully, the town fathers surveyed the shambles around them. Some felt that police action had only made matters worse. Others thought it time for calm evaluation of the situation. They decided finally to send for help—help to end the scandal and, perhaps, the homosexuality. It was worth a try.

In response to their appeal an expert arrived, a social scientist who had been dealing with homosexuals and homosexuality for thirty years.

He was not entirely accepted. Many regarded him as a prying old busybody, from the Sodom and Gomorrah on the Hudson. Unconcerned, he went about his job dissuading police from sensationalism, schooling mental hygiene and social workers. Apparently, he convinced even the doubtful that further arrests would serve no useful purpose. He suggested quiet arraignments and probation for those already arrested but not yet brought to court. He counseled psychiatric care, with aftercare by trained social workers and clergymen. He talked to judges, doctors, homosexuals and their families. He ventured into homes where relatives were mourning as though counting their dead. As he called at one homosexual's home, the wife was packing and preparing to leave with the children for her mother's house. The husband, released on probation, stood outside hopefully, awaiting her decision. She was adamant.

"You're not giving him much of a chance," the visitor said, "not as much as the law has."

The woman frowned. "I can't live with him any more," she said. "He's not the man I married."

The sociologist smiled. "That's where you're wrong," he said. "He's very much the man you married."

She was obviously puzzled. "What do you mean by that?"

"Let me ask you something," he countered. "How long have you been married?"

"Six years," she replied, still puzzled.

"Well," he said, "have you known any difference in him in all those years?"

As she began to understand, her face started to redden. "What," she demanded, "has that got to do with it?"

"Everything," the sociologist responded easily. "He's fundamentally the same man you've known since you were married. His homosexuality seemed to have little bearing on your marriage, when you didn't know about it. It was the accident of his arrest and disgrace that bothered you." He smiled. "But he's still the same man and now he needs you more than ever." He paused. "If *you* reject him," he said, "why should anyone else accept him?"

The housewife needed time to think it over. Several days later she sent the good word to her husband. "But I don't want to see that nasty old man again," she said.

Along with meeting immediate problems, the visitor felt it necessary to build up a foundation of understanding which would be helpful after he left. He stayed on for weeks, lecturing about the vagaries of the homosexual.

Like Dr. Henry, he distinguished between the homosexual whose conduct makes him principally a problem to himself and those who flaunt themselves, offending the sensibilities of society.

Homosexuals, he pointed out, often have nothing in common, not even their homosexuality. "No two are exactly alike," he said, "and while these cases are all problems of sexual maladjustment, it would be difficult to imagine some of these men sitting comfortably together in the same room for five minutes."

He asked understanding for those quiet, discreet homosexuals who were being punished, he said, not as breakers of the peace, but as nonconformists, whose last thought was to intrude their own nonconformity upon society. "Society," he said, "will not help these men by putting them in prison or holding them to scorn. They are individuals in need of care, rather than confinement in prisons, which, only too often, are breeding grounds for more homosexuality."

What is the answer to the problem? Who can say?

The psychiatrist feels it is psychotherapy.

The sociologist feels it lies in socially relating the homosexual to his environment.

The clergyman—and social philosopher—is confident that a moral resurgence is the answer, affecting not only the homosexual, but society around him.

And the homosexual, for the most part, thinks that legalizing his activities will solve everything.

Then there are the experts who believe that a happy combination of these approaches could relieve a problem, which, in its over-all impact, certainly affects more than just every sixth man.

Meanwhile, society, as some see it, will soon have to come to grips with this pressing problem. "The task will not be easy," one eminent authority pointed out, "for either the homosexual or society. The homosexual will have to learn a great deal about himself, and some of his knowledge will not be palatable. We must be prepared for him to stumble and even to fall. And we must face the fact, not always pleasant, that he is here to stay."